The Strategy Process

A Military–Business Comparison

Robert F. Grattan

Visiting Lecturer
School of Strategic Management
University of the West of England, Bristol

First published 2002 by
PALGRAVE MACMILLAN
Houndmills, Basingstoke, Hampshire RG21 6XS and
175 Fifth Avenue, New York, N. Y. 10010
Companies and representatives throughout the world

PALGRAVE MACMILLAN is the global academic imprint of the Palgrave
Macmillan division of St. Martin's Press, LLC and of Palgrave Macmillan Ltd.
Macmillan® is a registered trademark in the United States, United Kingdom
and other countries. Palgrave is a registered trademark in the European
Union and other countries.

ISBN 0–333–98445–5

This book is printed on paper suitable for recycling and
made from fully managed and sustained forest sources.

A catalogue record for this book is available
from the British Library.

Library of Congress Cataloging-in-Publication Data
Grattan, Robert F., 1931–
    The strategy process : a military–business comparison / by Robert F. Grattan.
        p. cm.
    Includes bibliographical references and index.
    ISBN 0–333–98445–5
    1. Strategic planning.   2. Business planning.   3. Military planning.
    4. Leadership.   I. Title.
HD30.28 .G724 2002
658.4′012—dc21   2002017698

10   9   8   7   6   5   4   3   2   1
11   10   09   08   07   06   05   04   03   02

Printed and bound in Great Britain by
Antony Rowe Ltd, Chippenham, Wiltshire

Contents

List of Figures

List of Tables

Preface

Strategy is a term used for a human activity that seeks to devise a way to achieve personal or organisational goals. In this sense, the word's meaning is the same in both military and business fields. This conclusion can be taken as the starting point for this thesis, which seeks to assess whether the strategy process in the business field also prevails in the military context, and what are the areas of similarity and difference.

Since the work focuses on process, the context and content of strategy are only of peripheral interest. The writings on military strategy, however, concentrate upon these latter dimensions, and little is written specifically on process. The methodology adopted for this study, interviews with strategists and some case studies, was used to focus upon strategy formulation in multiple contexts.

Strategic management theory has been subjected to considerable analysis by academics, and the conflicting views have been categorised here to permit comparison with military practice. Further to making this comparison, some influences were selected as a framework: organisation, leadership, risk, theory and context.

The military organisation is hierarchical and thus strategy formulation is more akin to that practised in bureaucracies than to that in entrepreneurial groups. Leadership is greatly prized in the military, and business has only recently accorded this facet the same amount of attention. The military are generally risk-averse, whereas an entrepreneurial spirit is valued in much of industry, particularly in small companies and in high-tech industries. There are some echoes of military theory in strategic management, but evidence is lacking for a complete mapping of one onto the other. Strategy formulation in both fields is dependent on the general context, in that there is a routine, regular process, which is punctuated by periods of crisis or urgency when the pattern of action undergoes change. In particular, in these periods of stress, leadership becomes a more potent factor, decision is taken at the top of the organisation and organisational politics are more subdued. Crisis, then, can be an advantage to the dominant coalition. A difference between business and the military is the importance accorded to aims. Selection of a precise aim is of central importance to the military whereas business leaders are content with more general strategic aims.

Leadership, being of such importance to strategy process, needs to be analysed, as far as is possible. The variety of human personality and traits, which are the focus of psychological studies, produces different forms of leadership. A particular role of leadership is the creation of vision for the organisation as a means of inspiring members to be more creative, and to give greater commitment.

If leadership is of such vital importance, then consideration must be given to how those leaders are identified, trained and nurtured. These processes are less structured in businesses than in the military.

The book concludes that there are significant parallels between the strategy process in business and the military. The military pay more attention than does business to the formulation of aims and goals. The military have a more formal system of training future leaders than in business, where it is often left to chance.

ROBERT F. GRATTAN

Acknowledgements

I would like first to acknowledge the help and forbearance of those eminent people who agreed to be interviewed to provide evidence for this study. They were unfailingly kind, generous and supportive, and I am truly grateful to them. I acknowledge one contributor who wished to remain anonymous but who gave considerable help on the IBM case study and was kind enough to provide additional information. Mr Richard Hatfield, who occupies a post of great importance and pressure in the Ministry of Defence, took the trouble to read the case study on the formation of strategy in the UK MOD and to correct some errors, thus earning my great gratitude. Air Vice-Marshal Professor Mason was also kind enough to cast an experienced, military eye over a draft of the paper and made a number of cogent and helpful comments. Mr Terry Soame kindly reviewed the case study on Alenia Marconi. The case studies and the whole work, however, remain my responsibility and any errors of fact or interpretation are mine.

Professors Charles Harvey and Julian Lowe, and Doctors Peter Taylor and Ken Russell gave me advice and encouragement which greatly improved the final work.

To my wife goes the martyr's crown for having had to live with me during the years occupied by the study.

ROBERT F. GRATTAN

The author and publishers thank the following for their permission to reproduce copyright material: Academy of Management for Tables 2.1 and 4.3; Alenia Marconi Systems for Table 3.3; Basil Blackwell Limited for Figure 3.2 and Tables 4.1 and 4.2; City University Business School for Figure 3.6; Elsevier Science for Figure 3.6; Emerald for Figures 4.3, 6.1 and 6.3; Her Majesty's Stationery Office for Figures 4.8, 4.9 and Table 4.7; International Thomson Business Press for Figure 4.2; MCB University Press for Figures 6.1 and 6.3; MIT Sloan Management Review for Figure 3.7; Pan Books for Figure 6.4; Pearson Technology Group for Figure 4.6; Prentice-Hall Inc. for Figure 6.2; Routledge for Figure 3.1; University of California for Table 6.2; John Wiley for Figures 4.4, 6.5 and Table 6.1. Every effort has been made to contact all the copyright-holders, but if any have been inadvertently omitted the publishers will be pleased to make the necessary arrangement at the earliest opportunity.

1
Introduction

1.1 The background

If it is legitimate for those in industry to use phrases like 'we have won the battle for industry leadership', 'we have successfully defended our market position', or 'we have made a killing on the stock market', there is a notional link suggested between military and business thinking. Both types of organisation are engaged in competition that threatens survival, physical in one case and commercial in the other. Both engage in cognitive activity, which seeks to identify a way of winning, and each defines this process as 'strategy'. Although the differences need to be acknowledged, there may well be parallels in the way that both these types of organisation reach the decision on their preferred course of action, and these processes are the subject of this study.

In a study of this nature, the choice of aims needs to be made between the normative and the merely descriptive. Should the study seek to say how strategy *should* be made or is it sufficient to investigate how it *is* made? Apart from the presumption of dictating to mature, experienced and talented strategists how they should pursue their craft, the evidence gathered here is more suitable for reporting, not prescribing. Nonetheless, the intention is to cast light upon a complex and esoteric human activity in the hope that a rising generation will be able to draw conclusions for themselves as to what strategy is and how it might, with profit, be made.

The present study grew out of the author's association with both the military and industry, during which periods the ideas from these areas of activity suggested a parallelism or, in some cases, convergence of underlying approaches to strategy. There is the possibility of similar parallels with the strategy process in the public sector, outside defence, but these will have to be considered by others.

The nature of the study

Some contend that the formulation of strategy is a rational, purposive activity, whilst others see strategy emerging over time in an unstructured way. Debate continues on whether the process is largely top-down or bottom-up in organisations. Many see strategy formulation as a 'political' process, which suggests that power and leadership may be significant factors. There remains the possibility that, although this study is being conducted from within a business school, there may be concepts, processes, techniques, and so on, which may be of value to the military. The underlying purpose of the study is to shed light on the strategy formulation process and to lead to greater understanding for the benefit of practitioners. Because the theoretical base of the strategy process will be seen to be more developed in management science, the approach will be to compare military practice with the view taken in business studies of strategy, its nature, models, paradigms, and so on. The study, being comparative in nature, permits widening the consideration of strategy to two different settings. The theories and paradigms from each area of study can be compared to reveal the fundamental ideas that drive an activity that is shown to have common roots.

Tranfield and Starkey (1998) drew attention to the concern over the pluralism – the profusion of theories and methodologies – in social sciences (and, thus, management studies). This diversity of opinion is reflected here in the debate on the nature of strategy and its various paradigms. For completeness, this study considers such issues as organisational behaviour, strategic leadership and the development of leaders, and the dilemma has been throughout one of comprehensiveness versus focus. In the terms used by Becher (1989), this work is 'rural': the broad territory has no sharp demarcation and there is a low people-to-problem ratio.

The research question

The advice given by Campbell, *et al.* (1982) was to study a topic that excites the researcher, is novel and has been discussed with as many colleagues or workers in the same field as possible. These criteria have been applied to this work, the aim of which is ... *to assess whether the strategy process in the business field also prevails in the military context, and if so, to focus attention on the areas of similarity and difference.* This, in itself, is not a question that can be simply answered, nor does it suggest research methodologies. If, however, this question is likened to a phylum in biology, it can be decomposed into 'species' that should point to an organisation of the research activity.

AIM	QUESTIONS	FACTORS
	What is the influence of organisation?	Size Power Politics
Assess whether the strategy process in the business field also prevails in the military context, and what are the areas of similarity and difference	What is the influence of leadership?	Training Experience Selecting
	What is the attitude to risk?	Entrepreneurship Luck
	What is the accepted underlying theory and practice?	Principles of war Appreciation method Military history Training Experience
	What is the influence of context?	Routine Crises Case studies

Figure 1.1   The research question as a phylum.

The supporting factors for the main question have been identified as: the influence of organisation and leadership, the attitudes to risk, the underlying theory and practice and the effects of context. Each of these can be further subdivided to yield the taxonomy shown in Figure 1.1. Another view is that these factors are drivers of the strategy process, which should be common, *mutatis mutandis*, to both military and business fields.

The hypotheses

The first hypothesis of this study is that 'strategy' is a concept that is used similarly in both business and the military. This can only be shown to be the case if the nature of strategy is first investigated and compared.

A second hypothesis is that the process by which strategy is devised is broadly comparable in each context. Demonstrating the truth or otherwise of this proposal is more complicated since there is no consensus in the business literature on how strategy is formulated. There is controversy on the underlying paradigms that influence the strategy process in business. The paradigms for military strategy are investigated and compared with the ideas in business.

A third hypothesis is that the strategy process is affected by contextual factors, particularly crisis, in a similar way in both business and the military.

Since the process of strategy formulation in the business field is the subject of continuing debate, the evidence here adduced is not likely to lead to the creation of new theories but may shed light upon the dialogue on this topic.

The nature of the question

Since much of this work is related to opinion and attitudes, the questions are not likely to be 'closed' in nature: that is, they are unlikely to have an unquestioned answer. Even consideration of 'what is the accepted underlying theory and practice?' is likely to have an equivocal answer. Although the question may be 'open', the research will search for where consensus exists and, alternatively, where divergences and controversies remain. Furthermore, the contexts and constraints that act upon the process of strategy formulation need investigation to form a view on their relative importance in the two fields considered, military and business. Above all, strategy process is a human activity, often undertaken by leaders, so leadership becomes a particular focus.

Limitations

Attempts have been made already to draw parallels between business and war (for example, James, 1984; Luecke, 1994) on a wider scale. Such texts sought to draw more extensive parallels with consideration of offence, defence, combat support, and so on, in both war and business. These may have proved useful to managers in particular circumstances, but often the similarities are overstretched and lacking in credibility. Galbraith, *et al.* (1996) shared this view and they commented on the general misapplication of military strategy literature to business. There is a significant difference between operations that can physically destroy the opposition and those that compete legitimately by methods short of death and destruction. Furthermore, these works have been primarily concerned with the *implementation* of strategy, rather than with its *formulation*. The present study is confined to the strategy formulation *process*, and does not seek wider parallels between the content and implementation of strategy in business and military practice.

Hofstede (1993) pointed out the influences of national culture upon the practice of management around the world and the same process can be assumed in military forces, all of whom are different in their approach and characteristics. It might be true that the strategy formulation in defence is similar in most countries, particularly those sharing common roots, but the assumption would have to be proved. The issue of national differences is not addressed in this thesis and the research is concentrated mainly on the strategy process in the military in Britain, and so the results are only valid for that area.

The approach

The methodology employed is described in detail in Chapter 2, but the study reviews the theory generated by successive academics in the field of business strategy. These theories are compared with the sparser material in the military field, where the emphasis has been on the *content* of the strategy, rather than how it is devised. 'Strategic studies' in the field of political science has an influence on military strategy and shows a preoccupation with considerations of 'grand' strategy, which, as will be discussed, sets the overall objectives and context for military action. Leadership is also influential in the strategy process and forms a theme that permeates this work, but the topic became so important that the final two chapters of this thesis are devoted to it.

Given, then, that the process of military strategy needs further research, the views of practitioners are the best evidence available, although deductions can also be made from case studies of actual campaigns. In certain cases, some military practitioners also have knowledge of operations at board level in commercial organisations and can offer their own comparison of the processes in the two fields. The general approach has been phenomenological in its design and relies upon the views of strategists in business and the military, and on case studies. This evidence, however, is compared with existing paradigms, theories and models in both fields described in the secondary evidence.

Strategy has to be seen in its historical context, as it is as much the outcome of what the organisation has become, its espoused values, its ethos, and so on, as the rational conclusions of a discussion as to the best way forward. Although some of this will be contained, in part, in anecdotes related in interview, the full richness of these influences are likely to emerge only in an extended case study. Four detailed case studies are provided to cover the temporal dimension of strategy formulation, two from each of the fields under study. Analysis of these data forms the basis of the final conclusions.

Implications

An implication of this comparative study is that the results are potentially of value to the two different fields under study, namely business and the military. The comparison will suggest areas where consideration can be given to adopting practices from the other field. For instance, the military insistence on clear and precise aims before considering strategy may cause a reconsideration of business practice. The intention, here, remains chiefly descriptive and analytical, not prescriptive.

1.2   What is strategy?

Introduction

Before a comparison can be made in answer to the research question, the meaning of the term 'strategy' must be shown to carry the same meaning in both the business and military fields.

Strategy is a construct that has evolved to signify an identifiable behaviour in humans. It is a term used in such diverse activities as war, business, sport and games. The idea is of great antiquity, and Isaiah, 14:27, attributed a strategy to God:

> The Lord of Hosts has sworn:
> In very truth, as I planned, so shall it be;
> as I designed, so shall it fall out:

Various descriptions and definitions of strategy are now presented, some of which take a process stance, that is, describing strategy by how it is done, and some a content view, that is, illustrating the nature by what results.

The military origins of strategy

The literature frequently reminds the reader that 'strategy' is derived from the Greek word for the 'art of the general', but this definition would seem to reveal more about the etymology than the meaning. What we can conclude, however, is that strategy has been a preoccupation of generals and statesmen for millennia. Cummings (1995) described the *strategoi* in Greek society of the fifth century BC who were the collective leadership responsible for decisions on behalf of the community and suggested that their roles were: to have vision, to articulate this vision effectively and to communicate it to the citizens for approval.

In the centuries immediately following the classical era, there is little evidence of formal thought on military strategy in the West, although tactics continued to develop slowly with the introduction of new weapons (for example, the longbow and body armour). Feudalism and chivalry were not conducive to strategic thought. If the *condottieri* in Italy had a strategy, it was to avoid casualties since horsemen were their principal assets.

Somewhat before Thucydides was writing *The Peloponnesian War* (about 400 BC) in Greece, Sun Tzu was producing his treatise on military strategy, *The Art of War*, (about 500–600 BC) in China. This remarkable document did not begin to influence the development of strategic thought in Western nations for many centuries, but still seems modern in many of its proposals to this day. For instance, Sun Tsu proposed that the most successful general was one that could win *before* the fighting had to start (echoes of deterrence theories); superior manpower, position, technology and so on would prevail (competitive advantage and the resource-based view); avoid what is strong, like water avoids high places (the indirect approach).

Niccolò Machiavelli conducted an analysis of the political and military situation in the sixteenth century AD and, with some perception, observed:

> Many are now of the opinion that no two things are more discordant and incongruous than a civil and military life. But if we consider the nature of government, we shall find a very strict and intimate relation betwixt these two conditions; and that they are not only compatible and consistent with each other, but necessarily connected and united together. (*Dell' arte della guerra* (1519–1520) in Gilbert, 1967, p. 3)

The author of *Il Principe* (1513) understood well the relationship between politics and war, and foreshadowed the *levée en masse* of the French Revolution with proposals for conscription. In practice, the growth of princely power and wealth precluded the early use of such democratic methods.

In the seventeenth century, the monarch was seen as ruling by divine right and as being the personification of the nation state: 'people commonly regarded any act of a monarch as just, no matter how capricious and arbitrary it may seem to contemporary observers. The king can do no wrong – including launching aggressive wars – if his authority derives from God's will' (Holsti, 1991, p. 55). Although by the end of the eighteenth century revolutionary movements, particularly in France, altered the nature of warfare by introducing both a nationalistic and ideological emphasis, war was still seen as an option open to the national leader in pursuit of his aims. This doctrine was brilliantly formalised into theory by Carl von Clausewitz, who produced the leading modern treatise on strategy, *Vom Kriege*.

From this brief overview, it is evident that, from the earliest days of history, rulers and generals have sought advantage through the development of strategies.

Grand strategy

The head of state needed to ensure the primacy of his nation or, at least, minimise the affects of aggressive moves by competitors. This strategic activity was, and often still is, conducted on a worldwide stage, will affect (and even cost) the lives of millions of people, will involve vast sums of money, and will influence the progress of human history. It is not surprising, therefore, that such activity is known as 'grand strategy'. It is considered further in Chapter 3.

Strategy and tactics

Below this level of national strategy, there are subordinate levels which usually qualify for the term 'strategy'. Thus, as an example, grand strategy determines the necessity for the conquest of India, but the way this aim is achieved will also require consideration of means, a method and a plan. So the process is applied at successively lower levels, but at some time the change from strategy to tactics will occur. The battalion commander faced with occupying a hill held by the enemy will have to evolve his plan which he may term his 'strategy' but which the corps commander would regard as 'tactics'. JWP 0–01 (Portillo, 1997) suggested that there is a Grand Strategic level with successively subordinate levels named Military Strategy, Operational and Tactical. Clausewitz provided the following definition:

> According to our classification, therefore, tactics *is the theory of the use of military forces in combat*. Strategy *is the theory of the use of combats for the object of the War*. (Rapaport, 1968, p. 173; italics in the original)

In a sense, though, the boundary may be arbitrary and lie in the eye of the beholder. If strategic thinking is brought to bear on a tactical problem, does it matter? A possible danger, though, is that, in worrying about wider issues, the proper operational duties are overlooked.

Possible military/business strategy differences

Sullivan and Harper (1996, pp. xviii–xix) tried to link military and business strategic thought. They identified three 'myths' which question the relevance of army (in this case, US Army) experience to the problems of business. They provide a military *apologia*:

MYTH NUMBER 1: 'IN THE MILITARY, GETTING RESULTS IS AS EASY AS GIVING ORDERS. IT'S NOT THAT SIMPLE IN CIVILIAN LIFE'

We would say that getting results is as easy (or as difficult) as giving the *right* orders, whether in the military or in business. Making the right decision and building a team to execute the decision is a challenge for a leader. Military leaders do have some tools business leaders do not have and vice versa – their environments are obviously not the same. But in both spheres, the leader must act through people.

MYTH NUMBER 2: 'AS A BUSINESSPERSON, I HAVE TO MAKE A PROFIT. IN THE MILITARY, YOU DON'T FACE THAT PRESSURE'
It is true that we in the military do not have to face the same kind of bottom line pressures that business face. But in the final analysis, the pressure that all of our organizations face is pressure to perform, to succeed and to win . . . in today's world, with political demands for accountability and efficiency reaching deep into every area of government, including the military, the Army has been forced to reduce its costs and improve its productivity as surely as any private enterprise – and under as much scrutiny.

MYTH NUMBER 3: 'IN BUSINESS, I HAVE TO STRUGGLE AND GET AND KEEP CUSTOMERS, BUT THE MILITARY IS A PUBLIC INSTITUTION – YOU DON'T HAVE TO GO OUT AND FIND CUSTOMERS'
Certainly, it is true that in the sense that America's citizens are our customers, we are in no danger of losing them. The danger is in failing them on the battlefield. In that sense, competition is at the core of the Army's being . . .

These are important justifications for a convergence of military and business thinking (to the profit of both) on matters strategic, and these are revisited throughout the thesis.

The impermanence of strategy

The military recognise that, at the level of grand strategy, victory is a transient state: a milepost in a long journey. As the Romans found, every time they extended their empire's boundaries through military victories, fresh conflict occurred at the new frontier. Thus as Magee (1998, p. 7) had it: 'Good strategy does not recognize the concept of victory.'

Strategy, then, is seen as the way to gain advantage in the current circumstances and as far ahead as it possible to look, but retaining the expectation that adjustments may have to be made. Businessmen would certainly recognise this problem.

The origins of strategy in business

Business interest in strategy only started in earnest in the 1960s, although there are some earlier allusions. In this period the military strategists were preoccupied with the problems of nuclear war and were applying game theory, probability theories and 'rational' methods in general to decide how to win (or, at least, to lose with minimum regret). Whether there are substantive parallels between the strategy process in the military and business is the research focus of the study, but, in its evolution, the concept of strategy has been derived from military origins, and has been later adopted by the business world. The various theories of business strategy are discussed in Chapter 3 but the argument is conducted below at the level of definitions in order to make comparisons.

Defining strategy

Definitions of strategy are many, and each can be placed in its temporal and theoretical context. Thus, consider:

- Strategy has been defined as '*the employment of the battle as the means towards attainment of the object of the War*' (Clausewitz in Rapaport, 1968, p. 241; italics in the original).
- Napoleon defined strategy as 'the art of making use of time and space' (in Jablonsky, 1993, p. 11).
- 'Strategy . . . is the art of distributing and applying military means to fulfil ends of policy' (Liddell-Hart in Freedman, 1981, p. xvii).
- 'Strategy is the pattern of objectives, purposes or goals and major policies and plans for achieving these goals, stated in such a way as to define what business the company is in or is to be in and the kind of company it is or is to be' (Hofer and Schendel, 1978, p. 16).
- 'Let's start by assuming that strategy actually embraces all the critical activities of the firm. Let's also hypothesize that strategy provides a sense of unity, direction and purpose, as well as facilitating the necessary changes induced by a firm's environment' (Hax in de Wit and Meyer, 1994, p. 9).
- 'Strategy is the creation of a unique and valuable position, involving a different set of activities. If there were only one ideal position, there would be no need for strategy' (Porter, 1996, p. 68).

Strategy can be seen, at its simplest, as 'the way to win', so winners must have a strategy, whether they acknowledge the need or not. The concept of strategy in the business and military fields appears to be defined in much the same way.

The nature of strategy

The view taken of the nature of strategy is very much influenced by the paradigm adopted by an author (of which more in subsequent chapters) and the theoretical position he or she has adopted. The following paragraphs illustrate the wide variation of opinions that have been advanced on the essential nature of strategy.

Five definitions of strategy

Mintzberg (1987b) maintained that a single definition can not capture fully the richness that is strategy. He offered five definitions, which describe strategy as being, severally: plan, ploy, pattern, position, and perspective.

- 'Plan' recognises that a common view is that strategy is a consciously intended course of action which is made in advance of the action and is purposeful.
- 'Ploy' suggests that strategy can be a manoeuvre intended to outwit or confuse the opposition.
- 'Pattern' identifies a consistency in strategic behaviour, whether or not intended, that over time becomes recognisable or even predictable.
- 'Position' means that strategy locates an organisation in an environment and is a mediating or matching force between an organisation and the outside world.
- 'Perspective' proposes that strategy is the way an organisation perceives the world, that is, its *Weltanschauung*. Strategy is seen here as an abstract concept, which shapes the behaviour of the parties involved.

The military would have no disagreement with these definitions, even with 'pattern' which might be seen to be undesirable since predictability of behaviour is not prized in war. Plans are deemed necessary for military operations, ploys that surprise the enemy are sought, position (in a geographical sense) is a primary concern of generals, and perspective arises from the staff system and their training. One can argue, however, that the plan is not the strategy, but the method for its implementation.

Strategy as competition

Strategy is needed to tackle opposition or competition. Strategies may be needed in non-competitive situations, but this use is not considered here. If, however, the intention of an organisation or individual is to win, to succeed, to do better than the rest, or whatever the objective is, then a way must be found to reach that objective. Thus Michael Porter (1980) constructed a whole theory around what is the way to beat the rest. He recommended that the first choice be of the game (industry, business, and so on) to be in because the 'attractiveness' (that is, the potential for profit) of the game determines and limits the success that is possible. Within that industry, the firm selects a strategy that optimises their position, given an understanding of the five forces acting upon them which determine industry attractiveness, and modifies to their own advantage, wherever possible, the forces acting upon them. These five forces were: New Entrants, Substitute Products, the Power of Suppliers, the Power of Buyers and Industry Competition. Thus, one can only do as well as the industry setting will allow, but the firm's task is to outdo others within those limitations. Similarly, the approach to military strategy is one of finding the winning formula in the struggle to compete against the aims and will of the opposing general.

Strategy as mission/vision

Schoemaker (1992) defined strategic vision as 'the shared understanding of what the firm should be and how it must change'. Mission, however, is defined by Campbell and Yeung (1991, p. 12) as: 'cultural glue consist(ing) of strong norms and values that influence the way in which people behave, how they work together, and how they pursue the goals of the organization'.

Campbell and Yeung went on to expand this into four elements – Purpose, Values, Behaviour Standards and Strategy (the so-called Ashridge Model). Although writers in this field concede that there are no agreed definitions of vision and mission, they assert that a clear understanding of the company's aspirations has to infuse the whole organisation and be accepted by everyone as the guide to their actions. On the other hand, the vision/mission cannot be seen to be a *strategy* as such, but as a means of implementation and of coordination of the efforts of the company, perhaps in the formulation of strategy itself.

In the military, mission is a term which is used extensively, and vision in strategists is highly prized. The military spend much time and effort in the definition of the aim of their operations, which is seen to be central to the achievement of success.

Strategy as order out of chaos

Recent discoveries about the complex behaviour of dynamic systems can be applied to human organisations. Implications of this connection are that: the specific long-term future is unknowable; nevertheless, the instability caused by chaos is bounded; self-organisation can generate a new order from chaos; and chaos is a fundamental property of non-linear feedback systems, including organisations. It follows that strategy can be seen as an attempt to counteract this systems behaviour and to create order out of chaos. Strategic thought has to take account of the unknowability of the long-term future and of the ability of organisations to generate a new order, provided that the structure permits the members to act strategically.

Again, chaos is well-known to generals and Liddell-Hart frequently referred to the confusing effect of the 'fog of war'. The starting conditions of a conflict may quickly deteriorate and lead to a loss of control, especially since many combatants are making individual decisions, all of which may have a chaotic effect on the war. Air Vice-Marshal Professor A.R. Mason recalled the views of Professor Sir Michael Howard to the effect that 'all previous plans have stood up for the first 48 hours, and that's it' (Interview, 14 November 2000). Military strategy, in part, seeks to limit the effects of chaos by making subordinate commanders autonomous within the bounds set by the intentions of the commander.

In this view of the nature of strategy, it is reasonable to characterise the activity as being the creation of meaning. The humans caught up in events use what can be deemed to be facts to try to make sense of and impose some order on a highly complex situation. Different humans may construct different meanings from the same facts. The construction of meaning can be done collectively by a group sharing their perceptions, or individually as in the 'great man' model of leadership.

Strategy as decision

Strategy is the choice, from many available options, of a way of succeeding. If there were no choice, that is, there was only one possible course of action, the resulting decision could not be seen as a 'strategy' but as a necessity. If, then, strategy is choice, the process must involve a decision, hence good strategies result from good choices, and bad ones result from poor choices. The decision needs to be rational, that is, conferring maximum advantage to the decision-makers, but without total, accurate knowledge of all the factors and influences, the rationality must be bounded. Part of this rationalisation is, as introduced in the previous paragraph, the creation of meaning and the definition of the nature of the problem. A solution cannot be effective if it sets out to solve the wrong problem. If the rationality is bounded by incomplete information, there must be a risk associated with the final choice.

The strategy, then, is influenced by the decision-maker's attitude to risk. Some will not move until there is as much certainty as is possible, whereas others will use their intuition to make 'inspired' (and, hence, risky) decisions.

Military officers are trained from the early stages of their careers to make decisions and the uncertainty of the future and knowledge of the risks are stressed as important factors. Risky plans are usually avoided.

Three-dimensional views

Pettigrew (1988) provided a further insight into the nature of strategy. He suggested that there are three, equally important, elements of strategy – content, context and process. De Wit and Meyer (1994) suggested that these three perspectives could be likened to a box's length, width and height, which analogy emphasises the three-dimensional nature of strategy. If the three are dimensions of the one entity, it follows that it is unlikely that one can be studied without consideration of the remaining two. Thus the context, for instance, the type and size of organisation, whether there is a crisis, and so on, will affect not only the measures adopted but also how the solution is actually determined. Clausewitz (Howard and Paret, 1976, p. 89) also used a three-dimensional concept in military strategy where the elements of 'this remarkable trinity' are the government, the military and the people. Although taking a different perspective from Pettigrew, one of Clausewitz's dimensions similarly cannot be taken in isolation from the others.

Multi-level

A further segmentation is to view strategy as being dependent on where it is being devised. Thus:

- *Corporate Strategy* determines which business, or businesses, the firm will be in.
- *Business Strategy* determines how the firm will compete in that chosen business or businesses.
- *Functional Strategy* determines how elements such as marketing, finance, and so on, will contribute to the achievement of business and corporate strategies.

Thus Grant (1997) suggested that corporate strategy is decided at head office, business strategy at divisional offices, and functional strategies within the divisions. Each subordinate strategy has to be nested within the next superior strategy in this hierarchy, but this necessity raises issues of organisation, communication and power.

Grand strategy is comparable to corporate strategy in that it determines the nature of conflicts that are likely. Military strategy is concerned with the ways and means to achieve grand strategy, and to provide the necessary guidance to 'functional' commanders of land, sea and air forces.

Holistic

At whichever level the strategy is formulated, its nature is to be holistic. Strategy in its fully developed state is seen in the literature as having to take account of:

1 Goals and objectives
2 Finance (capital formation, cost of capital, cash flows)
3 The environment (political, economic, sociological, technological)
4 The capabilities of the organisation (resources, knowledge, capabilities)
5 The interests of stakeholders (shareholders, leaders, managers, work-force, customers)
6 The nature of the organisation (multidivisional, entrepreneurial)
7 The culture of the organisation (for example, 'The Recipe' (Johnson and Scholes, 1997))
8 Ethics

To this list might be added the issue of whether the company is in crisis or not. If the requirement is to build upon and exploit previous success, the process of formulation is likely to be more measured and deliberate, whereas if the company is facing a crisis, which may be threatening its very existence, deciding on the strategy will be urgent and controversial and may necessitate a change of direction.

Military strategy is formulated in peacetime as well as while at war, and its holistic nature and the components listed above are all familiar to Ministries of Defence as well as to commanders. The formulation of peacetime strategy in the British Ministry of Defence is developed as a case study later in Chapter 4.

Theory of the firm

The view taken of the nature of strategy will be affected by one's view of the nature of the firm. Thus, an economist will have a mental model of the company as acting rationally to maximise its wealth (Pappas and

Brigham, 1979). On the other hand, Cyert and March (1963) proposed a behavioural view of the firm in which individuals pursued different goals and the conflict thus formed was only partially resolved. Furthermore, they saw rationality in the company as existing at the local, sub-unit level where the goals and problems are limited and the decision-makers avoid uncertainty by short-term horizons and negotiated environments. Organisations use acceptable-level goals and select the first alternative they see which meets those goals. The organisations make problemistic searches: that is, activity occurs only when stimulated by a problem and is directed towards finding a solution to that problem. This work can also be seen in the context of Simon's (1965) observations that managers do not maximise, but select aspiration levels which are seen to be attainable, characterised as the concept of bounded rationality, and his conclusion that man accepts the first satisfactory course of action: he 'satisfices' rather than maximises. It should be noted that these models only apply to large oligopolistic firms that face very little competitive market pressure. The economic model of the firm is not a concept that equates easily to military organisations but the behavioural model has applicability in both fields.

Resource-capability-based strategy

If strategy is as rational a choice as is possible, one of the constraints will be the resources available to the organisation. In this, one would hope that complete information is available but 'resources' can contain a conceptual, tacit element, such as the intellectual capability of the staff and their motivation, which is open to interpretation and, therefore, doubt. Stalk *et al.* (1992) took the view that competition is essentially based upon capabilities. Resources are, broadly, what the firm possesses and capabilities are what it can do. Prahalad and Hamel (1990) used a similar concept, the core competence of a firm, and advanced three tests to identify these competencies. The first test is whether a core competence provides potential access to a wide variety of markets; second, a core competence should make a significant contribution to the perceived customer benefits of the end product; and, finally, a core competence should be difficult for competitors to imitate. Strategic thinking from this perspective is based upon what a company is and can do but this thinking is also extended to include what the company can become through organisational learning.

The military organisation is also particularly suited to the resource-based view and this idea is developed later.

Strategy as a language game

Eccles and Nohria (1992) posited the view that managers live in a rhetorical world where language is used persuasively. They went on:

> Strategy should not be visualized as a cognitive activity that takes place at the upper levels of management and results in ingenious forward-looking plans for taking action that are in turn implemented at lower levels of organization with the hope of gaining a huge competitive advantage. Strategy is instead a complex system of acting and talking, a system that occasionally manifests itself in rational designs but more typically has to do with the entire network of conversations that exists within a firm – and with the way action is continually pursued through this network. (p. 60)

Strategy is seen to be an outcome of organisational interaction in which language is the mode of communication, but which can influence the thought patterns of others. The strategist is, therefore, a rhetorician and a manipulator. Although military strategy is often seen as emanating from the mind of the commander, there is in reality an organisational dimension to the strategy process and the description of it as a language game is not inappropriate.

Strategy as dialectic

Hampden-Turner (1990) took the view that strategy is the resolution of dilemmas, which can be likened to a dialectic process of thesis, antithesis and synthesis. This idea is developed in de Wit and Meyer (1994) where strategy was seen as coming to terms with opposites and resolving the conflict in order to find a way to success. These ideas are revisited in the discussion of process and decision in Chapter 3, where the similarities to military practice are considered.

Pennings's categories

Pennings (1985, p. 2) suggested that strategy has acquired three meanings:

1   It is a statement of intent that constrains or directs subsequent activities (*explicit* strategy)
2   It is an action of major impact that constrains or directs subsequent activities (*implicit* strategy)
3   It is a 'rationalization' or social construction that gives meaning to prior activities (*rationalized* strategy).

Strategy can be made explicit in the form of a plan or document, whereas implicit strategy requires examination of the history of the company to detect trends and patterns of behaviour. The 'rationalised' strategy suggests that there is no objective strategy but an understanding held in the minds of the organisation's members, and is recognised through myths, ceremonies and rituals. Pennings acknowledged the similarity of this taxonomy to the linear/rational, adaptive and interpretive [*sic*] models of Chaffee (1985) and the Rational Actor, Organisational and Political models of Allison (1971). In contrast to this view, the military would always wish to make their strategy explicit as a guide to all concerned. Nonetheless, the ethos of the services, their traditions and their operational doctrine all make for constraints on strategic choice.

Arthur Lykke

Colonel (Ret'd) Arthur Lykke of the US Army taught at the US Army War College and he averred that:

> strategy at any level consists of ends or objectives, ways or concepts, and means or resources . . . they [his students] can also appreciate the art of mixing ends, ways and means, using for each element the part subjective, part objective criteria of suitability, feasibility and applicability – the essence of strategic calculation. (in Jablonsky, 1993, p. 3)

Lykke's analysis of strategy works equally well in the business sphere as in the military.

Statecraft

Strategic studies, which is concerned with geopolitics and the efforts of nations to gain advantage over others, uses the concept of statecraft to describe the mindset of statesmen. Statesmen (and this term is taken to mean both male and female) are concerned to maximise the power and influence of their nation and, if it is true that 'trade follows the flag', then this includes economic advantages. Ultimately, it may become necessary to defend one's interests or to exert pressure to advance one's cause, and this has been the role of the military. Clausewitz (in Rapaport 1968, p. 119) recognised this process in his dictum 'War is a mere continuation of policy by other means', which he subsequently revised to the more significant, 'War is a continuation of politics with the addition of other means' (as pointed out by Professor Mason, Interview, 14 November 2000). Thus, statesmen determine the nation's objectives, its desired place in the world, which are analogous to the firm's mission or vision. This assessment is conditioned both by the environment and the nation's assets or resources. A risk assessment is necessary as nations often overplay their hands deliberately as a ploy (Hitler in 1938–9 and Saddam Hussein in 1990–1). The national strategy is, then, the outcome of a pragmatic formulation process, which seeks to take account of all the relevant factors, and to bring to it a subtlety and realism that Machiavelli would recognise. The combination of pragmatism, analytical skill, common sense and cunning are all valuable attributes of strategists in both business and military endeavours and enable them to hold in their minds the necessary holistic view. An example to illustrate a possible application of this process is the US policy of Lend–Lease adopted in 1940.

This example from the world of diplomacy looks at the strategic decision by the US government to provide war equipment to Britain under Lend–Lease arrangements. An object of US foreign policy in the late 1930s and early 1940s was to increase the power of their country, which necessitated a decline in the power and influence of the British Empire. The internal mood of the country, however, was for isolation from involvement in the power politics of the outside world. When the Second World War began, therefore, it was natural for the USA not to become involved on both of the above accounts. However, there was little point in exchanging a German empire for a British one and the statesmen in the USA saw their country's involvement as becoming inevitable in the longer term. The US government decided to accede to Britain's request for war *matériel* in the Lend–Lease programme. Strategically, this move met many of the USA's objectives:

- Selling the arms ate into Britain's financial reserves, thus weakening the Empire in the longer term.
- The supply of aircraft and ships enabled the USA to establish, or at least further develop, these industries which were important to the country's future economy and its war capability.
- The alliance gave the USA access to British technical developments such as anti-submarine warfare, radar and the jet turbine engine.
- The USA did not have to declare war (and thus anger its isolationists) in order to pursue its foreign policy aims in Europe.

The strategy was admirable.

If this idea of statecraft were to be applied to business strategy, the firm would be regarded as a nation state in a world of nation states each of which was trying to achieve competitive advantage. The firm would form alliances and coalitions, temporary or long-lasting, to further its aims. Its 'territory' would be the market that it is in (or seeks to invade) and they may have to protect themselves by making moves into the territory of others. The firm's strategists, whilst assembling as much 'intelligence' as they could, would acknowledge that they were always going to be less than completely informed, and some judgements would have to be made on the basis of their intuition and experience. Success is likely to be based upon some unique advantage the firm has or exploitation of some opportunity in the outside world. The statesman knows that luck plays a part in short-term success, but superior resources, coupled with insightful judgements, are the keys to long-term advantage. Although contextual factors, such as location, resources, unique skills and knowledge, are important, the path to sustainable competitive advantage is reached through superior statecraft, probably the only inimitable resource.

The following illustration, Nike, can be seen through the statecraft lens, which provides a more subtle interpretation of the events in that company than through using other business strategy ideas.

The circumstances of the Nike Corporation are described in the Harvard Business School cases 'Nike A' and 'Nike B'. In 1983, Phil Knights, the founder of the company, handed over short-term control of the company to Bob Woodell, whilst retaining responsibility for the longer term. The company was in a relatively poor state and it seemed it would get worse. After a short time, Knights returned to the company (like a *deus ex machina*) and took drastic action to reestablish Nike's fortunes.

It can be argued that Knights's action in handing his friend Woodell a poisoned chalice was a 'statecraft' move. If he had taken drastic action immediately, he would have attracted considerable criticism that would have adversely affected his long-term position and capabilities as a strategic leader. Allowing the company situation to deteriorate a little more enabled Knights to return as a saviour and the company employees would have, by then, realised the need for drastic action and would have accepted draconian measures.

The strategy enabled Knights to control the company effectively in the longer term, thus ensuring its survival at the cost of sacrificing his friend.

A possible objection

An objection to the concept of statecraft may be raised on the grounds that it is merely a restating of the holistic or the dictatorial approaches, whereas it is more likely that the nation is ruled by an oligarchy which debates the issues of grand strategy. Furthermore, the debate is quite open (at least in democracies) and a number of sections of society wield influence. The press, the churches, the political parties and academe are examples of bodies that contribute to the discussion. In the debates on nuclear strategy all of these contributed, and Kahn was a physicist, Schelling an economist and Kissinger a historian (Baylis *et al.*, 1975) so the input is interdisciplinary. Allison (1971) suggested that his Governmental Politics model, where decisions are the results of bargaining, is nearer the truth than his Rational Actor model (arguably introduced as a 'straw man'). In business, too, the influence of the press, the churches, political parties and academe provide comment on strategies for particular industries. The climate thus created may be normative. The constraints are largely ideational (and probably ethical) but are effective nonetheless. Not everyone, though, applauds the intervention of external strategists in the military field. General Meyer (1991, p. 156), in commenting on the growth of strategic leaders after the Second World War, asserted:

> The ranks of civilian–military strategists grew. They were very talented and very capable in understanding strategy, but they did not have their feet firmly planted in the mud, understanding what took place in the organization about which they were speaking.

(Meyer was reinforcing a point made earlier in his address, that strategists between the wars were technically knowledgeable about their profession.)

The statecraft mindset, however, does not imply a single decision-maker although the dictator model remains a special case in strategy formulation. Rather, the term is taken here to imply a mindset that can encompass the totality of the strategic issues and can form judgements in a disinterested, objective way. The issue of who takes the final decision is situation-dependent and concerns issues of leadership, but each of the participants in the decision can adopt the statecraft mindset. The greatest objection to the concept is that it demands too much of humans, who are almost inevitably doomed to partiality by their nature and limited cognitive ability.

Conclusion

This study investigates the process of strategy formulation by comparing business and military practice. Care has to be taken because war and business competition have different limits in permitted behaviour, but both are a struggle with opponents who may threaten the very existence of the organisation. Strategy itself has been variously defined but, at its most fundamental, signifies a means of achieving one's own aims whilst frustrating those of the opposition. In both of the fields addressed in this study, the complexity of, and interrelation within, the strategy process creates problems for the human mind, which, for all its power, has limitations. Strategy process involves the deriving of meaning from complexity, and this activity may be done collectively or individually. It is concluded that, since the business and military fields use the term 'strategy' in a similar way, a comparison is not invalidated. Since the formulation of strategy requires a broad vision and pragmatism in reaching the final decision, a comparison has been suggested with the thinking required to reach statesman-like conclusions that are rich in meaning and subtle. The search for parallels will be conducted in later chapters but the next chapter considers the sources and methods employed in constructing this thesis.

2
Sources and Methods

2.1 Introduction

The means by which the research question is answered must be related to the nature of the subject and the sources of the evidence used. This chapter will describe and justify the research methods chosen and the sources and treatment of data used for this work. In the chapter, the nature of the subject and sources and the choice of methodology are debated.

2.2 The research aims and scope

The aim of the research is *to assess whether the strategy process in the business field also prevails in the military context, and, if so, to focus attention on the areas of similarity and difference.*

This question cannot be answered simply but, if it is likened to a phylum in biology (see Chapter 1), it can be decomposed into 'species' that should point the way to organising the study. The supporting factors are seen to be: the influence of the organisation, leadership, theory and practice, and the effects of context.

Comparison can only be valid if the concepts of strategy and its formulation are sufficiently similar in both fields. Evidence was produced in Chapter 1 to support the view that such a comparison can properly be made. Consideration of the nature of strategy in Chapter 3 leads to a comparison of the paradigms of strategy, as a part of the search for a common ancestry and conceptual underpinning. Strategy can be shown to have developed its own language, which is revealing of its nature, and a comparison of this attribute in both fields is also made in Chapter 3. Chapter 4 focuses in more detail on the actual process of strategy formulation and explores the emerging description of strategy as being decision. Since leadership is a core topic in this consideration of strategy process, Chapter 5 is devoted to a consideration of the evidence and to the concept of strategic leadership, whilst Chapter 6 considers the characteristics of the leaders themselves. Chapter 7 goes on to consider how strategic leaders are developed in both the military and the business fields. The literature on military strategy is predominantly concerned with the *content* of the strategy, with less emphasis on the *process* used, so some conclusions from the historical evidence are inferential.

'Processes are embedded in contexts and can only be studied as such' (Pettigrew, 1992a, p. 9). This study is a comparison of strategy *process* in two different contexts, military and business. The *content* of the resulting strategies is of peripheral interest since the nature of war and the nature of business are sufficiently different as to require markedly divergent intentions and plans. Death and destruction are not legitimate activities for companies. Furthermore, the implementation of a selected strategy is taken here to be an operational matter, and thus outside the scope of this study.

Inherent in the research aim is the hypothesis that there *are* similarities, although proving the null hypothesis would still be a useful outcome. The argument goes that, if the concept of strategy in the military and business is comparable, one would expect that some similarities of process exist.

2.3   The nature of the subject

Strategy formulation is an intellectual process which results in a decision. This activity is often described as comprising several stages:

$$\text{Analysis} \quad \longrightarrow \quad \text{Choice} \quad \longrightarrow \quad \text{Implementation}$$

In addition, this sequence has been observed to be recursive, with or without the further inclusion of gap analysis as a trigger for another round. Whereas analysis and choice are likely to be comparable in the military and business fields, implementation is likely to be quite different in each context, so this latter step is deemed to be outside the scope of this study.

The strategist believes that he or she is being rational in the interpretation of facts, but a group or organisation, whose individual perceptions of reality may differ, often influences the strategy process, so that any consensus has to be socially constructed. There can be little doubt that a competing firm or opposing army exists, but the significance of the nature of the competition is open to interpretation, and this process can be approached rationally, heuristically or intuitively. The fact that the wrong strategy can be, and often is, chosen suggests that the choice process is neither algorithmic nor wholly rational. There would appear, therefore, to be an element of intuition or common sense which is applied in some strategy formulation situations. Thus the chosen study methods must be capable of shedding some light on which method was employed, and must yield valid, trustworthy conclusions.

2.4   Process

The word 'process' is derived from the Latin *processus* – a going forth, advance, course, progress – and is further defined in the *Chambers Twentieth Century Dictionary* as 'a sequence of operations or changes undergone'. Each definition is associated with a passage of time, and so it is necessary to study process over time, or longitudinally. Further, the context may affect the process – for instance, whether the organisation is in crisis or not – and so a comparison of approaches to strategy formulation can only be made where conditions are broadly the same.

This is the challenge posed by the research question. The complexity of the subject, however, leads to a further level of challenge: by which method is a valid answer to be found?

2.5   The importance of methodology

Sekaran (1992, p. 4) describes research as 'A systematic and organised effort to investigate a specific problem that needs a solution'. If research is indeed to be 'systematic and organised' then a clear plan and an appropriate set of research methods will be required. Kaplan (1964, p. 18) defined methodology as 'the study – the description, the explanation, and the justification – of methods, not the methods themselves'. Taken literally, methodology means the science of (or the study of) methods. In more general terms Bogdan and Taylor (1975) and Bulmer (1984) defined methodology as the way in which research is conducted to answer the research question while Sekaran (1992, p. 5) described research methods as 'the ways in which research studies are designed and the procedures by which data are analysed'. Hindess (1977, p. 5) linked the choice of methods to the validity of the results by arguing that: 'methodology lays down the procedures to be used in the generation or in the testing of propositions by those who wish to obtain valid knowledge. Scientific knowledge is thought to be valid only if its production conforms to the prescribed procedures.'

In this approach, knowledge is only valid if it has been obtained in accordance with the 'correct' procedures. Whilst scholars disagree as to which procedures can be considered appropriate, it is evident that the choice of methods is a highly important consideration in any research project.

2.6   Epistemology

For something to be acknowledged as 'known' generally requires some element of proof or supporting evidence. Burrell and Morgan (1979) concluded that each of us adopts a paradigm that determines what we will accept as valid evidence of knowledge. They went on to suggest that only one paradigm is acceptable, and incommensurability prevents acceptance of alternative views from different segments of their matrix, the dimensions of which are Subjective/Objective and the Sociology of Radical Change/Sociology of Regulation, which yielded four paradigms.

An alternative view is propounded here which suggests that the validity of the evidence is related to the nature of the phenomenon under scrutiny. Thus, the sniper's bullet is a hard fact whose existence might be denied, but whose effect is unavoidable and objectively observable. The motive of the sniper, however, which might be hatred, patriotism, pride in marksmanship, sense of duty, or compulsion is more difficult to determine other than subjectively. Even the sniper may not be able to untangle his emotions, self-justifications and thoughts, and one is left with the feeling that a single objective truth is unlikely. The two subjects, that is, the nature of sniping and the motivation of snipers, have a different nature, and it would seem logical that they are studied in different ways.

Jesus is reported (Mark 12:17) to have said 'Render to Caesar the things that are Caesar's, and to God the things that are God's', and perhaps the same philosophy pertains in considering epistemology. Such a theory would have us use the method appropriate to what was being studied, acknowledging that some knowledge can be gained objectively whilst other knowledge is subjective in its nature. A limitation on objective knowledge presented as physical laws is that one can only truly aver that the formulae have been shown to apply, *so far*, and it is not impossible that they will not always be true. But, until proved otherwise, these laws are a satisfactory explanation of the world we observe. On the other hand, although we might form a view of the likely motivation of the sniper instanced above, it would be impossible on the basis of that evidence alone to draw generalised statements about snipers' mind-states.

If enough evidence could be gathered from a number of snipers, then a working generalisation might be justified, but how many interviews is enough, and can one be sure that the interviewee is telling the truth?

The philosopher Locke's views were similar to the above stance. He propounded a dualist doctrine of primary and secondary qualities, in which the first were inseparable from the body, such as solidity, mass, and motion. The second quality could only be determined by the percipient. Thus the weight of an apple could be determined by a simple experiment, but the taste of the apple (and even its colour) was determined only by the percipient, who could not accurately share his or her views with another. Russell (1961) stated that Locke's dualism has been out of date since Berkeley and the advent of quantum physics, but the arguments are commonsensical and, perhaps, acceptable for a more prosaic study such as the present one.

Thorngate's (1976, p. 406) impostulate [*sic*], 'It is impossible for a theory of social behaviour to be simultaneously general, simple or parsimonious, and accurate', presents a problem. The research for this thesis is undoubtedly context-dependent, so how can generalities be derived that are not hedged about with lots of 'it depends'? The whole study is about comparing two sets of strategy process in two different contexts, the military and business. Care has been taken to identify similar circumstances (for instance, organisation structure, crisis or not) in making comparisons, but many differences, such as social milieu and military training, remain. Thorngate acknowledged the pessimism of his impostulate and went on to suggest that the 'insightful spectator will likely have more to offer than the plodding empiricist' (1976, p. 408) because, in studies of social behaviour, the accuracy of results plotted against effort is asymptotic. For this work, the dangers are acknowledged, but are taken to be insufficiently serious as to undermine the conclusions, provided context dependencies are properly identified.

Kahn (1960, p. ix) wrestled with the problem of 'quantitative or qualitative' research: 'Some people appear to be very suspicious of calculations – and correctly so. I have written extensively elsewhere on how quantitative analyses can lead either wittingly or unwittingly to error, but that does not mean that nonquantitative analyses are any more misleading.' He concluded that we should use numbers, but recognise that these give the *appearance* of great certainty but the effect has to be softened by the use of the conditional in text.

Easterby-Smith *et al.* (1991) suggested that there are two traditional approaches to social research methodology: phenomenology (or social constructionism) on the one hand and positivism on the other. Positivism proposes that the world exists externally, and that its properties can and should be measured objectively as proposed by Auguste Comte (1798–1857). Positivists, the product of the Enlightenment, use the empirical methods of the natural sciences. Quantitative methods are then used on the mass of assembled data to extract conclusions, which will validate or reject the hypotheses. The evidence is held to be incontrovertible because it is comprised of measured, observed facts that will remain, even when the observer has left the scene.

On the other hand, phenomenology holds that reality is socially constructed (that is, a particular group of people come to an agreement on the meaning of what they all experience), so the observer is part of the experiment. This approach has been attributed to Edmund Husserl (1859–1933), who held that the researcher should not be concerned with facts or with measuring the frequency of events, but with trying to understand and explain people's behaviour. Berger and Luckmann (1966, p. 3) believed that: 'specific agglomerations of "reality" and "knowledge" pertain to specific social contexts . . . these relationships will have to be included in an adequate sociological analysis of these contexts'.

Although students adopting either of the two paradigms seek to understand and to explain behaviour, the stance adopted will affect the methods they adopt to test their hypotheses. Unfortunately, the views from each camp have become markedly polarised into a qualitative versus quantitative debate, whereas a less dogmatic approach would favour applying positivistic measurement to suitable data (cash, inventory, populations) but using qualitative means when what is to be observed is imprecise and interpretative (human interactions and so on). The argument here is not on the *superiority* of positivism or relativism, but on their appropriateness. The representation of reality does depend, of course, on one's perception of the nature of the exterior world but the nature of the topic also influences one's view. Knights (1992, p. 516) attributed to Foucault the view that 'management knowledge is never independent of the power that managers and their corporations exercise'.

2.7   The epistemological stance in this study

Strategy is a human activity, which, so far, has defied attempts to turn it into an algorithm. The military use the appreciation format (discussed later in Chapter 4) to aid logical thinking, but judgement is still required to arrive at the solution. Those writers who prescribe a methodology for strategy formulation in business generally produce a sequence to be followed rather than a detailed account of the process. There is a diversity of views on strategic management theory, and academics approach the subject from an epistemological standpoint that is largely conditioned by the original discipline they studied, be it economics, organisational behaviour, psychology or whatever. There are no 'laws' proven in the subject, in the way that physical sciences have derived deterministic formulae like Boyle's Law, Ohm's Law and the like. Thus, if there is an objective entity that is 'strategy process', it has yet to be discovered.

Since humans conduct the strategy process, with all the infinite variety that that implies, there is unlikely to be a single description that can encompass and encapsulate it. Rather, the description of the process is likely to be affected by the observer, to be a constructed rather than an objective truth. It is likely that many strategists will be unable to describe adequately how the decision was arrived at, and may even distort the process in recollection. 'Who did what?' is likely to change each time the process is enacted and will be affected by the identity of participants. Seeking repeatable results, therefore, may be problematic.

Strategists may be filtering their view through the lens of their own biases, *amour propre*, conceits, or whatever. One can never be sure that what is being gathered is the 'truth' or a bowdlerised version, either because of this bias, or because of the limitation of language. On the other hand, it could be argued that a questionnaire yields positive data, but these are not immune from intentional or accidental falsification. The danger in this latter case is that digits imply exactitude and invite statistical analysis that seems to yield 'accurate' answers derived from opinion. The phenomenological approach may produce fuzzy, indistinct conclusions but they at least reflect the nature of the sources.

For these reasons, the stance adopted in this study is phenomenological.

2.8 Research design

The research design has two basic purposes:

(1) *to provide answers to research questions*
(2) *to control variance.* (Campbell *et al.*, 1982, p. 280; italics in the original)

Research questions have to be answered as validly, objectively and accurately as possible, and the research design is the framework that enables the aims to be realised. '*Validity* is the extent to which the research findings accurately represent what is really happening in the situation' (Hussey and Hussey, 1997, p. 57; italics in the original).

Objectivity requires an absence of bias and a reliance on fact. Accuracy is exactitude or, in practice, the maximum correctness permitted by the measurement method and the nature of that being measured. (In this respect, we need to be cognisant of the corollary of the Heisenberg principle, which suggests that it is not possible to measure something without changing it.) 'The main technical function of research design is *to control variance*. A research design is, in a manner of speaking, a set of instructions to the investigator to gather and analyze data in certain ways' (Campbell *et al.*, 1982, p. 284; italics in the original).

Variance in its statistical sense (that is, the square of the standard deviation and, thus, the measure of spread of data) is not an issue in this study since such methods are not used. The 'experiments', however, must be conducted in such a way as to yield results that are comparable and capable of producing meaningful results on analysis. The interviewees, therefore, should be given, as far as is possible, the same degree of guidance and the results analysed as objectively as possible. The case studies should address similar issues that have emerged over time.

The research question in this study seeks a comparison with processes that occur in two fields of human endeavour. Although the independent variables, the military and business, are known, the isolation of dependent variables is more problematical. The research might be designed around the study of particular dependent variables of strategy process (the influence of organisational structures and politics, the presence or absence of crisis, and so on) but such an approach would influence the data gathered. An alternative approach is to gather data from practitioners in the strategy field and to seek to discern a pattern that is valid and useful or, as Strauss and Corbin (1990, p. 24) described it, 'to develop an inductively derived grounded theory about a phenomenon'.

2.9   The chosen methodology

The research question will be answered by:

(a) A literature search of secondary data contained in writings on strategy
(b) Interviews with strategists
(c) Case studies from each of the two fields under study

Interviews

Since the approach adopted in seeking an answer to the research question is phenomenological, there is no attempt to assemble positivistic fact. It could be argued that a properly constructed questionnaire would yield more valuable results than a loosely structured interview. There are, however, objections to these arguments:

(a) The formulation of a questionnaire presupposes a series of contentions that need to be proved or disproved. Such a structured approach would determine the range of answers that will be received.

(b) How big should the sample be to be deemed statistically significant? Since a wide variety of approaches to strategy is already acknowledged in the literature, grouping the data could lead to bias, and to formation of a large number of groups each containing only a small sample.

(c) The answers received would be opinion, even though a numerical value was assigned in a scale of values. This criticism might seem to be applicable to all questionnaires, but the contention here is that the strategy formulation process is particularly unsuitable for the application of statistical techniques and an objective approach, simply because the subject is so diverse and difficult of description, even by the practitioners.

The principal method, therefore, was the use of loosely structured interviews with strategy practitioners. The researcher, however, gave a rough guide to the topics to be covered so that some comparisons could be made between the different interviews. The guidance given to respondents is attached as the Appendix to this chapter, and aimed to suggest some key questions (the first questionnaire was used for those with a military background, and the second for business). During interviews, the researcher attempted not to intervene, unless the point was being lost. In each interview, there were points in time when the silence needed to be broken and when the subject needed some prompting to proceed. Although some general guidance was given on broad topics within the field, the interviewee was free to make whatever comments or statements they deemed relevant. They were encouraged to describe their experience of the strategy process. Extended interviews enable the targeted person to expand on their views as a practitioner of the strategy process, and describe it in their own words. Any form imposed on the proceedings by the interviewer involves the risk of distorting the view of the interviewee and diverting the channel of his or her thoughts. There was the problem of balancing the wish to gather data around my assumptions and biases with allowing the interviewees to develop their accounts in their own terms. Some postulates were not of great interest to the interviewees so there was little point in repeatedly returning to these topics.

The choice of subjects for interview was random and depended greatly on who would agree to collaborate. The criterion for selection of interviewees was that they should have been closely involved in the strategy formulation process, either in the military or business, or preferably both. An attempt was made to include subjects from large companies and small, entrepreneurs and company men, and members of each of the three services, so that a variety of experience would be represented. In this attempt to represent 'business' or the 'military' the amount of evidence from any one field was reduced. This spread of results has affected the conclusions that can be reached in this study. Each interviewee was assured that the text of the interview would remain confidential, although quotations might be used. In general, the readiness of executives to participate was gratifying and those who were not able to agree to meet were apologetic. Only one eminent businessman and one eminent politician failed to reply to a letter of request.

Case study approach

There remains the requirement to study the strategy process in both fields with respect to the passage of time, since 'process' implies an activity occurring over a period. An additional approach is made, therefore, by using case studies 'to catch reality in flight' (Pettigrew, 1992a, p. 10). The approach used in this research is phenomenological and involves the interpretation of four case studies, arranged in two pairs with each pair containing a study from the military and one from the business field. One pair (to be found in Chapter 3) is 'The struggle for Europe, 1944–5' and 'The Alenia Marconi Systems joint venture', both of which are in the context of an attack by an international alliance on a well-dug-in enemy. The first arose from a reading of Irving (1982), which described the disagreements between the Allied commanders. The second suggested itself from a personal involvement with a part of the company, and from the decision to write novel case studies. The Alenia Marconi case was constructed from information provided by the company, and little if any detail could be found in the business press. The company is not quoted on the London Stock Exchange because the shares are retained by its parents, British Aerospace and Finmeccanica, and there is no published annual report. On the one hand, therefore, the case study is open to bias, but, on the other, provides information on an otherwise closed company. The second pair (in Chapter 4) is 'Military strategy formulation in Britain' and 'Strategy formulation in IBM', both of which illustrate the strategy formulation process in a bureaucratic context. The first of this pair arose from a personal involvement in the process whilst serving at the Ministry of Defence (MOD), and the second from the recognition of the similarity of their process with that of the British MOD whilst teaching IBM case studies written by the Harvard Business School. There is a disparity in the length of the cases, in that the military ones are much longer than the business ones. There is little written about the military strategy *process*, so it was deemed necessary to go into greater detail in this area, whereas the business theory is more highly developed, so these cases could be briefer.

The rationale for this choice of method has been debated in academic circles. Eisenhardt (1989a) describes the cases study as 'a research strategy that focuses on understanding the dynamics present within single settings'. The superiority of the case study strategy in this situation relates to the importance in this research of qualitative, as opposed to quantitative, research methods.

Eisenhardt (1989a) argues that there are three possible aims of case study research: to provide description, to test theory, or to generate theory. In this study, the case method is used for the first two of these aims, and adopts a deductive approach, rather than attempting theory generation by 'grounded theory' (Glaser and Strauss, 1967). In the terms used in Table 2.1, it increases the data collection methods, and, thus, provides triangulation of the evidence gained through interview.

Study of the process of strategy reveals that it has changed over time as society has experimented with new concepts. Behavioural norms have changed and national, organisational and personal relationships have become modified by these new ideas. The addition of a temporal dimension to the study is aimed at revealing aspects missed in a cross-sectional approach. A further advantage is the possibility of triangulating results obtained in other ways. There is the limitation of this approach identified by Cray *et al.* (1991, p. 228): 'The case study approach tackles the problem of intricacy directly, but at the expense of generalizability.'

Handling the evidence

The approach in this study has been, first, to analyse the existing theories of strategy formulation process in order to expose differences of opinion. Case studies from the military and business fields were written from secondary and primary sources to exemplify the processes in action. Although the accounts of what happened were recorded as objectively as possible, the cases were written with this study in mind, and to that extent were biased towards the research questions. The evidence here was related to the theories by commenting from business practice on military cases, and vice versa.

Table 2.1 The process of building theory from case study research

Step	Activity	Reason
Getting started	Definition of research question	Focuses efforts
	Possibly a *priori* constructs	Provides better grounding of construct measures
	Neither theory nor hypotheses	Retains theoretical flexibility
Selecting cases	Specified population	Constrains extraneous variation and sharpens external validity
	Theoretical, not random, sampling	Focuses efforts on theoretically useful cases – i.e. those that replicate or extend theory by filling conceptual categories
Crafting instruments and protocols	Multiple data collection methods	Strengthens grounding of theory by triangulation of evidence
	Qualitative and quantitative data combined	Synergistic view of evidence
	Multiple investigators	Fosters divergent perspectives and strengthens grounding
Entering the field	Overlap data collection and analysis, including field notes	Speeds analyses and reveals helpful adjustments to data collection
	Flexible and opportunistic data collection methods	Allows investigators to take advantage of emergent themes and unique case features
Analysing data	Within-case analysis	Gains familiarity with data and preliminary theory generation
	Cross-case pattern search using divergent techniques	Forces investigators to look beyond initial impressions and see evidence through multiple lenses
Shaping hypotheses	Iterative tabulation of evidence for each construct	Sharpens construct definition, validity and measurability
	Replication, not sampling, logic across cases	Confirms, extends and sharpens theory

	Search evidence for 'why' behind relationships	Builds internal validity
Enfolding literature	Comparison with conflicting literature	Builds internal validity, raises theoretical level, and sharpens construct definitions
	Comparison with similar literature	Sharpens generalisability, improves construct definition, and raises theoretical level
Reaching closure	Theoretical saturation when possible	Ends process when marginal improvement becomes small

Source: Eisenhardt (1989a, p. 533).

The interviews with strategy practitioners were taped, transcribed and then analysed around the framework suggested by the decomposition of the research question shown in Figure 1.1 (Chapter 1). The transcripts were read repeatedly and views noted under these heads. An attempt was made at coding and a statistical analysis of the findings, but mainly discarded because one could not be sure that like was being aggregated with like. Miles and Huberman (1994, p. 56), however, described the problem thus: 'A chronic problem of qualitative research is that it is done chiefly with words, not numbers.'

A formal analysis would have created a greater impression of certainty than could be justified by the nature of the evidence. Although the evidence is reviewed mainly in Chapter 5 below, comments from the interviews are woven, as evidence, throughout the thesis. Some issues common to most interviews, but outside the research framework, have been included as serendipity, and included in Chapter 5.

Reliability is a test of whether another researcher repeating this study would obtain the same results. Apart from the difficulties of matching accurately the methodology used and the sources consulted, it is conceded that the reliability here is low, particularly as the analysis of the data becomes more detailed. On the other hand, the research findings represent, as accurately as possible, the views of sources and persons consulted, and the validity can be claimed to be high. These characteristics are common to phenomenological research. If the results display some ambiguity and 'fuzziness', then this, it is claimed, is more to do with the nature of the subject than the diligence with which the study was conducted.

The analysis of the material gathered in this study has been more comparative than critical. Value judgements do emerge, and some prescriptions are made in the conclusion, but the approach in the book is mainly descriptive and comparative. The conclusions of this study are drawn from consideration of the ideas in the literature, the narrative of the case studies, and what was related in the interviews. These data were organised around the hypotheses proposed in Chapter 1 and the decomposition of the research question shown in Figure 1.1.

2.10   Methodology summary

The early part of this book has the nature of a literature review, which summarises what has been written on strategy process and categorises these works by studying the various paradigms adopted by previous researchers. This review was conducted for the two fields of business strategy and military strategy to provide a basis for comparison of process and to give an account of the relevant theory in both fields to underpin the evidence gathered by the research. Evidence of the processes used in the two fields covered by the study was gathered from loosely structured interviews conducted by the author with strategists experienced in either field and, in some cases, both fields (particularly senior officers who had retired from the military and had gone on to join companies). The interviews were tape-recorded and then transcribed on to floppy disk for printing.

Further evidence was sought from case studies, written by this author for the purpose, and contained in Chapters 3 and 4 of this book. These case studies provide an account of the strategy process at work, usually over a period of time, in a variety of contexts. Cases were written for both the military and business contexts and illustrated themes used in the analysis.

The evidence was then analysed using the structure shown in Figure 1.1. From this analysis, conclusions were drawn in answer to the research question.

Appendix

Proposed interview agenda 1

1 In your experience, is strategy formed:
   Top-down   ☐   Bottom-up   ☐   Combination of both   ☐

2 How does leadership affect this process?
   Strongly   ☐   Weakly   ☐   Not at all   ☐

3   Is the Military Appreciation used in practice?
    Yes   ☐   No   ☐   Sometimes   ☐

4   Are the 'Principles of War' consciously considered in strategy formulation?
    Yes   ☐   No   ☐   Sometimes   ☐

5   Is military history a useful guide in the practice of strategy formulation?
    Yes   ☐   No   ☐   Sometimes   ☐

6   Are biographies a useful guide to strategic thinking?
    Yes   ☐   No   ☐   Sometimes   ☐

7   Does the presence of a crisis affect the process?
    More top-down   ☐   More consultative   ☐   Other   ☐

8   How should one train future strategists? (Tick all that apply)
    Staff College ☐ Other academic ☐ PSO ☐ Planned career   ☐

9   How does the strategy process in business compare with that in the military?
    Very similar   ☐   Somewhat similar   ☐   Dissimilar   ☐

10 In what ways are they similar and in what ways are they dissimilar?

11 Is the LTC/Departmental Plan process in the MOD the way military strategy is routinely formulated?
    Yes   ☐   No   ☐   Partially   ☐

Many thanks for your assistance in my study.

Proposed interview agenda 2

1 In your experience, is strategy formed:
   Top-down ☐   Bottom-up ☐   Combination of both   ☐

2 How does leadership affect this process?
   Strongly ☐   Weakly ☐   Not at all   ☐

3 Are formalised procedures for deciding strategy used in practice?
   Yes   ☐   No   ☐   Sometimes   ☐

4 Are theoretical business ideas consciously considered in strategy formulation?
   Yes   ☐   No   ☐   Sometimes   ☐

5 Are case studies a useful guide in the practice of strategy formulation?
   Yes   ☐   No   ☐   Sometimes   ☐

6 Are biographies a useful guide to strategic thinking?
   Yes   ☐   No   ☐   Sometimes   ☐

7 Does the presence of a crisis affect the process?
   More top-down ☐   More consultative ☐   Other   ☐

8 How should one train future strategists? (Tick all that apply)
   Universities ☐ Experience ☐ PSO ☐ Planned career ☐

9 How does the strategy process in business compare with that in the military?
   Very similar ☐   Somewhat similar   ☐   Dissimilar ☐

10 In what ways are they similar and in what ways are they dissimilar?

11 How is the final decision made?
   By the CEO ☐   By the Directors   ☐   Other   ☐

Many thanks for your assistance in my study.

3
War, Business and the Language of Strategy

3.1 Introduction

Both war and business are concerned with competition and how to succeed in the face of determined adversaries. As a result of the arguments in the preceding chapters, it has been concluded that the concepts of strategy in the military and business fields are virtually identical, and, thus, the comparison can proceed. In each case, resources (physical, human and moral) are applied at the critical point in an attempt to achieve the aim. Such a perspective raises issues of 'what resources?' and 'how much?' and also what is meant by 'critical point' and how it is identified. Of prime importance is the selection of the aims of the enterprise for these will define what 'succeeding' means. The argument in the study moves on in this chapter to consider military strategy and then to review the various paradigms of strategic management. The chapter continues with a comparison of the common language of strategy from the two fields. The chapter ends with two case studies and the subsequent comments.

3.2 Military strategy

The development of military strategic thought

The military origins of the concept of strategy have already been described in Chapter 2 and this base is developed by looking in greater detail at the theories underlying the formulation of military strategy. As noted earlier, a basic difficulty is that much of the writings concern the *content* of strategy and less is written about the *process* of formulation, which is often assumed to be the sole province of the commander. Indeed, the great commanders of the past were expected to decide what to do and many would have considered that seeking the advice of others was an unacceptable sign of weakness. Leadership style is a cogent factor in military strategy formulation and is discussed later, in Chapter 6. The development of military strategy is now considered from a historical perspective.

Greece

The Greek language provides the word 'strategy' from *stratos* (army) and *agein* (to lead) (Cummings, 1995). In Athens in 508 BC, ten new tribal divisions were formed, each headed by an elected *strategos*. 'The creation of the position of *strategos* reflected increasing military decision-making complexity. Warfare had evolved to the point at which winning sides relied no longer on the deeds of heroic individuals but on the co-ordination of many different units of men fighting in close formation' (Cummings, 1995, p. 23). *Strategoi* were not only selected for their wisdom, but were also required to have first-hand experience of battle. Pericles, a famous *strategos* of the mid-fifth century BC, saw the leader's tasks as to have a vision, and to articulate and communicate it. Thucydides records examples of the orations of *strategoi* attempting to convince the population of their suggested course of action, and Pericles' reply to the Spartan ultimatum is a masterly appreciation of the political and military situation. He knew, too, the influence of chance upon human affairs and the limitations of human rationality: 'There is often no more logic in the course of events than there is in the plans of men, and this is why we usually blame our luck when things happen in ways that we did not expect' (Thucydides, trans. Warner, 1954, p. 52).

Thus, at the time of the Peloponnesian War (431–404 BC), because the *strategos* produced a proposed strategy, which was then debated and approved (or rejected) by the tribe, he had to be both a clear thinker and an expert rhetorician (echoes of Eccles and Nohria, 1992).

In the next century, the battle of Chaeronea (338 BC) resulted in a victory for the forces of Philip of Macedon and his son Alexander. Mintzberg *et al.* (1998) use this battle to draw parallels with current management concepts:

- Philip and Alexander had very clear goals.
- They used an indirect approach.
- They used deception.
- They had a well-developed contingency plan.
- They exploited their top-down command structure, whereas the Greeks relied on the more cumbersome democratic system.

- They analysed their strengths and weaknesses, and used their strengths to offset their weaknesses (particularly their mobility).
- They attacked their opponent's weakness.
- They concentrated their forces at the critical points.

Although this analysis imposes a contemporary look on these far-off events, there is evidence of recognisably strategic thinking by the Macedonians to achieve superiority over the numerically stronger Greeks.

China

Sun Tzu wrote his treatise *The Art of War* some time between 500 BC and 300 BC in the Kingdom of Wu where he had become the general commanding the forces of King Ho Lu. This book appears to be the first written formulation of principles of strategy, and his precepts have been much quoted in recent years in the business context. Sun Tzu, first, stresses the value of planning:

> The general who wins a battle makes many calculations in his temple before the battle is fought. The general who loses a battle makes but few calculations beforehand. Thus do many calculations lead to victory, and few calculations to defeat; how much more no calculation at all! (Sun Tzu, trans. Clavell, 1983, p. 11)

He recognises the value of timing:

> The value of time – that is, being a little ahead of your opponent – has counted for more than either numerical superiority or the nicest calculations with regard to commissariat. (ibid., p. 13)

The concept of war as a contest of wills of the opposing generals is enunciated:

> To fight and conquer in all your battles is not supreme excellence; supreme excellence consists in breaking the enemy's resistance without fighting . . . Thus the highest form of generalship is to balk the enemy's plans. (ibid., p. 15)

He anticipates the strategy of the indirect approach:

> Military tactics are like unto water; for water in its natural course runs away from high places and hastens downward. So in war, the

way is to avoid what is strong and to strike at what is weak. (ibid., p. 29)

Sun Tzu also emphasises mobility:

Speed is the major factor in successful competitive action. You must take advantage of the situation before your competitor arrives. Exploit his lack of readiness. Attack his weakest spot. (Krause, 1995, p. 89)

He also identifies leadership and morale as important attributes of successful forces, together with many other observations still relevant today. During the Ming period (AD 1368–1644), however, the influence of Confucianism led to war and violence being frowned upon. Furthermore, under a series of weak emperors, the strategy process became increasingly political, in an organisational sense. Waldron (1994, pp. 102–3) observed:

Although the Ming had experts on frontier and defense policy who usually combined a first-rate classical education with common sense and border experience, such people had more and more difficulty in making their voices heard. Foreign policy instead became an area for the factional politics of the Ming court. Unqualified people made military proposals, and the ultimate decisions on them reflected intrigue rather than deliberation. This was natural, given that the first emperor had weakened and divided the bureaucratic hierarchies which might otherwise have made policy in a systematic way.

The sophistication of the Chinese system thus affected the strategy formulation process by diminishing the role of the commander in favour of a more bottom-up approach.

Rome

Rome developed in a period when warfare could still be seen as a collection of individual combats. Rome's contribution, the introduction of legions, discipline and organisation, was largely tactical, although the cumulative effect of many wars produced a strategy and, subsequently, an empire. Frontinus did write his *Strategematicon* but again this work is largely a tactical description of how to deal with the Silures in Wales. Caesar's *De Bello Gallico* is similarly concerned principally with the techniques and tactics of military life in Gaul and lacks consideration of strategic issues. Rome suffered from Hannibal's thinking at the battle of

Cannae when the Carthaginians defeated the legions by encirclement. Although this plan was tactical (being confined to a single battlefield) the concept was strategic since it confronted the Roman approach of annihilation of the opposition with the use of manoeuvre. The Romans were ruthless and warlike, habits ingrained in the nation from the bitter battles for survival in the early years. The Senate made the strategic decisions and directed the state, but senators were not only politicians, because 'no Roman could stand for political office until he had served on ten annual military campaigns' (Bernstein, 1994, p. 62). Like the *strategoi* of Greece, the Roman strategists knew from first hand about military operations. Luttwak (1987, p. 137) summed up the Romans' problem in the later years of the Empire:

> The Romans did not face a single enemy, or even a fixed group of enemies, whose ultimate defeat would ensure permanent security. Regardless of the amplitude of Roman victories, the frontiers of the empire would always remain under attack, since they were barriers in the path of secular migration flows from north to south and from east to west. Hence Roman strategy could not usefully aim at total victory at any cost, for the threat was not temporary but endless.
>
> The only rational goal was the maintenance of a minimally adequate level of security at the lowest feasible cost to society.

These conditions anticipate the problems of modern corporations, which cannot win by single battle, but face an endless war of attrition in which only the most efficient will survive. The search for maximum security at minimum cost is still conducted in modern Britain.

Japan

Miyamoto Musashi wrote his treatise *The Book of Five Rings* (translated by Cleary, 1993) in AD 1643 as a guide to the duelling samurai, and focuses attention on the 'psychology and physics of lethal assault and decisive victory as the essence of warfare' (1993, p. xvi). As such, the book may be seen more as concerned with the tactical issues of combat, particularly duelling. Yagyu Munenori completed *The Book of Family Traditions on the Art of War* in AD 1632 and made use of the concepts and teachings of Zen Buddhism. He divided his work into three main sections:

> *The Killing Sword* – represents the use of force to quell disorder and eliminate violence.

The Life-Giving Sword – represents the preparedness to perceive impending problems and forestall them.

No Sword – represents the capacity to make full use of the resources of the environment. (1993, p. xvii)

Munenori's book, then, is more strategic than Musashi's (which is still widely used in martial arts) and recognises the concepts of war as an extended act of policy, the merits of deterrence, and strategy as a harmony of the army (or company) with its environment.

The development of strategy in later history

After these early beginnings, strategic thinking seems to have waned. The known world comprised nation states, which raised feudal armies or bands of mercenaries when necessary to impose their will on another state. Technological developments (the knight in armour, the longbow, gunpowder) affected the conduct of war and the armed forces gradually became better organised and more professional. These effects, however, were largely confined to the field of battle.

Eventually, in part due to the developments in technology, attempts were made to formalise ideas on the use and conduct of war, leading to a more detailed development of the idea of strategy in an attempt to understand and control the powerful forces released by war.

Machiavelli

Niccolò Machiavelli would not have understood the term 'strategy' in its current usage, but would have thought of it as Frontinus used the word, to denote a stratagem, that is, a plan for deceiving an enemy. Nonetheless, Machiavelli introduced concepts and ideas that influenced later thinkers on the subject, such as Clausewitz. First, Machiavelli linked military action and political aims. The purpose of military means was to overcome the enemy's state. Second, he introduced the concept of a decisive battle and the committal of all available means to its winning. At that time of great social change, war had moved from a feudal duty to a business conducted by mercenaries whose interests were often best served by the *avoidance* of battle. (Machiavelli observed satirically in his *Istorie Fiorentine*: 'In the battle of Zagonara, a victory famous throughout Italy, none were killed except Lodovico degli Obizzi, and he together with two of his men was thrown from his horse and suffocated in the mud' (Gilbert, 1967, p. 12).) Next, being a man of the Renaissance, Machiavelli harked back to the days of ancient Rome and stressed discipline and organisation as essential to armies. He emphasised the necessity of teaching individual soldiers to obey words of command, and he addressed the problem of subdivision of the army into more flexible, mobile units. He based his advice on the latter on the Roman legion and suggested the largest unit should be the *battaglione* of 6000 to 8000 men. Another striking innovation that similarly looked back to Ancient Rome but also was a precursor of Napoleonic practice was the introduction of conscription. Finally, this Renaissance man tried to consider war rationally and attempted to discover rules and laws governing war. The proposition that war is an art, rather than a science, was to be developed after Machiavelli's death, but a case can be made that he was the originator of modern strategic thought. In particular, linking war and politics recognised the importance of an aim, a desired condition *post bellum*.

Clausewitz

Carl von Clausewitz was born in 1780 and experienced war at first hand through service with the Prussians, French and Russians. He was, however, of a philosophical turn of mind and attempted to analyse his experiences to produce a theoretical basis for the conduct of war. He lived when the Enlightenment was, through science, revealing more of the secrets of the universe. It was thus a natural extension to apply science to war. On the other hand, Berkeley and Hume were proposing that man created and moulded the world through his own consciousness. Thus Howard (1983, p. 14) observed:

> Intellectually Clausewitz was very much a child of his time. For him war was not an activity governed by scientific laws but a clash of wills or moral forces. The successful commander was not the one that knew the rules of the game, but the one who through his genius created them. The uncertainties and hazards that made war so unpredictable and uncontrollable were not barriers to be eliminated but opportunities to be grasped and exploited.

His ideas, expressed in his posthumously published book *On War* (*Vom Kriege*), have been influential in most of the European nations and in America. Rapaport (1968, p. 13) commented:

> Clausewitz views war as a rational instrument of national policy. The three words 'rational', 'instrument', and 'national' are the key concepts of his paradigm. In this view, decision to wage war 'ought' to be rational, in the sense that it ought to be based on the estimated costs

and gains of the war. Next, war 'ought' to be instrumental, in the sense that it ought to be waged in order to achieve some goal, never for its own sake; and also in the sense that strategy and tactics ought to be directed towards just one end, namely towards victory. Finally, war 'ought' to be national, in the sense that its objective should be to advance the interests of a national state and that the entire effort of the nation ought to be mobilized in the service of the military objective.

Nonetheless, he realised that the purpose – the objective – of a war was political. Howard (1983, p. 16) commented on the stark fashion in which Clausewitz expressed his views:

The political object of war can be of two kinds; either to totally destroy the adversary, to eliminate his existence as a State, or else to prescribe peace terms with him.

Clausewitz observed contemporary practice and so believed that strategy is the province of the commander. Thus:

An immense space lies between a General ... and his Second in Command, for the simple reason that the latter is in more immediate subordination to a superior authority and supervision, consequently is restricted to a more limited sphere of independent thought. This is why common opinion sees no room for the exercise of high talent except in high places. (Rapaport, 1968, p. 155)

He sought to analyse the difficulties of high command and dwelt on the qualities required for a general. He also investigated the nature of the problem facing the strategist (that is, the commander):

In the lower ranks the spirit of self-sacrifice is called more into request, but the difficulties which the understanding and judgement meet with are infinitely less. The field of occurrences is more confined. Ends and means are fewer in number. Data more distinct; mostly also contained in the actually visible. But the higher we ascend the more the difficulties increase, until in the Commander-in-Chief they reach their climax, so that with him everything must be left to genius. (Rapaport, 1968, p. 190)

Clausewitz's legacy, then, is the association of war with a desired, political outcome, and the idea that strategy formulation is more art than a science. There is, then, little point in seeking to remove *all* doubt by the application of rational thought. In his view, the general is responsible for the development of strategy.

Jomini

Antoine Jomini was born in 1779 in the French part of Switzerland. Although having had no formal military training he achieved by various means the rank of brigadier general in Napoleon's army and the post of chief of staff to Marshal Ney. He spent much time in writing on the theory of war and his books were used as military textbooks into the 1860s. A product of the Enlightenment, he sought rational explanations and underpinning theory in the study of war, much of which was based upon the campaigns of Napoleon. He defined strategy, tactics and logistics for the first time and decided that the fundamental principle of strategy consisted in:

1   Bringing, by strategic measures, the major part of an army's forces successively to bear upon the decisive areas of a theater of war and as far as possible upon the enemy's communications, without compromising one's own;

2   Maneuvering in such a manner as to engage one's major forces against parts only of those of the enemy;

3   Furthermore, in battle, by tactical maneuvers, bringing one's major forces to bear on the decisive area of the battle-field or on that part of the enemy's lines which it is important to overwhelm;

4   Arranging matters in such fashion that these masses of men be not only brought to bear at the decisive place but that they be put into action speedily and together, so that they may make a simultaneous effort. (Brinton *et al.*, 1967, p. 85)

Jomini, therefore, held out the hope of rational solutions, and this idea would have been welcome to those working on the idea of a specialist military staff (see section on Prussia–Germany below).

Delbrück

Hans Delbrück (1848–1927), in his *Geschichte der Kriegkunst* (published in Berlin in 1900; see Craig, 1967, p. 263) proposed two forms of warfare.

The first, *Niederwerfungsstrategie* (the strategy of annihilation), had as its sole aim the decisive battle as proposed by Clausewitz. The second strategy was named *Ermattungsstrategie* (the strategy of exhaustion) in which 'the battle is no longer the sole aim of strategy; it is merely one of severally equally effective means of attaining the political ends of the war' (Craig, 1967, p. 273). The first was the application of maximum force at the decisive point but the second, being predicated upon the possession of limited resources, was more subtle:

> The decision [which of several means of conducting war to employ] is therefore a subjective one, the more so because at no time are all circumstances and conditions, especially what is going on in the enemy camp, known completely and authoritatively. After a careful consideration of all circumstances – the aim of the war, the combat forces, the political repercussions, the individuality of the enemy commander, and of the government and people of the enemy, as well as his own – the general must decide whether a battle is advisable or not. (ibid.)

Delbrück suggested that Pericles followed this approach in the Peloponnesian War and, when Cleon chose the *Niederwerfungsstrategie*, disaster overtook Athens. *Ermattungsstrategie*, he suggests, is the modern approach to war and such it proved to be in the First World War (1914–18), when technology (particularly the machine gun) made *l'offensive à l'outrance* a strategy of exhaustion.

Strategy process – some historical examples

The dynastic form of state predominated in the early to middle years of the last millennium and the king, in theory, was the absolute ruler and decision-taker. In practice, the ruler usually had to balance the intentions of the ruling house against the power of the aristocracy. A turning point was reached in 1792 when the French Revolution swept away many of the prevailing assumptions and structures upon which much of society was built and the national form of state replaced the dynastic. In military matters, citizen armies replaced professional armies and the limited war of siegecraft and ingenious manoeuvre was replaced by an aggressive, mobile strategy of mass armies. During this period, too, technology in the form of improved artillery, better road-building and cartography opened up new possibilities for the conduct of war. The development of a new style of strategy process can be detected in the following examples.

Habsburg Spain, 1556–98

Geoffrey Parker (1994) provided a powerful analysis of strategy formulation under Philip II of Spain. He began by pointing out that Philip believed that, since God was on his side, he could disregard obvious threats and failures because of that belief. Parker observed, 'A better example of cognitive dissonance would be hard to find. Upon such rocks of blinkered intransigence, rational calculations of Spain's strategic advantage foundered' (Parker, 1994, p. 130). There appeared to be no organisation for high-level strategic planning, although a complex network of councils advised the king, but their responsibilities remained only for routine matters. The councils' responsibilities were strictly defined and the only person to have a complete picture was the king, who devised three devices to overcome the fragmentation:

(a) A number of his key advisers served on several committees and for particular operations Philip would form a special committee. One such, the Committee of Presidents, had eight senior councillors to consider a financial crisis.
(b) Second, the king allowed his ministers to write to him directly on important matters.
(c) Third, the king saw all letters that went out in his name. On some days he would sign 400 letters and, on average, he resolved 30 petitions a day.

The result was predictable. The king became bewildered by all the detail and overwhelmed by the sheer volume of paper with which he had to deal. When the king fell ill, decision-making stopped. Since the king deliberately ensured that he was the only one in possession of the complete picture, the administration was powerless without him, and then could only react to events.

Philip saw his strategic mission as furthering the cause of religion and it was axiomatic to him that God would be on his side in such a noble cause. The king permitted no discussion of Spain's strategic needs and he remained the source of final decision. As he aged and became ill, his mental powers declined, yet he continued to place his total confidence in God. The system he created effectively prevented any alternative solutions, since he was the sole creator of strategy.

France, 1661–1715

John Lynn (1994) traced the strategic process under Louis XIV, 'a larger-than-life monarch and . . . his quest for *gloire*' (p. 178). Of the strategy formulation process in this period Lynn's conclusion was:

> In substance and style, Louis XIV embodied absolutism, but his power was scarcely absolute: it acknowledged tradition and necessity as limits. Nevertheless, in matters over which he claimed authority, he brooked no interference. Paramount among the king's life-long concerns were foreign affairs, his army, and the conduct of war; in these areas he set and managed policy on a daily basis. (1994, p. 179)

The strategy process was top-down, and the top was the king. There were only a very few trusted advisers. Louis saw his role as making decisions based on common sense and he took counsel from his four secretaries of state – foreign affairs, war, navy and royal household. The highest body was the *Conseil d'en haut* or Council of State, which met when the king decided it should. Within the Council, discussion was open, but strictly confidential. Thus, ministers could criticise the king in private, which they could not do in public. Decisions were usually by majority, but the king could decide to the contrary. Inevitably much work fell to the king and it worked only because he had a great appetite for work. The system was not to everyone's taste, and the army, which had become accustomed to a high degree of autonomy, chafed at the bit of Louis's autocracy and interference. 'Generals might lobby for their own plans, but they did not dictate actions' (Lynn, 1994, p. 183).

Again the limitation of autocracy can be seen in the overloading of the king's mental capacity, and his reluctance to delegate.

Prussia–Germany

Frederick the Great, King of Prussia in 1740, wrote his *Militärisches Testamen von 1768* on the art of generalship and the following extract shows his approach to strategy formulation:

> The general can even discuss the war with some of his corps commanders who are most intelligent and permit them to express their sentiments freely in conversation. If you find some good things among what they say you should not remark about it then, but make use of it. When this has been done, you should speak about it in the presence of many others: it was so and so who had this idea; praise

him for it. This modesty will gain the general the friendship of good thinking men, and he will more easily find persons who will speak their sentiments sincerely to him. (Phillips, 1943, p. 188)

The officer in the Prussian army of that time, drawn almost exclusively from the upper class, was bound by a personal oath of loyalty to the sovereign and the system demanded immediate and unquestioned response to orders. Hence Palmer (1967, p. 85) wrote: 'No one reasons, everyone executes; i.e. the thinking is done centrally, in the mind of the king.' Frederick was an absolute monarch who made the strategic decisions himself and did not feel constrained to take advice from anyone.

Later, during the Napoleonic era, France had combined the creation of a democratic army and technological advances to introduce innovations such as mobilisation and logistics. Napoleon had divided the French army into divisions and corps which meant some degree of tactical delegation to subordinate commanders who may not always have been in communication with the overall commanders. Thus Walter Millis (in Goerlitz, 1953, p. ix) commented:

> *It was still just possible in Napoleon's time for individual genius (aided by such improvisations as the divisional system of command and the embryonic staff officer) to direct the new forms of military action which were coming into existence; but even with genius, the results were not too happy ... The inevitable answer – in war as in commerce, industry or civil administration – was system, organisation and specialised training.* (Italics in the original)

As early as 1640 the Prusso-Brandenburg army had appointed quartermasters to handle problems of supply, military law, transport and military police but these, although precursors of the true Great General Staff, were not involved in strategy formulation. In 1803, the King of Prussia ordered the reorganisation of the quartermaster's staff and the reform, undertaken by Scharnhorst, resulted in the creation of a general staff in 1813. This organisation had sections or *Abteilungen* responsible for: strategy and tactics; internal administration; reinforcements; mapping; and artillery and munitions. The chief of staff aimed to become the *alter ego* of the commander but stood in the background, advised, warned and guided. Goerlitz (1953, p. 41) observed:

> It was Gneisenau who quite deliberately developed the conception of the joint responsibility of the various Chiefs of Staff for any decision

which the army commanders might take. The object – it was of prime importance – was to ensure the spiritual unity of the General Staff and to enable it to assert its will as a unitary organism against army commanders who were refractory and difficult.

Superficially this might seem to suggest that the chiefs of staff of the armies had power of decision, but the context is important in understanding the relationships. Prussian officers swore an oath of allegiance *to the king*, not the state, and to him alone were they obedient. The chief of staff to the king had the responsibility of controlling the subordinate chiefs of staff, who had the right of direct access to the king over the head of their respective commanders. Thus the chiefs-of-staff system ensured obedience to the will of the supreme commander.

Staff officers were trained to be loyal, efficient, knowledgeable and faceless. The study of military history was a required preparation for entry into the staff. Von Moltke in 1871 wrote to try to explain the staff system:

> Fundamentally, the secret of his [Moltke's] school was that it had no secret. In war, he said, nothing is certain except the commander's capital in will and energy. Situations often cannot be fully foreseen in advance and strategy is nothing but a system of *ad hoc* expedients, the value of which must be judged by their capacity to achieve their object, whatever that object may be. (Goerlitz, 1953, p. 96)

The general staff had been moulded into a 'unique instrument combining flexibility and initiative at the local level with conformity to a common operational doctrine and to the intentions of the high command' (Rothenburg, 1986, p. 301). Dandeker (1990, p. 87) commented that, with the development of the general staff system, 'the "brain" of military organizations became collectivized'. What was novel in this system was the creation of a source of ideas, rather than a willing, but subservient, collection of officials. The highly expert staff officers could develop strategies for the consideration of the commander. In the period 1871–1918, the control of the army at higher level was not so well-organised. Holger Herwig (1994, p. 243) pointed out:

> The war minister held an impossible position entailing great responsibility but little power. As an active officer he was directly responsible to the Prussian king for the combat readiness of the Prussian army, yet as minister he was plenipotentiary to the Bundesrat

(Federal chamber) and as such had to answer to the Reichstag (Parliament) on fiscal matters.

But, as Herwig goes on to explain, the inability of Kaiser Wilhelm II to act as the final arbiter of policy differences in this Byzantine world resulted in the general staff exercising *de facto* control of national strategy.

Von Moltke (the elder) agreed with Clausewitz that, since strategy is an art, not a science, the political and military problems of war could not be totally resolved by calculation. Schlieffen, however, differed by placing his faith in rationality and calculation: 'he was a specialist who favoured concrete calculations over abstract speculation' (Rothenburg, 1986, p. 311).

After the Armistice in 1918, the Allies decreed, in the Treaty of Versailles, the dissolution of the general staff, but the *Truppenamt* was, in truth, the same thing under a different name, but now penetrated by officers with political ambitions, a phenomenon abhorred in the original body. Adolf Hitler came to power in 1933, and he believed that the Prussian officer corps was largely to blame for the outcome of the First World War. He said, 'the General Staff is the only Masonic Order that I haven't yet dissolved ... those gentlemen with the purple stripes down their trousers sometimes seem to me even more revolting than the Jews' (Howard, 1970, p. 112). There was a mutual distrust between Hitler and his generals, many of whom regarded him as a 'facile amateur'. In fact, Hitler had read widely, as Strawson (1971, p. 51) recorded: 'The campaigns of Frederick the Great, Clausewitz's *On War*, the theories and practices of more recent successful Commanders-in-Chief, Moltke, Schlieffen, Seeckt – he had studied them all voraciously.'

Bullock (1993, p. 725) confirmed this view and draws attention to Hitler's technical skill. The disadvantage of this knowledge, combined with his poor opinion of his generals, made Hitler vulnerable as Strawson (1971, p. 234) pointed out: 'whereas in the earlier years of the war, he conducted his military conferences with moderate restraint, seeking opinion, feeling his way, success bred both confidence in his own strategic genius and contempt for others, worst of all contempt for fact'.

Hitler readily admitted that many of his decisions were intuitive and guided by his *Vorhersehung*, his foresight, but Goerlitz (1953, p. 484) recorded General Manteuffel's opinion that 'he [Hitler] occasionally had flashes of insight, but ... denied that he had any real strategical or tactical talent or even any schooling in that direction'. Hitler gradually assumed even more power over the German military machine. Graeger (1998, p. 64) commented:

> Thus the command levels and responsibilities were distorted by Hitler's accumulation of functions. Not only did he take over strategic and operational command and control, but also involved himself in tactical command. Hence even field marshals who were appointed as Commanders-in-Chief for the individual theatres of war became commanders at the tactical level.

Thus the German system for strategy determination (which has been dealt with at length because of the wealth of relevant detail) moved from an autocratic system, where the leader had personal authority and decision-making power, through a system of broadly-based advice from experts available to guide the commander, and back to an authoritarian who assumed even more power than had been the case under Frederick the Great. Hitler's judgement was also distorted by the effect of his singular personality, his inhuman ideology and his Nietzschean belief that the strength of his will could determine the outcome of the war. The general staff worshipped 'efficiency' as the logical outcome of nineteenth-century rationalism and positivism, and applied the developing technology to formulate complicated plans. Hitler relied more on his intuitive judgement. The first approach (detailed planning) failed in the First World War and the second approach (intuition) failed in the Second World War.

Strategy development in recent history

The carnage of the First World War left an indelible mark on Britain (and many other nations), and the British military came to realise that the power of the defence that came from the mass-produced, effective weaponry, rendered impractical the *offensive à l'outrance* (attack at any cost) ideas. The strategy of attrition and the horrors of trench warfare had been the result. The significance of the tank as a means of attack at the critical point was grasped by such as Major General J.F.C. Fuller and B.H. Liddell-Hart (if not by the British general staff). Liddell-Hart proposed the strategy of the indirect approach, even though the outstanding example of this method from the First World War, Gallipoli, had been a tactical disaster in practice. The eight maxims proposed by Liddell-Hart in his work *Strategy* (quoted by Nickols, 1999) are worth summarising here because they echo the mistakes of the First World War and resonate with business practice too:

1 Adjust your ends to your means.
2 Keep your objective always in mind, adapting plans to circumstances.
3 Choose the line (or course) of least expectation.
4 Exploit the line of least resistance (providing it leads to the ultimate objective).
5 Pursue a line of operation that offers alternate objectives – keep the opponent guessing.
6 Make sure your plans are flexible.
7 Do not take the offensive when the enemy is on guard.
8 Do not renew an attack along the same line that has once failed.

Air power was now a new factor and one which used an element that covered the whole world and knew no boundaries. Extravagant claims were made for the effectiveness of this new arm, which only in the closing decades of the twentieth century was being realised, when the technology conferred new orders of accuracy on air strikes. Then, in 1945, the explosion of the atomic bomb was deemed to have invalidated all previous concepts, and led to a strategic debate that bordered on the metaphysical, as complex theoretical structures were built upon conjecture.

The process of strategy formation developed, too, and increasingly, views were heard from others than the politicians in power and the military. Academics, both from scientific and political disciplines, increasingly made an input to the development of national strategy as technology played an increasing part in military affairs and the interactions of nations were viewed more as a 'game'. Grand strategy is necessary in peacetime as well as in war, and attempts were made to provide a theoretical basis for these considerations (for example, Mahan, Mackinder, Liddell-Hart, J.F.C. Fuller, Howard) but this trend was never more evident than in the debate on nuclear weapons (for example, Morgenstern, Brodie and Kahn), which was an attempt to argue out rationally the principles and likely conduct of a war that no one could win. Equally significant, military strategy was now being debated by academics, not men in uniform. The advent of computers made available techniques of war-gaming through which military plans could be tested using probabilistic, statistical techniques. But, as Allison (1971) deduced, the only example available (the Cuban Missile Crisis) shows that the strategy process was not that of the Rational Actor, but fitted better either his Organisational Process Paradigm or the Governmental Political Model.

Moskos, *et al.* (2000) suggested that, in recent years, the development of military thought could best be understood through the typology that defines *Modern* as the period from the nineteenth century to the end of the Second World War, *Late Modern* as extending from the mid-twentieth century to the end of the Cold War in the early 1990s, and *Postmodern* as referring to the contemporary period. Their book as a whole investigates the armed forces of twelve Western nations in these three periods under eleven aspects of these forces. Attention was drawn to the changing roles of the military, particularly the emphasis on peacekeeping, and how aspects like force structure, mission definition and perceived threat had changed in the three periods. The one aspect of particular relevance to strategy formulation (not a topic considered as such) is the nature of the dominant military professional, which was described (Moskos *et al.*, 2000, p. 15) as:

- *Modern*: combat leader
- *Late Modern*: manager or technician
- *Postmodern*: soldier–statesman; soldier–scholar

This development would suggest that the military leader of the future will need different skills and a wider view than has been needed in the past. In which case, the training of the senior military will need to be adjusted to prepare them for these new, wider roles. The idea expressed earlier in this book (Chapter 1, section on 'Statecraft') of the strategist as practising 'statecraft' would seem to be particularly relevant to the post-modern military. Conversations with contemporary, British military leaders as part of this study have tended to echo some of these thoughts, especially those of Dandeker (2000), but the evidence is insufficient to offer any proof or disproof. Bellamy (1997) wrote in similar vein on the changing roles of the military from peacemaking to peacekeeping.

Military strategy – a summary

Process paradigms are not so clearly identified in the military strategy literature. The evidence from history shows that, over time, strategic decision has passed from being centralised in the monarch to a broadly-based coalition, and, as a result, has become more political (in an organisational sense). (Hitler's return to centralised, autocratic decision-making is an aberration in this historical trend.) Those involved stressed the rationality of military strategy, but examples, such as the Cuban Missile Crisis, tend to show elements of dominance by doctrine and organisational influences, and the horse-trading of politics. Following the development, first in Germany, of the general staff system, the general is not the sole creator of the strategy, although he may well be the instigator of the ideas from which the plan develops. The general, however, will still take the final decision and bear the responsibility for the outcome. Intuition plays a part in strategy, because it is this factor that separates the brilliant commander from the pedestrian. At the highest level, that is, 'grand' strategy, there is less emphasis on planning but, as the actual scene of combat is neared, the need for carefully integrated plans becomes paramount. The planning process is detailing implementation, and not devising the strategy. The strategy in the theatre of operations, where it blurs into tactics, is more likely to be incremental and reactive, even though it is highly planned. The complexity of modern war and the wide geographic spread of many conflicts necessitate a high degree of delegation, and theatre commanders are given an aim, rules of combat and the resources thought necessary, and might be largely free to choose their methods of tactical operation. Schwarzkopf (1993, p. 357), however, described his experience in the United States armed forces: 'A regional commander can't simply promulgate any war plan he pleases. The Joint Chiefs of Staff dictate his mission in accordance with the stated national strategy. This comes in the form of a slim secret document, the Defense Planning Guidance.'

3.3 Business strategy

Structuring thought on business strategy

In contrast to the development of military strategy, the progress of business strategy process theory has produced a series of paradigms to organise thoughts on the subject. The concept of a 'paradigm' seems to have emerged from the writings of Thomas Kuhn (1962) in which he envisaged one meta-theory replacing another in a series of revolutions by which scientific enquiry proceeded. Kuhn was not consistent in his use of the word but for the purposes of this book, a paradigm will be deemed to mean 'an organising principle' or a 'mindset'. This guiding principle will determine the nature of the process adopted for strategy formulation and the conduct of the resulting strategic analysis. This chapter suggests an ordering of the variously available paradigms in a working typology.

The nature of strategy revisited

Our environment is characterised by complexity and uncertainty. The strategy process can be seen as human beings trying to understand the complexities of their environment and their organisation, to identify the uncertainties, and to take a decision on the best course of action in order to achieve their objective.

What one means by the word 'strategy' can be conditioned by one's paradigm, but there are some characteristics that are unlikely to be contested. First, strategy has to be practical. Choose the wrong course of action and, at the limit, the firm may fail, or at least the operations will be suboptimal. Second, strategy is about decision. After all the analyses, debates, arguments and so on, the strategy represents a choice from the options available. Third, strategy is holistic. It has been described as a 'helicopter view' of the firm. The decision on strategy must have considered the relevant factors of a complex situation for it to be considered comprehensive and valid. Fourth, strategy, to be understood, has to be approached longitudinally, rather than being seen as an isolated decision bereft of historical context (Pettigrew, 1992a, p. 10). Finally, strategy is about achieving competitive advantage or, in other words, is the way to win.

The theoretical approach to defining and understanding strategy in business has been conditioned by the knowledge bases of the theorisers. Thus, a large body of theory has been generated by academics whose knowledge is in economics while another body has its roots in social science studies. The search was not only for an explanation of what was thought of as 'strategy', but also to develop prescriptive guides for practitioners in the field. One is that, while claiming to be holistic, the subject seems to lack any integration of the economic and behavioural disciplines. Neither, on its own, seems fully to account for the richness of strategy content and process, although each has yielded powerful analyses – as far as they have gone.

Whittington (1993) identifies four generic approaches to strategy: classical, evolutionary, processual and systemic, which he combines with processes and outcomes to form the perspectives illustrated in Figure 3.1. This model suggests that there is an interaction between the content of the strategy and the way in which it is determined – the process. There are, at the limit, only two generic outcomes that are considered – profit-maximising and pluralistic – and these can be linked to the economics and social science studies streams of thought respectively. An alternative way of describing these outcomes is to regard them as aims or objectives, which are an important part of the strategy process since they define what the strategy has to achieve.

Pettigrew (1988) suggested that strategy could be understood to have three dimensions – context, content and process (see Figure 3.2). He stressed that these are not separate identities, but dimensions of strategy, in the way that height, width and length define a box. One might

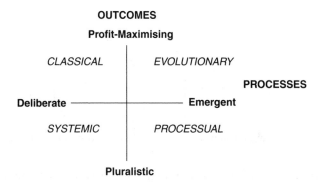

Figure 3.1 Generic perspectives on strategy.
Source: Whittington (1993, p. 3).

add the longitudinal dimension of time to envisage context, content and process existing over a period, which view would also suggest the emergent outcome defined by Whittington.

Consideration of many of the paradigms in the strategy literature seems to be appropriate mostly to the content dimension. There are paradigms associated with strategy process (which will be discussed shortly) and these arise principally from the literature on decision-making. If strategy were little more than an investment decision, then the content paradigm could safely be economic/financial. If, however, an additional 'lens' were to introduce consideration of leadership (dominance), and organisational structure (politics) and chance (stochastics), the economic/ financial approach would be seen to be an incomplete and inadequate explanation of the strategy process. The relationship can be depicted in the alternative form shown in Figure 3.3, which also introduces the decision element. In this view, the strategy process is seen as taking

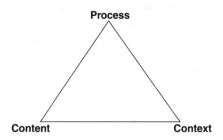

Figure 3.2 The three dimensions of strategy.
Source: Pettigrew (1988).

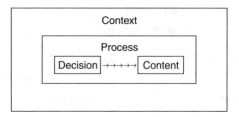

Figure 3.3   A diagram illustrating the context/process/content relationship.

place within a given context culminating in a decision as to the content of the strategy. Process at the limit becomes primarily concerned with decision-making and the employment of the various options open: game theory, intuition, statistical methods, 'garbage can' (Cohen *et al.*, 1972), and, in the temporal dimensions, deliberate or emergent, introduced by Mintzberg and Waters (1985).

Given the complexity of strategic management, it is, perhaps, unlikely that one meta-theory will be devised, but the search will likely continue, particularly to associate content and process paradigms.

A paradigm problem

Burrell and Morgan (1979) said that paradigms arise from one's funda-mental view of the world. The implication of this argument is that one can adopt only one paradigm, which will be incommensurable with theories arising from alternative world-views. Thus, they held, the theories of positivists, for instance, cannot be reconciled with those advanced by phenomenologists. If incommensurable, are the theories considered here also irreconcilable? Are they alternative views or mutually exclu-sive interpretations of the phenomenon of strategy? A further problem is introduced by Peters and Waterman (1982) who concluded that the successful company is one in which the strategists can hold opposing views at the same time, but still resolve this dilemma to produce a single course of action (an idea developed by Hampden-Turner, 1990). If we were constrained by our paradigm to a single view of the world, then Peters and Waterman's prescription would be impossible.

A further complication is that the above description is only one possible approach to the way we think about the world. Joyce and Woods (1996) offered the following alternative framework:

- *Modernist*: 'Modernist thinkers see strategic management as the prov-ince of the decision-making elite within the corporation ... These top decision makers, guided by their analytical tools and measurements, determine the new strategic moves. They carry out rigorous (analytical) assessments of their situation and choices and undertake, ideally, quantitative forecasts of the organization's environment' (p. 34).

- *Postmodernist*: 'The post-modernist style thinkers see top management and the formal institutions of strategic decision making as, at best, creating the context in which spontaneous action by others at lower levels can occur and then ensuring successes are backed... Consequently, the top managers discover – make sense retrospectively – of action produced spontaneously by others' (p. 38). This view encompasses both chance and experimental action (that is, learning).

- *New Modernist*: '...new modernist strategic management resembles the modernist paradigm in its positing of strategic management as a rational and intellectual process, but it recognizes that there are significant limits on knowing and controlling... The spirit of new modernism is probably best captured in Mintzberg's (1987) metaphor of strategic management as a "craft"' (p. 44). Given this limited knowledge and understanding (bounded rationality), top management cope with events in an incremental fashion (Quinn, 1978).

This alternative view based on intellectual movements might be a useful triangulation in the search for enlightenment, but the problem of incommensurability remains unsolved. Those who hold firm and fixed views as to the nature of business (and, indeed, of the world) are least likely to surrender their position and will not countenance a view at variance to their own. Those, however, who can view the varying paradigms as alternative views of the same reality that all agree is 'strategy' can apply these paradigms to investigate situations to judge which sheds the most light. There may be a parallel with the parable of 'The Six Blind Men and the Elephant' (John Godfrey Saxe in Mintzberg *et al.* (1998)) who each felt a part of the animal and derived their image of the whole from their partial impression. If that is a valid comparison, then no one is in a position to comprehend the whole that is 'strategy', because they are all limited by their own paradigm. The approach adopted here is to construct as complete a view as possible by using all the 'lenses' available, and to use these different theories to evaluate the evidence collected. Incommensurability is not seen as preventing this approach.

Content paradigms of strategic management

When strategic management first began to be studied in the 1960s, it was considered that the process of strategy formulation was a rational act and that the optimum course of action could be determined from a logical analysis of the facts about the firm (which was deemed to be a profit-maximising body) and the environment. A challenge to this view came from Cyert and March (1963) who opposed the economists' theory of the firm by proposing a behavioural theory of the firm. Bodner and Thomas (1993) suggested that there is a link with organisational behaviour (OB) and they use this term to contrast the I/O (industrial/organisation) approach. Nonetheless, the early development of strategic management thought was dominated by the I/O paradigm which had originated in economics and engineering. McWilliams and Smart (1995) used the S–C–P (structure–conduct–performance) paradigm from economics as a further model. Thus, at an early stage, both the economics and social science streams were much in evidence.

Prahalad and Hamel (1990) suggested a link between the core competences of the firm and its strategy. Stalk *et al.* (1992) took the view that competition is based essentially upon capabilities. Barney (1991), Teece, *et al.* (1997) and others developed the theory of the resource-based view (RBV) of the firm. A further variant of this theory (that the optimum strategy for the firm is as much conditioned by the assets the firm possesses as by the environmental conditions) is the knowledge-based view of strategy (and knowledge can be seen as a resource). If the I/O paradigm represents an outside-in view of strategy, the resource-based view takes an inside-out stance.

Prahalad and Hamel (1994, p. 11) suggested: 'Theories of war and diplomacy provide good models for thinking about competition and collaboration.' They clearly accept an analogy between the competition of business and the struggle for power and position in the world. Although these 'grand' strategies are thought of as being approached from a linear/rationalist point of view, Allison (1971) illustrated that, in practice, this is not necessarily the method that produces the strategy. The selected course of action often involves the 'intuition' of a statesman, probably because the problems are too complex for a human (even with computer assistance) to solve (hence the 'bounded rationality' of Cyert and March (1963)). Furthermore, Allison discovered that organisational routines and politics had more influence on the strategy selected than the ideas of the 'great man'.

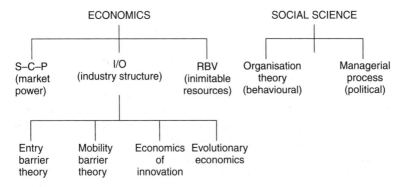

Figure 3.4 A family tree of business strategy theory.
Source: Rumelt *et al.* (1991).

Figure 3.4, which draws heavily on Rumelt, *et al.* (1991), illustrates one way of viewing the antecedents of various views of business strategy.

By contrast, Galbraith *et al.* (1996) described the content of military strategy as comprising:

(a) *The Direct Approach*: The concentration of resources in time and space at the decisive point.
(b) *The Indirect Approach*: A process of dislocating an opponent's psychological and physical balance by operating on other than the expected line of approach.
(c) *The Protracted Approach*: A slow but increasing tempo of territorial or economic control. The term 'attritional' is not inappropriate to this category.

This taxonomy adopts a completely different view of the content of strategy illustrated in Figure 3.4, and so one cannot be mapped onto the other. There are hints of similarities, like market power and attrition, but the relationship can hardly be called a parallel.

These theories or paradigms reflect various views of the nature of strategy and are mainly concerned with the *content* of strategy, but they are drivers of the strategy process, which is the concern of this thesis.

Process paradigms

The paradigms considered so far are concerned with what is driving the process of formulation to decision. When all the analyses and arguments about the nature of strategy and what drives it are over, a choice has to be made from the identified options available. Because one is expected to make a rational decision, the process is similarly expected to be conducted in a predictable, ordered fashion. If a decision is taken by intuition, should it be considered irrational or should we accept that, although we cannot trace the process, it is still possible for it to be rational? In either case, we have to be mindful of the limitation imposed by human 'bounded rationality' (Simon, 1965). Eisenhardt and Zabaracki (1992) viewed the processes used in strategy formulation as being: rational (but boundedly so); power and politics; and the 'garbage can' theory of Cohen, *et al.* (1972). Ellen Earle Chaffee (1985) separated the process into linear, adaptive and interpretive [*sic*] modes. Allison (1971) proposed, from his study of the decision-making processes of the Cuban Missile Crisis, three models: the Rational Actor; the Organisational Process; and the Governmental Political. The position adopted here is that there are three categories (paradigms?) of strategy process, each of which lies on a spectrum between deliberative and emergent modes:

(a) Linear/rational
(b) Organisational
(c) Anarchical

These three categories form the major subdivisions illustrated in Figure 3.5.

Linear/rational

Mintzberg criticised what he described as the 'Design School' of rationalists, both for their belief that it was both possible and desirable to devise strategies from the 'facts' of the environment and the internal workings of the firm, and for the separation in this theory of strategy formulation and implementation. Adherents to this school, however,

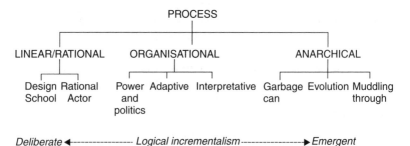

Figure 3.5   A family tree of strategy process models.

believe that a planned and systematic consideration of the strategic position of a company is feasible. In the main, the initial proponents of this theory were engineers and economists, who might be expected to adopt a positivist stance. Allison (1971) included consideration of a 'Rational Actor' model in his study but, arguably, the model was introduced as a 'straw man', rather than as a serious suggestion that strategy was formulated in that way.

Organisational

The interaction of people in the organisation, the distribution of power and the nature of the organisation will all affect the formulation of strategy. Three groups of theories are included under this heading: power and politics, adaptive and interpretative.

Power and politics   If the strategy process is essentially decision-making, the strategist(s) must have the power to ensure that their decisions are accepted. 'Organizations operate by distributing authority and setting a stage for the exercise of power' (Zaleznik, 1970, p. 48). This power can be conferred upon the strategists by their place in their organisation and by the consent of the people. Zaleznik (ibid., p. 50) observed, however, 'One of the most common errors executives make is to confuse compliance with commitment', that is, just because the people appear to do as instructed, it does not necessarily mean that they are committed to this course of action and are giving it their full support and energies. Strategists can also acquire their power through political manipulation of the organisation. Organisational structures do not actually exist, but are constructs of the people working within them, so it is possible for individuals or groups to aggregate power to themselves based upon knowledge or political skill, or under the protection of the senior levels in the company. The decisions that emerge, therefore, can be ones that suit an individual or clique, and may not be the disinterested, logical solution that is best for the company. The power of disaffected groups is illustrated in the following mini-case (Zaleznik, 1970, p. 54).

Interpublic Group

In November 1967, the directors of the Interpublic Group, a $700 million complex in advertising and public relations, moved for the resignation of the leader and chief executive officer, Marion Harper, Jr. Briefly, Harper had managed over a period of 18 years to build the

Box (*Continued*)

world's largest conglomerate in market services, advertising and information on the base of a personally successful agency career. In expanding from the base, Harper made acquisitions, started new companies, and widened his orbit into international branches and companies.

As often happens, the innovator and creative person is careless in controlling what he has built so that financial problems become evident. In Harper's case, he appeared either unwilling or unable to recognize the seriousness of his financial problems and, in particular, the significance of allowing cash balances to go below the minimum required in agreements with lending institutions.

Harper seemed careless in another, even more telling, way. Instead of developing a strong coalition among his executive group, he relied on individual ties to him in which he clearly dominated the relationship. If any of the executives 'crossed' him, Harper would exile the offender to one of the 'remote' branches or place him on partial retirement.

When the financial problems became critical, the aggrieved executives who had once been dependent on Harper and then cast out, formed their own coalition, and managed to garner the votes necessary to, in effect, fire the head man.

Thus, Harper overestimated his power and failed to recognise the need to engage the support of the other influential executives. The ruthless leader still needs the support of some willing associates.

Prahalad and Bettis (1986) considered the strategy process in diversified companies and suggested that the upper management of such companies had to come to terms with the characteristics of diversifying acquisitions in order to manage them. The writers developed the idea of a 'dominant logic' or an accepted prescription for managing the particular concern, which was applied to problems, often without a detailed appraisal of the circumstances. Thus, the dominant coalition at the head of the company reacted by applying mental maps that had been successful in the past or were accepted as the way to proceed.

Adaptive.   Chaffee (1985) used the term 'adaptive' as a classification for those strategies that were: 'concerned with the development of a viable match between the opportunities and risks present in the external environment and the organization's capabilities and resources for exploiting those opportunities' (a quotation from Hofer, 1973 p. 3). The problem with this definition is that it still leaves a large question mark as to *how* this state is achieved. It is, therefore, more a statement as to the *nature* of the strategy, rather than the process of arriving at it. Nonetheless, it describes an attitude of mind, or an approach, to the issue of arriving at a winning solution that seeks to adapt the firm to its environment.

Interpretive   The term 'interpretive' would be described in Britain as interpretative. Chaffee (1985 p. 93), using this paradigm, defined strategy as: 'Orienting metaphors constructed for the purpose of conceptualizing and guiding individual attitudes of organizational participants'. Again we are left a little in the dark as to *how* this is to be achieved but the term describes a situation in which the members of the organisation collectively construct and agree upon their view of the nature of the external context of the firm. From this construct, the participants devise ways of achieving their firm's goals.

Anarchical

The anarchical hypothesis rejects the proposition that strategy is formed through logical thought and with a structured method.

Garbage can   There is a view that the concept of a formal process in strategy is mythical and that, in common with many activities involving humans, it is messy and unstructured. Cohen *et al.* (1972) suggested that organisations can be anarchical, at least for periods of time if not permanently, and are characterised by three general properties:

(a) The preferences of the organisation, which are more a loose collection of ideas than a coherent structure, are inconsistent and ill-defined.
(b) The processes of the organisation (which they term the 'technology') are not understood by its members, who operate on a simple trial-and-error basis.
(c) Participants vary in the amount of time and effort they devote to different domains, so the boundaries of the organisation are uncertain.

If organisations are vehicles for problem-solving, bargaining and interpretation, then they can be seen as: a coalition of choices looking for problems; issues and feelings looking for decision situations; solutions looking for issues to which they might be the answer; and decision-makers looking for work. The authors view a choice opportunity as:

> a garbage can into which various kinds of problems and solutions are dumped by participants as they are generated. The mixed garbage in a single can depends on the sorts of cans available, and the labels attached to the alternative cans, on what garbage is currently being produced, and the speed with which garbage is collected and removed from the scene. (Cohen *et al.*, 1972, p. 2)

Since this phenomenon occurs when preferences are problematic, technology (that is, process) is unclear, and participation is fluid, it is antithetical to the deliberative process. Most of the 'garbage can' research seems to have been conducted in universities, which, it could be argued, are a special case.

Evolution   Henderson (1989, p. 139) drew attention to Gause's Principle of Competitive Exclusion: 'No two species can co-exist that make their living in the identical way'. Thus, when two similar organisms competed for the same food supply, sooner or later one displaced the other. This mechanism cannot be described as 'strategy', since success is largely a result of a chance mutation rather than the will of the organism. An important corollary of Gause's Principle is that the best strategy for success is differentiation, or the possession of some unique attribute, be it invention, skill, knowledge, or whatever. Another implication of the evolutionary view of strategy is that chance can dominate an outcome, despite the machinations of humans. Chance, however, is also influential in all fields of human endeavour.

Muddling through   Lindblom (1959, p. 84) took the view that 'limits on human capacities and on available information set definite limits to man's capacity to be comprehensive'. In which case, he argues, policy has to be formulated by a process of successive limited incremental changes not only because of man's intellectual limitations, but because we do not have adequate theory to apply to problems in policy areas. Thus the Rational–Comprehensive (or Root) method is simply not feasible and we progress satisfactorily by the Successive Limited Comparison (or Branch) method. We compensate for our inabilities by small, safe steps from existing policies, knowing that we can repair the damage easily because the steps taken have been small and limited. Mintzberg's (1987a) idea of 'crafting' strategy can be placed in this category. Mintzberg used the analogy of a potter working on the wheel, and suggested that strategy is formed in the same way, intuitively but incorporating all of his or her knowledge and experience.

Deliberate/emergent

An additional dimension to the structural theories considered above is the temporal spectrum, the poles of which are 'deliberate' and 'emergent'. The argument here is whether strategy is, or should be, determined as a routine, structured, programme set in a fixed temporal routine, or whether it is a continuous process. As shown in Figure 3.5 above, this dimension, based on time, is separated from the ideational paradigms and could apply to most of the three major divisions discussed previously, but the linear/rational mode is least amenable to a continuous process and the anarchical most likely to be emergent.

Deliberate Strategy formulation is deliberate when a formal, organisational routine is initiated for that purpose. Often, the routine requires actions from various individual functions at set times in the year and, after a period of data-gathering and analysis, the strategy is selected, usually by the executive or the CEO. Unless some crisis occurs, the strategy is not reviewed until the next annual cycle begins. Since plans are drawn up by and for business units during this process, it is often called Strategic Planning, although strictly speaking the plans are to do with implementation, not strategy selection. In the military, the planning process is used as a validation of a strategy, so every option considered will be thoroughly worked out before the final selection is made of the best option.

Emergent Mintzberg and Waters (1985) and Quinn (1978) have mounted important challenges to the idea that strategy is formulated as a deliberate, rational act at a point in time. The former considered that strategy is a pattern in a stream of decisions, and that the following three criteria must be satisfied for a strategy to be perfectly deliberate:

(a) The organisation must have precise, articulated intentions;
(b) The intentions must be common to all actors in the organisation;
(c) These intentions must have been realised exactly as intended, which requires that the environment was predicted perfectly or was totally benign.

Emergent strategies, they argued, required consistency in action over time but a lack of intention in the organisational players. Mintzberg and Waters regarded both situations as unlikely to occur in their pure forms, so 'deliberate' and 'emergent' form the poles of a continuum.

Logical incrementalism

Quinn (1978) adopted a similar stance at the outset by observing that, on the basis of his research, strategy formulation is seldom conducted using a rational/analytical system as suggested by the literature. Although his main findings question the validity of either 'formal systems planning' or the 'power-behavioural' explanations for strategy formulation, he does see strategies emerging over time from what he terms 'strategic subsystems'.

The implication of these ideas for a study of strategy process is that the context can extend over a period of time, which could be quite lengthy. This view is consistent with Eisenhardt's (1989a) work on the use of case studies in strategy research. Arguments about these methods revolve around issues such as: can accurate forecasts be made particularly in turbulent environments? Is it sensible to consider strategy annually when the business situation is fast-moving? Are the strategists able to comprehend the complexities of their business sufficiently to make rational analyses? Can continual review of strategy lead to 'strategic drift'? These issues are considered later in the light of the evidence gathered.

Alternative analyses

Idenburg (1993, p. 133) reviewed the contending theories of strategy process and summarised them as shown in Figure 3.6. His observations can be summarised:

(a) *Rational planning*: The process is structured, quantified and iterative. A deep involvement by top management. Assumes the world is more or less predictable. Minds and hands are separated.

(b) *Learning process*: Tries to introduce mental models of reality for discussion. A common image of reality, a common language and the joint acquisition of new insights are as important as defining exact goals. The world is unpredictable and the tensions thus caused stimulate creativity. Strategy development and managerial development go hand in hand.

(c) *Logical incrementalism*: Planned implementation is an illusion. The process develops in phases, but each is linked to earlier phases. Organisational power and politics are a reality, and play their part in the strategy process, which involves internal negotiation. The

Goal orientation (what?)

	Strong	**Weak**
Strong **Process orientation** (how?) **Weak**	Logical incrementalism	Guided learning
	Rational planning	Emergent strategy

Figure 3.6 Four views on the process of strategy development.
Source: Idenburg (1993).

process is not just rationality but is a question of emotions, doubts, worries, intuition and stress.

(d) *Emergent strategy*: The environment is unpredictable and so explicit objectives are infeasible. The company needs to be reactive, flexible and opportunistic. Companies are often overtaken by events and must 'muddle through' as they are presented with the unexpected.

Although Idenburg encountered all of these processes in one company, the actual method used varied as to context.

In attempting to classify and explain observed strategy process behaviour, theorists have identified a rational–creative spectrum. Langley (1995, p. 63) identified dangers associated with both of these methods: 'In their decision-making activities, managers need to tread a fine line between ill-conceived, arbitrary decisions (extinction by instinct) and an unhealthy obsession with numbers, analyses and reports (paralysis by analysis).' She classifies the results of her research in the diagram reproduced as Figure 3.7. It can be noted that this taxonomy introduces the element of intuition in strategy formulation as an *alternative* to rationality, and does not consider intermediate situations.

Mintzberg (1990a) offered a different analysis of the contending schools of strategy when he identified ten schools of thought (see Table 3.1). He acknowledged that not of all these schools were of the same type, in that he describes the first three (design, planning and positioning) as prescriptive, that is, more how strategies *should* be formulated rather than how they *are*. He also averred that the third is more concerned with content than process, but this confusion has already been

**Risk of extinction
by instinct**

                                    **Risk of paralysis
                                    by analysis**

Participation

Limited —————————————————— Widespread

Power

Concentrated —————————————— Diffuse

Opinions/motivations

Convergent ———————————————— Divergent

Leadership style

Autocratic ———————————————— Consensual/passive

Cognitive style

Intuitive ————————————————— Analytical

Figure 3.7   Factors that affect the quantity of analysis produced.
Source: Langley (1995).

encountered. The following seven are claimed to be more representative of how strategy is formed, although it seems possible that more than one of these could be evident at the same time.

This attempt to combine the previous analysis and that of Mintzberg is not as tidy as one would wish it to be, but, since unconnected analyses are being combined, there is no reason why they should fit neatly. Even scientists cannot always agree which species a particular plant or animal belongs to and these decisions are frequently changed. Furthermore, the construction of the matrix is by the author, and so Mintzberg, and

Table 3.1   Classifying strategy process paradigms

School	Process	Linear/rational	Organisational	Anarchical
Design	Conceptual	*		
Planning	Formal	*		
Positioning	Analytical	*		
Entrepreneurial	Visionary			?
Cognitive	Mental	?		?
Learning	Emergent		*	
Political	Power		*	
Cultural	Ideological		*	
Environmental	Passive			*
Configurational	Episodic			*

Source: Mintzberg (1990a).

others would probably come to different conclusions. This confusion reflects the complexity of the subject and also the relatively early state of its development. The greatest difficulty, however, is with the process adopted by the entrepreneurial and cognitive schools because each encounters the problem of the role of intuition. This important factor is considered further in Chapter 6 in a closer investigation of the *actual* process.

Context paradigms

The debate in academe does not, so far, appear to have attempted to define paradigms for the strategy context. Perhaps this is for the very good reasons that there are none. Given the great diversity of situations encountered in different sectors of business, different countries, at different stages of the economic cycle, and so on, this lack is not surprising. There are, however, conditions that do affect how the strategy process is conducted, and they may well affect the content. The following conditions are states of the context that have been identified for this thesis and that will, to varying degrees, affect the outcome of the strategy process:

(a) Whether the organisation is in crisis or not. Is the process being conducted at a time when the organisation feels threatened or is it a routine reappraisal of the strategy?
(b) Does the organisation have a strong dominant leader (perhaps an entrepreneur) or is the power of decision more distributed and democratic?
(c) What is the effect of leadership?
(d) What is the attitude to risk of the strategy-forming coalition or leader? If the organisational culture is risk-averse, some strategic options will be deemed to be not worth consideration.
(e) The specific factor of risk is only one aspect of the general culture of the organisation (but sufficiently important to be separated).
(f) There is, however, the overall influence of organisational structure and culture on the strategy process.

General environmental conditions, often analysed under the headings of political, economic, social and technological, will have an effect on the content of the strategy, as will other factors such as market conditions, customer attitudes, competitive conditions, and so on. In the wider context, there is the issue of turbulence in the environment and Drucker (1980), Brown and Eisenhardt (1998) and others have considered the measures that companies are forced to take in these conditions. This particular issue is not addressed in this study because it is more related to the context of strategy than the process.

Interim conclusions

The literature suggests that there are various forms of process which can be used by an organisation needing a strategy. Variables are issues like the degree of rationality involved, the amount of social involvement in the process, and whether the actions taken are deliberate or emergent in style. Whether one form of strategy process is superior to another will depend on the success each method achieves, and that judgement is inevitably after the fact. The context in which the strategy is decided is influential. For instance, the degree of uncertainty present in the environment will affect the confidence that can be placed in strategies for the longer term. Furthermore, the effect of context means that it is very uncertain that a successful strategy copied from somewhere else will work, unless many factors (such as environment or organisation culture) are the same. Attempts by academics to relate the degree of success to the various forms of strategy process have been inconclusive, so the arguments continue.

The two-by-two matrix in Figure 3.8 suggests a way of classifying the forms of strategy process in business that is suggested by the preceding sections. The theory of strategy process in the military has not been studied and classified in the same way, but evidence in the following case studies will suggest that the deliberate/rational is favoured for the ongoing formulation of defence policy and an element of the deliberate/ intuition arises in time of war. These interim conclusions are discussed

	Deliberate	**Emergent**
Rational	Design school	Logical incrementalism
Intuitive	Adaptive	Interpretative

Figure 3.8 A matrix for classifying strategy process paradigms.

at greater length as the argument in this thesis is developed. In particular, the possible effect on the selection of a strategy process of the following will be considered:

(a) The mindset of the strategist(s) and issues of leadership;
(b) The type of organisation involved;
(c) The distribution of power within the organisation;
(d) The effect of context, particularly the effect of crisis.

3.4   The language of strategy

So far, this chapter has considered the ideas surrounding strategy in both military and business fields and has tried to order and classify the various theories. As a further aid to the comparison of strategy in business and the military, the meaning of the language used in these fields is compared. The chapter ends with two case studies, one from each field under study, and these are compared.

The problem of semantics

Words are the vehicles we use to convey ideas, and rational, constructive thought would not be possible without them. On the other hand, we cannot be totally sure that the concept expressed by a word is entirely replicated in the mind of the recipient. The more abstract the concept, the more ambiguity will exist. The problem is relatively simple when there is something physical that can be indicated, but the shades of meaning of words and their context can make understanding uncertain when the object is intangible. Terms like 'leadership' have value connotations and may be seen by some as a beneficial way of releasing the capabilities of a group of people, but by others as a form of dominance. Each subject of human interest quickly develops its own vocabulary, which carries the potential problem of making the subject entirely incomprehensible to an outsider. The more abstract the concepts, the more danger that what purports to be a dialogue is, in truth, parallel statements of mutually incomprehensible positions.

Because of the nature of strategic thought, ideas and vision are often communicated by metaphor or symbol. Steve Jobs organised the Apple office around a central foyer in which stood a grand piano and a BMW. 'I believe people get ideas from seeing great products', Jobs claimed (Wise, 1984, p. 146). One remembers, by contrast, the negative effect of hearing the general manager extol the virtues of his new company car at a time when the company had serious cash-flow problems. The executive leader personifies the organisation and communicates in non-verbal ways through example, and by symbolic means, like a poet or an actor. The process is interactive to the sensitive leader, who draws ideas from those whom he leads.

Particular care is needed in a study that seeks to draw parallels. Do the words used in each field actually convey the same meaning? When military strategists use the term 'aim', does it mean the same thing as 'mission' or 'strategic intent' in business? In order, therefore, to lessen the likelihood of semantic problems, a comparison of the language of strategy in both military and business fields is necessary and meanings are proposed for the various concepts used.

The contexts compared

Before comparing the process of strategy formulation in the military and business fields, the differing contexts should be considered. War is usually seen as a temporary alternative to the state of peace, but in business the conflict with competitors may abate temporarily, but never ceases. On the other hand, grand strategy continues through peacetime. War, in this case, can be seen in Clausewitzian terms as a continuation of policy by other means. In business, the state of competition may be punctuated by 'campaigns' arising from initiatives or innovations, which seek to gain advantage over the rest. Some of the competition may disappear as a result, like a defeated nation, but anti-trust laws prevent a company from sustaining a complete hegemony over a particular market. So, the comparison between war and business will always have limitations, but, it is contended, the concept of strategy in the two fields is sufficiently similar to bear comparison.

Purpose and aims

The military stress the primacy of the aim in their operations. The logical sequence is seen to be: *Aim* (what is to be achieved) – *Strategy* (how the aim is to be achieved) – *Plan* (how the strategy is to be implemented). 'Selection and Maintenance of the Aim' is the prime principle of war, and much time is spent before embarking on armed conflict in establishing the exact end that is required. In particular, the conditions that are required *post bellum* are carefully defined. In the business field, such precision is less often sought, and what are described as aims, objectives, missions and the like can be, very often, vague. On the other hand, Mee (1965, p. 61) stated the importance of objectives in business: 'Before initiating any course of action, the objectives in view must be clearly determined and understood and stated.'

The need for clarity is illustrated in the following example from Brodwin and Bourgeois (1984, p. 143):

> A major diversified manufacturer concluded that a steady stream of new products was the most important factor in improving the stock price, yet the performance measures and management reports imposed on the division heads stress quarterly profit. As a result, division managers don't make the long-term investment required for successful new product development.

Harrison and Pelletier (1997), however, found that a 'closed' process was associated with fixed and predetermined objectives, whereas an 'open' system used dynamic objectives and levels of aspiration. (The degree of openness was associated with the level of involvement of those outside the dominant coalition at the top of the company.) This observation confirms the assertion above that fixed and unequivocal aims are not seen in business as necessarily desirable.

It can be taken as axiomatic that a company wishes to make as much profit as it can, but is that the only objective? A particular problem for the company is satisfying the often conflicting aspirations of its 'stakeholders'. If the shareholders, the owners of the company, are given priority by maximising dividends and share prices, then this may be at the cost of lower wages and salaries for the employees. Directors, customers and suppliers are also stakeholders in the company and demand their benefits too. So it may be very difficult for aims to be set for the company in the way that the Cabinet sets war aims, although there are still stakeholders in the national context. On the other hand, the prospects for a winning strategy must be much reduced unless this dilemma of aims can be resolved. The military would never go to war without a clearly defined aim and if the politicians whose role it is do not set these aims, then the military will.

Hamel and Prahalad (1989, p. 3) used the concept of strategic intent in the business context:

> On the one hand strategic intent envisions a desired leadership position and establishes the criterion the organization will use to chart its progress... At the same time strategic intent is more than just unfettered ambition... The concept also encompasses an active management process that includes: focussing the organization's attention on the essence of winning, motivating people by communicating the value of the target, leaving room for individual and team

contribution, sustaining enthusiasm by providing new operational definitions as circumstances change, and using intent consistently to guide resource allocation.

A military person could well have written this passage, so closely does it follow their doctrine and practice. 'Unfettered ambition' unrelated to hard realities can eventually lead to nothing, as Alexander the Great, Hitler and Stalin all found to their cost.

Sullivan and Harper (1996, p. 104; italics in the original), who offered the following definition, reflected this view of intent: '*Strategic intent* is *what* you are working to accomplish. Strategic intent is more specific and limited than vision, as well as more quantitative.' Vision, according to Bennis and Nanus (1985), is the leader operating on the emotional and spiritual resources of the organisation. In which case, the aim or objective operates on the tangible and measurable. The vision, however, has to be realistic even when it is demanding of and stretching the organisation.

Simpson and Burnard (2000, p. 235) concluded that 'the primary role of senior managers is to identify and clarify what to focus on and then to direct energy into that focus', but they acknowledge that this activity is conducted in 'the place of unknowing'. This term they used to define the area in which the situation is uncertain and there is a lack of agreement on what to do, which accords with the intuitive view that, in a known, factual context where everyone is agreed on the required course of action, there is no need for the leader to provide focus. Even so, the leader may be required to provide the vision and aims for the organisation.

Vision

In addition to the need for purpose and aims, organisations need a sense of the future, a desired state or aspiration that draws the people forward with a common purpose. Magee (1998, p. 16) described vision as ' the image of "what ought to be" for the organization to position it for success in a futuristic environment'. A problem of definition surrounds 'mission' and 'vision'. Campbell and Yeung (1991) suggested that vision is more associated with a goal, whilst mission is more a guide to behaviour. They portrayed in their Ashridge Model that 'mission' arises from purpose (why the company exists), values (what the company believes in), behaviour standards (policies and behaviour standards that underpin the values) and the strategy. The importance of vision is the corporate sense of being and the enduring purpose that it creates. Vision is only important strategically when it is accepted and used by everyone in the organisation, and so it needs to be articulated as part of the strategy formulation process. This task is the responsibility of the leader, a topic that will be addressed in Chapter 6. There it will be seen that vision arises from a logical and collective organisational process that involves key members whose efforts are orchestrated by the leader. Carey (1996) supported this last idea by describing the military approach to teamwork, which does not create leaderless groups floundering towards knowledge and decision, but combines sharing of ideas with guidance from a leader responsible for the outcome. Again, there is little difference in the application of this concept in business and in the military.

Thus, those who are being led must espouse the vision so that it will inform and guide their actions. The stated purpose may not necessarily be the one that the leader secretly intends, and the leader can use it to manipulate behaviour. So Hitler used the humiliation felt by the Germans over the terms of the Treaty of Versailles after the First World War as a rallying cry that led eventually to the leadership by the Nazis.

Risk

Both businessmen and generals have to take account of risk. The businessman will assert that risk must be congruent with the expected return, and the military will have no problem with that concept. In business, it is only rational to accept a high risk of failure if the profit from success is very high. The military are trained to be cautious and only to take risks when forced to do so, or when there is a real prospect of winning a battle. The individual entrepreneur is more likely to take risks than a corporate dominant coalition, because the bold decision is more difficult to have accepted by a team than by a single decision-maker. The 'entrepreneurial' general, such as Patton, is more likely to take the bold, risky decisions than the cautious, 'staff' man, such as Montgomery (see the case study that follows this section). Flexibility, however, is a factor that can be used to reduce risk. If a plan can include possible outcomes or sequels, preparations can be made for contingencies and thus reduce the risk of being bound into a rigid plan. The skill lies in knowing when to take risks because an entirely safe plan will probably underachieve. Foss (1997, p. 6) observed:

> The commander who makes no mistakes and takes no risks probably does not accomplish very much – nor does he have soldiers with great confidence in the unit or its leaders. The commander who

centralizes everything in an attempt to be strong everywhere is, in fact, strong nowhere. But worst of all, his chain of command and his junior leaders will never develop responsibility and initiative.

Strategy and tactics

A battle can be lost, and yet the war still won, so differentiating the strategic from the tactical is important. Strategy is the way of achieving the overall, and usually long-term, aims, whereas tactics are concerned with the more immediate and local. The summation of tactical moves, however, either achieves or prejudices the strategy. Events at the tactical level can also become strategic. The bomb from an aircraft that goes astray, like the one that killed refugees fleeing from Kosovo, can result in a strategic reappraisal. The military commander must allow subordinates considerable freedom of action, because the local action frequently needs rapid decision in a situation often confused by what Liddell-Hart termed the 'fog of war'. The local commander must, then, know the intentions of his commander so that, locally, he can make decisions that are in accordance with the senior commander's wishes. Delegation is part of the military commander's acquired skills. Modern communications facilitate the exchange of information, which has made delegation more difficult. The availability of information leads to the danger of senior commanders making tactical decisions that properly belong to the more junior level. This tendency is present in business. Proper delegation and empowerment at working level are the solutions to centralisation.

Command and control

The military high command is ever concerned with issues of command: who ultimately has the power of decision, and who has control within specified parameters, such as time and space? This issue is linked to that of strategy and tactics. Such concerns may seem, superficially, to be pedantic and egotistical, but they seek to avoid the situation which so often occurs in business when someone is put in charge, but not permitted to exercise the power of decision that they need to accept the responsibility. Tight control may be necessary both in business and in the military, but it becomes counterproductive when the subordinate is not allowed to act without clearance from above. The strategy specifies the ultimate end and the way this will be achieved. The plan allocates the required means to carry out the strategy, and the subordinate leader must be trusted to perform the assigned role in the full understanding of what the commander intends. In this way, junior leaders perfect their tactical skills and are introduced to strategic issues. Managers in large, bureaucratic firms are often given profit targets, but are not allowed to take tactical decisions (prices, overseas travel, marketing initiatives, and so on) that bear upon reaching these targets. Learning opportunities are thus denied by the misunderstanding of command-and-control issues.

Strategies for change

A strategy might call for a continuation of the current mode of operations, but it is more likely in today's turbulent environment that a change will be necessary. Successful strategies are often those that exploit discontinuities or change the accepted rules. Sullivan and Harper (1996) illustrated the idea of transformation through a rule change by showing how the record for the high jump in athletics improved gradually during the time that the 'scissors' technique was in vogue, but witnessed a steep improvement with the introduction of the 'western roll'. More steady improvement in the record occurred until the 'straddle' was introduced which was followed in turn by the 'Fosbury flop'. Playing by the rules can lead to improvements, but a transformation through a revolutionary strategy is likely to yield more positive results.

The strategist's mindset in both fields under consideration here seeks the 'different' solution. Following the same strategy as everyone else leads to a struggle of attrition, whereas the different or indirect approach can open a free path for advance. The Apostle Paul advised the Romans (12:2): 'Adapt yourselves no longer to the pattern of this present world, but let your minds be remade and your whole nature thus transformed.'

There are limitations to the rational approach so often associated with strategy, and the addition of dogma, doctrine and 'the way we do things here' can all lead to stereotyped solutions. Although the military are often characterised as rigid, routine thinkers, business is no better, and often worse.

Statecraft

The idea of 'statecraft' was introduced in Chapter 1 above as a concept of wise, comprehensive thinking about strategy. The term 'statecraft' is taken to imply:

(a) A set of values which underpins the approach to strategic thinking. One would hope that these are ethical but the pressure for pragmatism often leads to the ends justifying the means.

(b) A vision of a future desired state, which is formed in as much detail as is necessary for the current purpose.

(c) This vision is condensed into a series of aims that the finally selected strategy has to achieve.

(d) The process is as rational (that is, based on 'hard' fact) as it can be in the circumstances, but experience, wisdom and judgement are necessary because the future is unknown and possibly turbulent.

(e) A dominant coalition who, whilst operating under organisational and political constraints, arrive at the decision and bargain their way to a solution that is deemed to be the best that can be achieved, given the current circumstances.

(f) The decision-maker(s) will know their business in the round and from personal experience. Thus the military commanders need the ability to encompass the differing requirements of war on land, sea and in the air. Businessmen need to be able to think holistically, too, without a fixation on one function (finance, marketing, production, and so on). The strategist(s) will be able to project the implications of their chosen course of action into the future, will have a plan to counter likely opposition moves and will have considered the required moves under certain contingencies.

(g) The leader(s) will be able to communicate their strategy in such a way as to achieve acceptance by and the full support of those who are to implement it. The leadership must inspire and motivate the organisation.

(h) The leader will know how to manoeuvre and manipulate to achieve their ends.

Given these attributes, statecraft does not fit neatly into any one of the categories derived from the literature. Statecraft is cognitive but only partly rational, pragmatic but driven by ideals, and holistic, based on a hands-on knowledge of the 'business'. In real life, the process may be chaotic and disjointed, bearing some resemblance to the 'garbage can' (see p. 67) and may be a mixture of the planned and the incremental.

The nearest parallel to the idea of statecraft discovered in the literature is that of 'strategic thinking'. Liedtka (1998) discovered that this term is used in a variety of ways and has not generally been accurately defined. She defined the term as a particular *way* of thinking and suggested that it contains the following five elements:

1 *A systems perspective*: A strategic thinker has a mental model of the system of value creation, and understands the interdependencies.

2 *Intent-focused*: Strategic thinking is intent-driven, which is similar to the ideas of strategy's relation to goals and vision.

3 *Intelligent opportunism*: The well-articulated strategy must not deter the thinker from recognising alternatives better suited to the changing environment.

4 *Thinking in time*: Strategic thinking connects past, present and future.

5 *Hypothesis-driven*: Like the 'scientific' method, strategic thinking generates and tests hypotheses. In this way, analytic and intuitive thinking are combined.

These ideas are not the same as those proposed for 'statecraft' but do represent ideas of the type of holistic thinking required of the strategist.

Conclusion

The common language of strategy describes ends, ways and means. Strategy is a human activity, so is affected by mental limitations, frailty and issues of personality. The process can use rational or intuitive thinking, and can be deliberate or emergent in style. These categories come from strategic management theory and do not appear in military texts. Leadership is required but, as discussed in Chapter 6, need not require a 'great man' style. Strategy requires clarity, subtlety and lateral thinking. The great strategies are original and break the mould of currently accepted thought. The evidence collected for this study will be compared to the paradigms and theories discussed in this chapter.

3.5 Case study 1: the struggle for Europe, 1944–5

Introduction

The planning for and implementation of the D-Day landings in June 1944 and the subsequent campaign culminating in the surrender of the German government are of interest, not only for the scale of the enterprise, but for the interplay of the principal actors. The way the strategy was decided is an illustration of the military strategy process. The evidence presented here is largely from the biographies of the commanders involved, and so readers are dependent on these authors for the facts and information made available. Some replay their differences with colleagues, perhaps seizing the opportunity to put their point of view without immediate contradiction, and others choose to forget the arguments and take the safer route of praise. Much information, however, has been revealed.

The big decision

The first decision, that the continent of Europe would be invaded via north-west France, was the big one and was not without controversy. Eisenhower (1977) recalls that studies for the invasion of Europe were conducted in the early part of 1942, shortly after America's entry into the war and when the initiative was firmly in the hands of the Axis powers. Attacking Germany through the Mediterranean was thought to be unattractive because of the mountainous terrain of the approaches in northern Italy. On the other hand, General Alan Brooke (later Field Marshal Viscount Alanbrooke), the British Chief of the Imperial General Staff (CIGS), regarded these Italian operations as an essential means of drawing German troops away from Russia and north-west Europe, a concept which he could never make the Americans understand fully. Attacking alongside the Russian forces was impractical because the only access was through Murmansk and the capacity of this port was insufficient for the vast supplies needed in logistic support of a major fighting force. Plans for attacking through Norway, through Spain and Portugal were also studied in detail.

The US Chief of Staff, General Marshall, and the President's representative, Mr Harry L. Hopkins, left Washington on 7 April 1942, and discussed the strategy with the British government and Chiefs of Staff. General Brooke argued against 'premature and inadequately supplied offensives against Hitler's Western Wall, but recommended striking at the Axis in the one theatre where, because of salt water and geography, logistics could enable the still comparatively minute land-forces of the allies to exert an influence out of all proportion to their size' (Bryant, 1957). He meant North Africa.

The decision was 'to make the attack across the English Channel the principal offensive effort of the two governments in Europe' (Eisenhower, 1977, p. 48), but the date was put back from 1942, first to 1943 and then to 1944. Brooke used as a planning assumption that no more than twelve German mobile divisions should be present in France at the time of the invasion, whilst the Russians pressed for the invasion in 1942 to take forty German divisions from Russia. The Americans were anxious to take the offensive against the Germans and to commit their troops to battle and felt that the British were reneging on the joint decision. A mission was sent from Washington to London in July 1942 to seek adherence to the joint decision rather than deferring action through the force of current circumstance. However, the reality was that the Allies had insufficient shipping, particularly landing craft, to transport a decisive force to the shores of France. The objective of a landing in France was endorsed at the Casablanca conference in 1943 and detailed planning begun. In the autumn of 1943 at the Cairo conference, however, Mr Churchill dwelt at length on one of his favourite subjects – the importance of assailing Germany through the 'soft underbelly', of keeping up the tempo of the Italian attack and extending its scope to include much of the northern shore of the Mediterranean.

> He seemed always to see great and decisive possibilities in the Mediterranean, while the project of invasion across the English Channel left him cold. How often I heard him say, in speaking of Overlord prospects: 'We must take care that the tides do not run red with the blood of American and British youth, or the beaches be choked with their bodies.' (Eisenhower, 1977, p. 194)

Thus, although the decision (to invade north-west Europe – but not yet) had been made, the support from Britain was, at times, less than total. Final agreement between the two allies was reached at the Quebec conference in August 1943, by which time Sicily had been conquered and Italy was about to be invaded. The Americans felt that the British were at last committed to the landings when their allies came to the conference in August 1943 with definite plans for the invasion of France. Although the two allies were now working together 'in increasing confidence, cordiality, and frankness' (Parker, 1990, p. 127), 'some American soldiers thought the British irresponsibly ready to sacrifice long-term plans to present opportunities, while some British soldiers thought the American naively rigid in their attachment to their plans' (ibid., p. 126). At the end of this conference, Brooke confided to his diary, 'I am not really satisfied with the results. We have not really arrived at the best strategy, but I suppose that when working with allies, compromises, with all their evils, become inevitable.'

The principal military actors

The strategy formulation process was in the hands of a relatively few players. The Supreme Commander for the invasion (Operation Overlord) was the American General Dwight D. Eisenhower who was guided by General Marshall, the Chief of Staff of the American Armed Forces, who was based in Washington. Combined Chiefs of Staff Committee exercised formal control of the strategy, but, just as Eisenhower took guidance from Marshall, General Sir Bernard Montgomery (later Field Marshal Viscount Montgomery of Alamein) kept in close touch with

General Alan Brooke. Mr Churchill, the British Prime Minister, also interfered in the operations to a greater extent than his American counterpart, Mr Franklin D. Roosevelt. Although Brooke was always able to sustain the military point of view, Churchill refrained from exercising the dictatorial powers he undoubtedly possessed (although Brooke commented in his diary, 'He is the most difficult man to work with that I have ever struck' (Bryant, 1957, p. 723)). Add in the efforts of General Charles de Gaulle, leader of the Free French Forces, and the web of command of the operations in north-west Europe was complex, if not tangled.

General Eisenhower

Irving's (1982) description has Eisenhower as 'quintessential American. With his open, warm, Great Plains manner, his wide, ready grin, his tangy and colloquial speech, he seemed like a figure out of a Western pulp novel...And yet behind all this homeliness there was a subtle, relentless intelligence.' Eisenhower had graduated from West Point in 1915 and, during a successful career, spent nine years with General MacArthur in the Philippines. After the Pearl Harbor attack in December 1941 and the entry of America into the war, he was summoned to Washington by General Marshall to head the War Plans Division. In June 1942, having been heavily involved in strategic talks between President Roosevelt and Prime Minister Churchill, he assumed the post of commander of ETOUSA (European Theater of Operations, United States Army). In that capacity, he commanded the American invasions in Morocco and Algiers, moving his headquarters first to Gibraltar and then North Africa. He commanded the Allied forces in the invasion of Sicily and, when President Roosevelt met him whilst on a visit to Tunis, in December 1943, was informed, 'Well, Ike, you are going to command Overlord' (Eisenhower, 1977, p. 207). He chose General Omar Bradley as the ground commander of the American ground forces for this campaign and the British nominated General Montgomery (General Alexander, preferred by Eisenhower, was deemed unavailable and was to remain commanding the Allied forces in Italy). Later, Eisenhower appointed General George S. Patton to command the US Third Army when the storm aroused by the conduct in Sicily of that controversial and impulsive figure had died down. The Air Commander (and deputy Supreme Commander) was Air Chief Marshal Tedder who had served Eisenhower as air commander in the Middle East. The naval commander-in-chief was British Admiral Ramsay.

General Alan Brooke

General Alan Brooke was born in Northern Ireland in 1873 but was brought up in France. He emerged from the 1914–18 war as a Royal Artillery brevet lieutenant colonel with a Distinguished Service Order (DSO) and Bar, a Croix-de-Guerre and six Mentions in Dispatches. In the between-wars period he held a variety of important posts both in the artillery and in military colleges. At the outbreak of the Second World War, he led the Second Corps of the British Expeditionary Force in France, and his accomplished handling of the defence of the northern flank after the collapse of the Belgian Army made possible the evacuation of Dunkirk. He knew the German Army's capabilities and never underestimated them. He records in his diary in 1940, 'There is no doubt that they are most wonderful soldiers' (Bryant, 1957, p. 118), and he knew that an early return to the Continent would only be at the cost of a great number of lives. In 1941, he was appointed Chief of the Imperial General Staff, coinciding with the assumption of the premiership by Winston Churchill. Brooke was abrupt in manner, quick-minded, resolute and seemingly imperturbable. The Americans tended to distrust him for his lack of obvious warmth and utter concentration on the task in hand, but he eventually achieved a good working relationship with them. He lacked small talk but his diaries show him to be sensitive and capable of warm affection. His statue, which stands in Whitehall Gardens outside the present Ministry of Defence, bears the legend 'Man of Strategy'. He had difficulty in conveying to the Americans his strategic concepts and thus gaining the acceptance of his ideas, which covered the whole canvas of the World War picture and which viewed the Allied operations as an integrated and interdependent whole.

General Montgomery

General Bernard Law Montgomery was born in November 1887 into a harsh household regime imposed by his mother. He was not a good team member, and at Sandhurst was seen as something of a bully. He won the DSO whilst a subaltern at the battle of Ypres in the First World War. He was an unorthodox officer: austere, dedicated and eccentric. Montgomery did not tolerate 'bellyaching' by his senior commanders in the desert, but employed these methods himself when serving under Eisenhower. Dixon (1976) gave a psychologist's view of this complex character: 'a leader who cared about the welfare of his men, who was human and possessed of a sense of humour . . . he possessed . . . initiative. He may have been unbearably autocratic but he was not authoritarian'

(p. 357). 'Montgomery's regard for human life, [was] a potent factor in the over-cautiousness of which some historians have accused him' (p. 358). The war he had seen in the trenches in 1914–18 was very different from his rival Patton's experience in 1918. His lapses included 'An inability to get along with many of his military colleagues'(p. 359); [he sometimes allowed his own desire for personal glory to influence his planning' (p. 360). 'For a man who was adept at simplifying the apparently complex, whose ability to extract the essentials from a host of irrelevant factors was second to none, who could communicate his intentions and issue orders to his subordinates with a lucidity that left no room for misinterpretation, and who could write his memoirs with a style that puts most generals to shame, it is extraordinary that he should have been almost incapable of explaining himself to those *above* him' (p. 361). Dixon concluded 'that Montgomery's generalship was marred by the effects of his unhappy childhood' (p. 361).

General Omar Bradley

General Bradley was a personal friend of General Eisenhower, dating back to the time when they were at West Point together. Eisenhower selected him for the post of American Army Group Commander (in preference to General Patton) after they had worked closely together in the North Africa and Sicily campaigns. Eisenhower (1977, p. 215) comments on 'his ability and reputation as a sound, painstaking and broadly educated soldier... he demonstrated a real capacity of leadership. He was a keen judge of men and capabilities and was absolutely fair and just in his dealings with them. Added to this he was emotionally stable and possessed a grasp of larger issues that clearly marked him for high office.' His American colleagues respected Bradley, and Farrago (1979, p. 147) records that

> Patton admired Bradley's talents as an all-round foot soldier – his professorial approach to tactics; his masterly synchronization of intelligence, operations and logistics; his thorough execution of plans. And he, who was so boisterous and profane, respected Bradley's saintly personality. In Tunisia he found his Deputy Corps Commander self-effacing, impeccably honest, loyal, and industrious.

For Overlord, Bradley became Patton's commander.

General George S. Patton

General Patton was born into a rich family on 11 November 1885 near Pasadena in California. His father was a cultured man who read the classics to his children but denied them formal education in their early years. Thus George Patton was illiterate when he eventually went to school at the age of eleven. After he left West Point in 1909, he served with some panache in the cavalry with General Pershing in Mexico, and his career proceeded at an astonishing rate. He was promoted to lieutenant colonel in 1918. Later that year he was made a full colonel commanding a brigade, leading the operations of the first tanks to see service in the US Army. The *New York Times* gave a succinct summary of his character in 1945 (Farrago, 1979, p. 563):

> Long before the war ended, Patton was a legend. Spectacular, swaggering. Pistol-packing, deeply religious and violently profane, easily moved to anger, because he was first of all a fighting man, easily moved to tears because underneath all his mannered irascibility he had a kind heart, he was a strange combination of fire and ice. Hot in battle and ruthless, too, he was icy in his inflexibility of purpose. He was no mere hell-for-leather tank commander but a profound and thoughtful military student.

Dixon (1976) unfortunately does not include a psychological profile of this intriguing, complex character. One would intuitively conclude that Patton and Montgomery would not get on – and they did not. (Montgomery (1958, p. 262) quoted a reported remark of Patton's to Bradley at Argentan: 'Let me go on to Falaise and we'll drive the British back into the sea for another Dunkirk.')

General Charles de Gaulle

Charles de Gaulle was born in 1890 and attended the academy at St Cyr. He was taken prisoner by the Germans at Verdun in 1916 and became a lecturer at St Cyr on his repatriation. At the beginning of the Second World War he was appointed Under-Secretary of War but left France to put himself as head of the Free French Forces and operated from London. There his dictatorial intentions became evident when it was discovered that 'Frenchmen in Britain who were reluctant to join de Gaulle were deported to a remote French colony and "quietly dropped from view," as a source phrased it in a report to the American government' (Irving, 1982, p. 132). Irving went on to record that de Gaulle hated the Anglo-Saxons, was surrounded by anti-American advisers, and hated the British. This situation was hardly a good basis for trust and cooperation during the liberation of France from the Germans, and on the assumption of dictatorial powers by de Gaulle.

Conclusion

Eisenhower, the gregarious skilful soldier, had the task of supreme command of the Allied forces and had the difficult task of maintaining harmony and unity of purpose. He had to deal with Churchill, Alanbrooke and Montgomery on the British side, and the latter, in particular, was both eccentric and egotistical. Marshall, Bradley and Patton were the principal players on the American side. The first was Eisenhower's patron and mentor, the second was a stable individual and friend, and Patton was idiosyncratic, egotistical and vain. Apart from the dislike between the cautious infantryman (Montgomery) and the dashing, bold cavalryman (Patton), there was an undercurrent of distrust between the Americans, the British and the French. Interestingly, two of the principal players (Eisenhower and de Gaulle) both later became the political heads of their respective nations.

Stakeholders

It is important in the strategy process to consider the bodies that had a stake in the operations and what were their aspirations. The concept of stakeholders is one that is used in strategic management theory and can be usefully applied here.

Politicians

Von Clausewitz's famous dictum that war is merely an extension of political activity would indicate that the statesmen and politicians would be seeking advantage from the struggle for Europe.

(a) *Britain.* The British had entered the war, ostensibly through their treaty obligations to Poland, but also through considerations of the balance of power in Europe (a constant preoccupation of British foreign policy for centuries). In 1945 the British Empire was still intact and had provided essential supplies (particularly of manpower) for the war effort. Nonetheless, the cost of the First World War and much of the Second had dissipated the accumulated wealth of Britain and its predominance on the world stage was sure to be eroded in the subsequent peace. Britain, then, needed to salvage as much power and position at the end of the war as it could.

(b) *America.* By contrast, America prewar had isolated itself from world events and did not wield as much political power as its great wealth would suggest. The attack on Pearl Harbor in December 1941 forced a violent reappraisal of its *Weltanschauung*. The USA was forced onto the world stage and emerged from the Second World War as the most powerful nation on earth. The need for the *matériel* of war had necessitated a rapid development of industry and, given the large resources and wealth available and the native skill in production techniques, American industries, particularly aerospace, moved to world dominance. The Second World War conferred, formally, the status of 'superpower' on the USA.

(c) *France*. France had been humiliated by the Germans in 1940 and needed to restore her self-esteem and her world position. This restoration could only be achieved by military participation in the war and, like Britain, the French made full use of their colonial forces. De Gaulle had to fight his corner with the other Allies to achieve the perception of relevance to the cause and he proved a difficult ally. Participation in the military operations was seen as a means of ensuring France's presence in the peace settlement and in the postwar world political scene.

(d) *Soviet Union*. Although not present on the Western Front, their sacrifices on the Eastern Front determined the satisfactory outcome of the war for the Allied cause. Initially concerned to repel the invader from their territory, the latter stages became an opportunity to extend their hegemony over much of Eastern Europe. These moves can be seen both in the context of the spread of Marxism–Leninism and the traditional concern from tsarist days of securing their western boundary in the absence of any natural geographical boundary.

Military command

All of the generals, admirals and air marshals in the war were professionals, and their status in the profession of arms was dependent on their securing victories and acclaim. Their position in command was the result, in the main, of their dominant personalities and their acquisition of the necessary technical skills. Naturally, those of the necessary predisposition became obsessed with their own achievements or *la gloire* and were quick to take offence if they felt they were assigned a secondary role.

Military fighting men

In contrast to the aspirations of their commanders, the majority of the fighting men were not in the war for glory. They desired first their survival and, second, victory to release them to normal life. The strategy that would satisfy these demands had to result in low casualties and speedy victory. Eisenhower (1977, p. 467) recorded that Marshal Zhukov told him the Soviet practice for dealing with minefields:

> There are two kinds of mines; one is the personnel mine and the other is the vehicular mine. When we come to a minefield our infantry attacks as if it were not there. The losses we get from personnel mines we consider only equal to those we would have gotten from machine guns and artillery if the Germans had chosen to defend that particular area with strong bodies of troops instead of with minefields. The attacking infantry does not set off the vehicular mines.

Most soldiers would have preferred the American and British methods even if the resulting Soviet advance were quicker in achieving its object.

The Populace

The population of the countries of Western Europe suffered greatly and these privations had begun for some as early as 1938. The French were occupied and humiliated. Although some collaborated with the Germans, the majority looked for liberation. The British population had accepted that war with Germany was inevitable and looked for a complete victory that would remove the possibility of a similar conflict in the future. The population had to endure bombing, rationing and the loss of their relatives, both male and female. Their war had begun in 1939 and they expected the fruits of victory to be theirs. By contrast, the Americans entered the war in late 1941 when forced by Japanese action (although there had been for some time a strong lobby in Washington for entry into the European war for grand strategic reasons). When the build-up to a war footing was complete, the US forces greatly outnumbered any other ally (Eisenhower observed that at the end of the war in Europe he was commanding three million American troops). The populace in the USA were not subjected to bombing (apart from one raid on California by the Japanese) and did not suffer the same material privations, but had in common with their allies to endure the tragic loss of relatives. The populations of the allied countries, then, looked for complete victory and the acknowledgement of the suffering they had endured. They collaborated as allies, but were sensitive to the claims of others that *theirs* was a more important contribution.

The Enemy

The enemy's stake in the war was initially based upon the Nazi ideology, which promised *Lebensraum* and an empire that would last a thousand years, which were the rights of a Nietzschean master race. The Nazis, however, also capitalised on the feeling of the majority of Germans that they had been wronged after the First World War. The Nazi Party was prepared both physically and mentally for the outbreak of the war. In contrast, the British were still seen to be developing their war capability as late as 1942 (Kennedy, 1957). The German superiority in forces, equipment and generalship quickly resulted in successes. The British alone were unlikely to be able to secure victory in the shorter term and were hard pushed even to take the initiative, a necessary precursor of victory. The attack on Russia and the entry of the USA into the war sealed Germany's eventual fate. As time wore on, the more percipient in Germany saw the long-term situation as hopeless, and the generals, who had always had an uneasy relationship with Hitler, were early in this recognition. The German people suffered great privations, and were only induced to continue by the appeals to their nationalism and by the force of will of their leader. Von Clausewitz had conceived of war as a clash of wills: 'War therefore is an act of violence intended to compel our opponent to fulfil our will' (Rapaport, 1968, p. 101). The German's stake moved from world domination to survival.

Conclusion

All the stakeholders wanted early victory, but, for some, the way the battle was won was important for reasons of grand strategy or national and personal prestige.

The situation in 1944

Although the decision to invade north-west Europe had been taken in 1942, the support from the British was still equivocal at the Casablanca conference in January 1943. The result of that conference was a decision approving 'the plans for the invasion of Sicily, and [resolve] to press on with the preparations for opening a front in France at the earliest possible moment' (Kennedy, 1957, p. 285). In October 1943 the British were still lukewarm on the invasion. 'There is still a distinct cleavage of opinion between us and the Americans as to the correct strategy for Europe. C.I.G.S. feels very strongly that we should exploit the openings in the Mediterranean and extend the range of our offensive operations to the Aegean and the Balkans' (ibid., p. 307). Meanwhile the

Soviet Union was agitating for an invasion of the Continent to relieve the pressure on them. After a 'spoof' operation off Dungeness in September 1943, the Germans recognised the bluff and continued to withdraw units from France to bolster their operations in Russia. The determination to perform Overlord was sustained by the Americans, whilst the British continued to be concerned about possible casualties.

Conclusion

There continued to be differences of approach and opinion between the Allies, who came to different conclusions from their analyses of the situation. The British had had first-hand experience of the fighting power of the Germans and were resource-limited. The Americans geared up their powerful nation for war (although this took longer than they had thought), were anxious to seize the initiative, and assumed that their superior forces entitled them to the dominant role in the Alliance.

Command and control

The organisation for command and control of the Allied war effort is important because the structure determined the way that strategy was decided.

Political Control

The highest level of control of the war effort was invested in the two national leaders – President Roosevelt of the USA and Mr Churchill of Great Britain. The President, by virtue of his office, was the Commander-in-Chief of the American armed forces, and thus held the ultimate power of decision. Mr Churchill was both Prime Minister and Minister of Defence and thus held a similar power, but Bryant (1957, p. 27) observed that 'though he had the power to be a dictator in the day-to-day conduct of the war, he refused to be one...he never once overruled [Brooke] and the Chiefs of Staff in a major military decision'. The enemy leader, Hitler, was a dictator and commander-in-chief and interfered constantly in the direction of the German military effort.

Military command

The British system for the higher direction of the war used a Chiefs of Staff Committee (COSC) comprising the heads of the three services, one of whom acted as chairman. This committee had a Joint Planning Staff to conduct studies and to provide planning effort in support of the strategic decisions. The COSC met daily during the war, and reported and conferred with the Prime Minister at the same frequency.

When the Americans entered the war, following the attack on Pearl Harbor, the cooperation with the British became closer and more formal. Brooke was dismayed at the lack of integration of the effort of the American land and sea forces (the air arm was under the command of the US Army), and their unpreparedness for the rigours of war against the Axis powers. Following discussions between the two nations, the British system of control was adopted by establishing a Joint Chiefs of Staff Committee, comprising the professional military chiefs of both nations. This committee, and its associated planning staff, was located in Washington and the British appointed Field Marshal Sir John Dill (the previous Chief of the Imperial General Staff (CIGS)) as head of the British military delegation there. Brooke greatly admired Dill and their association was harmonious and effective. These senior officers were responsible for giving strategic advice to their political masters, the President and the War Cabinet respectively.

The Joint Chiefs of Staff Committee prepared directives for the theatre commanders, who were given considerable freedom in implementing these orders. When the Americans and British established their close integration, the theatre commander became a supreme commander for all the Allied forces. General Eisenhower, for instance, was Supreme Commander Allied Powers Europe, whilst General Alexander commanded similarly in Italy. In turn, these commanders had subordinates, who were themselves very senior officers, who commanded armies, corps and divisions, and who had a part to play in the strategy formulation process and its implementation. A significant concession gave commanders access to their own national authorities when they felt it necessary.

Conclusion

The British experience was useful in providing a sound structure for the command and control of the Allied effort. The politicians controlled the military, and a joint decision-making body provided a forum for agreement on strategy (even though some of the staff arguments were hard-fought) and the deployment of resources. Within the political and overall military frameworks provided by this organisation, the Supreme Commander had considerable freedom of action in achieving the objectives defined by his directive. A weakness was the direct access to national authorities granted to senior military commanders in the field (mainly invoked by Montgomery), which weakened the power of the Supreme Commander.

The strategy process

The process by which strategy was decided was complex, understandably, considering that the fate of nations and millions of human beings hung on the decisions. In the case of the British, strategy was hammered out between the Prime Minister and the military chiefs, so the personalities affected the outcome. Churchill, given his dominant personality and strong interest in strategy, made life difficult for the COS and Sir John Dill's health was adversely affected by the constant battles in Whitehall.

Churchill and Brooke formed a winning team, not only because the CIGS had the strength of character to stand up to Churchill's hectoring, but also because of the complementarity of their personalities. Bryant (1957, pp. 24–5) observed:

> In contrast to [Churchill's] sweeping Edwardian impatience for inconvenient details and 'method of suddenly arriving at some decision as it were by intuition without any kind of logical examination of the problem', Brooke's whole career had been a training in adapting means to ends. He had the imagination to see what was possible and the practical knowledge to know how, when and where it could be made so. He saw the war steadily and never, whatever the pressure of the moment, lost sight of the global picture. He had the ability – the hallmark of the born strategist – to grasp all the essentials of a problem at once.

Grand strategy, the selection of aims and the overall ordering of the Allies' approach to the war were decided by the political leaders at a series of high-level conferences: Washington, Casablanca, Cairo, Teheran, and so on. The military staffs, however, were present at these meetings and contributed to the discussions and decisions deploying arguments developed by their respective staffs. Thus, at Casablanca, the British argued for a Mediterranean-based strategy whilst the Americans favoured an early assault on the north-west coast of Europe.

The strategy for the conduct of the invasion of Europe and subsequent operations was in the hands of the Supreme Commander, who received advice from all sides. Thus, General Montgomery presented the invasion plans that had been devised by the Joint Planning Staff under his direction.

Table 3.2 Strength of the German Forces

	Enemy strength opposite First US Army			Enemy strength opposite Second British Army		
	Panzer divisions	Tanks	Infantry battalions	Panzer divisions	Tanks	Infantry divisions
15 June	–	70	63	4	520	43
20 June	1	210	77	4	430	43
25 June	1	190	87	5	530	49
30 June	½	140	63	7½	725	64
5 July	½	215	63	7½	690	64
10 July	2	190	72	6	610	65
15 July	2	190	78	6	630	68
20 July	3	190	82	5	560	71
25 July	2	190	85	6	645	92

Source: Montgomery (1958, p. 259).

Strategic issues

The strategy process has been described, in general, above, but the following issues were points of controversy that help to illuminate how the strategy emerged.

The Breakout in Normandy

The plan for the development of the D-Day bridgehead was the work of Montgomery and called for the British and Commonwealth (21st Army Group) forces to tie down the bulk of the German forces at Caen, whilst the American (12th Army Group) on the right flank was to achieve the breakout. Montgomery (1958, p. 259) provided the data (shown in Table 3.2), the purpose of which was probably to support Montgomery's argument that his strategy never intended a breakout on the British front, whose role was to be the hinge of an envelopment. Eisenhower (1977, p. 266) conceded this point: 'From the beginning it was the conception of Field Marshal [*sic*] Montgomery, Bradley and myself that eventually the great movement out of the beachhead would be by an enormous left wheel, bringing our front onto the line of the Seine.'

The broad front strategy

Eisenhower became responsible for land operations (see below) and was immediately faced by a dilemma. His decision (20 August) was '12 Army Group to be directed towards Metz and the Saar, where it could link up with the Dragoon force' (advancing from the south)(Montgomery, 1958,

p. 267). Montgomery, however, countered with his opinion that the strategy should be 'for the great mass of the Allied armies to advance northwards, clear the coast as far as Antwerp, establish a powerful air force in Belgium and advance into the Ruhr' (ibid.). On 20 August, Patton's 3rd Army had captured Orléans and was advancing on Troyes, and he called Bradley, 'Damnit, Brad, just give me 400 000 gallons of petrol and I'll put you in Germany in two days' (Farrago, 1979, p. 384). Liddell-Hart (1970, p. 562), commented: 'Eisenhower was now in the uncomfortable position of being the rope in a tug of war between his chief executives'. The compromise was to give priority to Montgomery with the American First Army covering his right flank. On 31st August, the 7th Armoured Division of the 3rd Army established a bridgehead across the Meuse at Verdun and then stopped because Patton had no petrol and other essential supplies. After the capture of Antwerp on 4th September, the 3rd Army was given supplies but now the resistance they met had stiffened. The outcome of the arguments between the commanders was a decision to maintain the broad-front strategy designed by Eisenhower before the invasion, with no army group being given the priority. This compromise satisfied no one and some commentators aver that it delayed the date of victory and conceded large amounts of territory to Russian occupation. Liddell-Hart's view was that the strategy was appropriate against an unbeaten enemy, but was wrong in the face of an army beaten and disorganised after the severe defeat and losses sustained in Normandy. The German General Blumentritt endorsed Montgomery's plan, 'He who holds northern Germany holds Germany' (Liddell-Hart, 1970, p. 565).

Resources

Resource availability had a dominating effect on the Allied military strategy. Despite the decision to defeat Germany first, in the beginning of 1944 there were thirteen American divisions in the Pacific to ten in the United Kingdom (Bryant, 1957). Only 29 divisions would be in Britain for the invasion in May 1944, and even that number assumed the transfer of seven British divisions from the Mediterranean in November 1943 (Parker, 1990). Of the 19 000 assault vessels built in America in 1943, only 1000 were allocated to the invasion of Europe, and Admiral King (USN) had concentrated 90 per cent of America's landing craft in the Pacific (Bryant, 1957). The planners had to assume that ports would not be available in the early months after D-Day, either because they would be stoutly defended or, if abandoned, they would be comprehensively destroyed and mined (as the Germans had left Tripoli). The mobile harbours, Mulberry, and the undersea pipeline, Pluto, had to be constructed to rectify this shortcoming.

After the invasion, supplies for the armies were crucial but difficult to maintain. Many of the Channel ports were still controlled by the Germans some time after the invasion (Lorient held out until the final German surrender) and re-supply had to be effected via the Normandy beaches. The air bombardment had virtually destroyed the French railway system, so supplies had to go by road. The 'Red Ball' express highway was established, operating 24 hours a day, and patrolled by military police to keep all other traffic away. The very successes of the advance across France, particularly by Patton's 3rd Army, exacerbated the supply situation to the extent that the decision of where to attack was conditioned by how much petrol and ammunition were made available and to whom. Irving (1982, p. 275) illustrated the scale of the operation: 'On August 30 1944, Eisenhower sent a congratulatory message to the Navy Department on the unloading so far: in the British area, 806 559 troops and 201 200 vehicles; in the US area, 1 197 897 troops and 219 947 vehicles. And a total of 3 153 476 tons of stores' (and the war had nine further months to run). Montgomery complained that in September he was importing only 6000 tons a day, half his daily needs. On 31 August, the 7th Armoured, followed closely by the 5th Division, established a bridgehead across the Meuse at Verdun. On the same day, Patton received a report that no petrol had been received and the Third Army was bone dry (Farrago, 1979).

The strategy for the advancing armies was decided by the availability of supplies and the allocation of them.

The issues of command

On D-Day, General Eisenhower was the Supreme Commander Allied Forces and Air Chief Marshal Tedder was his deputy. The command of the Allied ground forces for the assault was vested in General Montgomery, and General Dempsey commanded the Second British Army on the left, and General Bradley (Commander First US Army) the Americans on the right flank. On 1 August 1944, the command structure was radically changed, Montgomery assuming command of the 21st Army Group and Bradley the 12th Army Group. The 6th Army Group joined these groups after ANVIL (the operation that had delivered American and French troops into the south of France on 15 August 1944). Eisenhower was the Supreme Commander and also assumed command of land operations on 20 August, an arrangement that was challenged by Montgomery. Montgomery maintained that the Supreme Commander could not also command the land operations, but should have a deputy for this purpose in the same way as he had Tedder commanding Air Operations and Ramsay the naval forces. Montgomery, with typical lack of modesty, proposed himself for this task (although he did say that he would serve under another). Despite the force of the argument for such an appointment, Eisenhower knew that Bradley and Patton would refuse to serve under Montgomery. Not only were issues of command influenced by personalities but also the strategy itself was affected by the interaction of determined, egotistical individuals.

Conclusion

The Overlord landings and subsequent operations in north-west Europe were of a scale that almost beggars belief. Millions of men, millions of tons of stores, all costing many millions of pounds/dollars were in the control of a few men whose decisions affected the course of history and the lives (and deaths) of thousands of human beings. It is unsurprising, therefore, that some decisions were less than perfect, particularly when they were argued over by strong-willed, egotistical men who were convinced that *they* were right and held the keys to success. The strategy process was affected by national politics, organisational politics, personalities and resources. No business will ever deploy such resources nor play for such high stakes, but this case was written to shed some light on the process by which decisions were taken, to suggest parallels for business strategy theory.

3.6   Case study 2: the Alenia Marconi Systems joint venture

(Note: The case study was prepared using information supplied by Alenia Marconi Systems and outside information, other than general comment on the industry, was not available.)

Introduction

The defence industry has proved to be very profitable over a number of years, particularly during the years of the so-called Cold War. Even the collapse of the Soviet Union and the subsequent reduction of international tension have not seriously affected the volume of defence business, although competition has increased worldwide. In response to this increased competition, the defence industry in the United States of America has sought to improve its performance by increased concentration into fewer firms. Now, the likes of Boeing and Lockheed Martin are huge, and have a wide range of in-house capabilities, strong financial backing and economies of scale. Europe's defence industry, by contrast, continued to be fragmented into companies that could not match the scale of the American giants. During the 1990s, the companies, with political encouragement from the European Union, began a process of exploring possible mergers.

Seeking partners

The larger players in the European defence industry were to be found in France, Germany and the United Kingdom, although Italy, Sweden and Spain, among others, had a significant capability. Much of the French, Italian and Spanish defence industry was state-owned and some restructuring of companies like Aerospatiale and Thomson-CSF had been put in hand in anticipation of the expected concentration of the European industry. The Italian holding company Finmeccanica was similarly being broken up with deals like the joint venture in helicopters between the Italian Agusta and GKN Westland in the UK. Much attention was focused on British Aerospace and, at one time, it was expected that they would come together with DaimlerChrysler Aerospace (DASA) in Germany, as a step towards a European Aerospace and Defence Company. In the event, British Aerospace took the unexpected step of purchasing the defence arm of Britain's General Electric Company (GEC). As part of the deal, BAe acquired a part-share of Alenia Marconi Systems.

The Alenia Marconi Systems joint venture

Alenia Marconi Systems was created in December 1998 as a joint venture between Finmeccanica of Italy and GEC of the UK. The commercial arrangement is unusual in that it is a 50/50 split of ownership: that is, there is no dominant partner. The company operates a dual headquarters: one part in Rome and the other in Chelmsford.

The reason for forming the Alenia Marconi Systems joint venture is similar to the military logic: 'Whilst the reasons for adopting a multinational (coalition or alliance) response may vary, the aim is usually to accomplish an objective which a nation either does not wish to, or could not, achieve unilaterally' (Defence Committee, 2000, p. xxxi). The aim of the joint venture was 'to become across the sector the number one defence company outside of the States' (Interview with Mr Terry Soame, 24 January 2001).

The company structure comprises a series of corporate functions and four operating divisions: (a) Naval Systems; (b) Land Systems; (c) Missile Systems; and (d) Air Traffic Management Systems. In each of these

Table 3.3   Alenia Marconi Systems – key figures (in £ million)

	1999	2000	2001
Order intake	1480	1700	2060
Sales	930	1140	1310
Order book	3500	4060	4810

divisions there are Italian-based and UK-based companies, so nationally-based Italian and UK divisions have been avoided by choosing a functional structure. Although this arrangement avoids national 'blocs', there are differences of business practice between the two countries which now come into play. For instance, the UK operations are nearer to American practice and rely more heavily on documentation, whereas Italian business is less formal. The senior managers in Italy are more likely to be engineers than is the case in the UK. These differences, and others, have been confronted by the integration into functional, rather than national, divisions which will, it is hoped, benefit from best practice in each country.

The joint venture is only two years old and acquisitions are still being made, so the company has yet to achieve its final, stable organisation structure. The necessity for continuing change is more familiar to the UK workforce, and the joint venture foresees constant development as necessary for the foreseeable future. An imminent development is the transfer from BAe Systems to Alenia Marconi Systems of Combat and Radar Systems (CARS). When that acquisition has been made, Alenia Marconi Systems will have overtaken its European rival, Thales, and will have become the largest company in the world defence systems market, excluding North America and missile markets.

The joint venture is also achieving organic growth as shown in Table 3.3.

The defence market

The defence market has some special characteristics that affect the strategy and the strategy formulation in Alenia Marconi Systems. The customers are government departments or agencies who are under pressure to buy at the lowest price. More recently, the shortcomings of concentrating on the purchase price alone have given way to a search for a more complete approach, such as through-life-costing. In any event, it is a highly competitive market in which the customer is technically well-informed and competent. Business is conducted by competitive tender, which complicates business planning because either a substantial amount of business is won or there is no input at all. This contrasts with consumer marketing where production is continuous and revenue can be forecast to a better degree. Defence contracts have a long gestation period, maybe five years or more, and, the product may remain in service for fifteen to twenty years. Nevertheless, innovation is still a factor. Whenever the specification allows, commercial components will be used which are being developed continuously by the specialist suppliers. Currently, computing power is doubling approximately every 18 months. Customers demand the latest technology as 'future-proofing', and this hardware will have an effect on software production by Alenia Marconi Systems.

In contrast to the past, the significant value-adding process is software production, rather than hardware, and Alenia Marconi Systems are increasingly willing to rely on trusted hardware suppliers. Development across the board of all the hardware involved would no make commercial sense for Alenia Marconi Systems. Research and development and system improvements have to be continuous and the integration of R&D within the joint venture is still incomplete. Rationalisation of R&D is essential and is proceeding within the joint venture, because duplication of effort must be avoided. The American market has special characteristics, not least that the US suppliers are sometimes technically ahead of Europe, but also there is a natural tendency for the huge demands of the US armed forces to be met from US suppliers. Thus, Alenia Marconi Systems will work with US suppliers, but will generally avoid trying to sell into that market, for reasons of cost coupled with low expectations of success.

The market for air traffic control (ATC) equipment is a little different, although the customers are, again, usually government-controlled bodies. It is possible, however, in this case to make products for off-the-shelf purchase, in contrast to military systems, which are often bespoke to particular customers. The air traffic control market is also highly competitive and subject to continuous development as the demand for air travel continues to grow.

The two partners, thus, had similar competencies, which has aided joint working and synergies, although harmonising working practices and developing a new culture is taking time. Both partners, however, are very experienced in the defence and ATC markets.

The strategy process

The company begins the process of formulating its strategy by clearly defining its aims, and these not only define the required direction for the joint venture, but also serve to satisfy the expectations of the share-holders, Finmeccanica and British Aerospace. The details of the aims need not be considered in a discussion of strategy process, but the joint venture is broadly committed to growth and leadership within the defence and ATC systems markets. Its intentions, however, are specified in much greater detail in the formulation of their strategy.

The process adopted by Alenia Marconi Systems is an adaptation, endorsed by the shareholders, of the methods that were used in GEC Marconi. Under this system, the company strategy is reviewed annually, because Alenia Marconi Systems are required to report every year to their shareholders (Finmeccanica and BAe). Issues which require the shareholders' input can be raised as a part of this process, but generally there is little interference by them in the day-to-day running of the joint venture. The formal strategy process is guided by a corporate function, Corporate Strategy, which has offices in Rome and Chelmsford. The divisions provide staff to work in the strategic planning group that is responsible for generating both the strategy and the associated plan. The strategic planning group operates at director level under the guidance of the corporate strategy staff, and the divisional representative supply specific data, such as marketing information, and also their views on where the business should be going. The process is not entirely bottom-up, since the board will also add their views as the discussion reiterates between them and the strategic planning group. Agreement is finally reached on the strategy and the strategic plan, but the equal split between British Aerospace and Finmeccanica often results in a lengthened discussion until the negotiations are completed and agreement is finally reached. These negotiations by equal partners do affect the outcome, since agreement on radical changes in strategy would be difficult to achieve.

When the strategic plan is completed, the results are subjected to sensitivity-and-risk analyses. The business is too diverse for failure on one single contract to prejudice the survival of the whole business, but it is clearly important to know which parts of the plan are likely to suffer in the event of predictions and assumptions proving to be incorrect. Scenarios are generated and contingency plans considered, leading to an overall assessment of the nature and source of risk in the programme. These results are presented, with the plan, to the shareholders, who are also given a comparison of the predictions and outturn from the previous year to give an assessment of confidence in the process.

Although the defence systems sector moves relatively slowly, the company finds that an annual cycle is too infrequent, so a monthly cycle is superimposed upon it. Every month, the environment is scanned for new trends, the assumptions in the strategic plan are reviewed, and assessments of progress from the divisions are considered. Crucial orders and projects would have already been identified and progress in these areas is monitored for possible remedial action. This regular appraisal of progress on the strategic plan adds an emergent dimension to the annual, formal planning cycle, but is also an instrument of management control.

The company is aware of the need to secure the commitment of the entire workforce in the strategic plan. Widespread knowledge of the details of the company's strategy and its implementation may lead to a loss of security, such that this information might leak to competitors. There is, then, a dilemma between ensuring ownership of the strategy by the joint venture workforce and the risk of the plans being known by the opposition. There is no simple answer, although, it might be argued, the competitors' analysis of the joint ventures' plans would, in any case, reveal much of what is in the plan. On the other hand, there is a natural reluctance to provide them with free confirmation of their analysis. The support of the joint venture workforce has been deemed to be so important that information on the company strategy in detail sufficient for the employees is being published in the company newspaper. Furthermore, employees are encouraged to comment on the strategy by e-mail to a designated company website.

The strategy, then, is decided by an iterative process between the strategy planning group and the main board, which is under the overall guidance of the Corporate Strategy staff at the headquarters. The annual process is formal and deliberate, and continues into the production of a strategic plan for the year. The strategy and the plan are reviewed monthly, when modifications of an emergent nature can be made. The involvement of all employees is encouraged through a dedicated website, but whether meaningful inputs will be made is still to be discovered. On the one hand, the horizons at lower levels may be more tactical than strategic, and, on the other, the workforce may view strategy as something that the board should do.

Implementing the strategy

Implementation is not an issue central to the actual formulation process but, in this case, the outcome of the strategy process in Alenia Marconi Systems is a management plan. Ownership of this plan by those involved is important to its successful implementation. If managers think that what is written in the plan does not match their perception of the realities they face, the resulting dissonance could lessen the enthusiasm for achieving the defined targets. The managers have to believe that the targets, although maybe challenging, are achievable, otherwise they may become demotivated. The plan may also be seen principally as a method of control from above. The value of the plan may well, therefore, depend on the inclusiveness of the strategy formulation process.

Alenia Marconi Systems acknowledge the link to management control methods, but their view is that, as the organisation structure matures, as acquisitions are absorbed, and as experience in joint venture working is gained, the need for control will be reduced. The company is well-aware that control can stifle the innovations which might confer competitive advantage. Alenia Marconi Systems have already reduced to seven the layers in the organisation between CEO and the lowest level, and further reductions are not ruled out. The Italian element of the company is not accustomed to such formality in the strategy process, and there is some need for education of the British groups as well. Cultural changes are notoriously slow to be achieved, and acceptance of the strategy process has to be rooted in the hearts, minds and attitudes of the company workforce, but particularly the management.

Conclusion

Alenia Marconi Systems is a young company, which, nevertheless, is influenced by the culture and practices of its component parts, which have a long and proud tradition of successful defence contracting. The equal split of shareholding can slow the negotiated decision process, since no party has the casting vote, but results in a robust plan that is not overdependent on one nation. The strategy process adopted is a development of the formal, deliberate methods used in GEC Marconi, but an emergent element is superimposed to prevent the annual plans becoming inappropriate. Although final decisions are made at board level after a period of exchanging views with the staff, the lower parts of the organisation are encouraged to proffer their views. In any event, the strategy process will have to develop in consonance with the changes in the organisation and staff, but particularly as this young company develops a culture which, hopefully, will benefit from the best practices of two nationalities.

3.7   A commentary on the cases

Introduction

The case 'Struggle for Europe' concerns a series of military operations involving allies. The Alenia Marconi Systems case is about business conducted in an alliance. These events can be seen through the lens of strategic management theory in a search for parallels.

The linear rational view

The strategy that required an invasion of France in 1944 was the outcome of intense negotiation, during which the case for the primacy of operations in the Pacific was strongly argued. There was little doubt, however, that Europe would have to be invaded before Nazi Germany could be defeated. The approach to the operations was very rational and planned, and the preconditions for launching the assault were carefully defined. No evidence was found of intuitive judgements.

Alenia Marconi Systems adopt a similar approach to strategy in that the process requires a careful appraisal of the facts by staff drawn from the divisions. Intuition may be used, although this is not evident, but the analysis is generally based upon facts and agreed predictions.

These two cases concern large bureaucratic organisations. The evidence supports the theory that such bodies use linear, rational methods.

The emergent view

The overall aims of the war were not in dispute, but the means to that end remained controversial. From the earliest period of the Alliance the Americans wished to have a definite date fixed for the invasion. The British stalled until they felt that the overall balance of advantage had swung positively in favour of the Allies, although this approach led to accusations of lack of commitment to the cause. There is some evidence that the British adopted a 'muddling through', incremental approach to the strategy, whilst keeping the final aim clearly in view.

Alenia Marconi Systems, on the other hand, use a deliberate, annual process, combined with a review held every month. There is, therefore, an attempt to gain the benefits of both a deliberate and an emergent process. The British tried to avoid the constraints of a planned strategy by deferring decisions as long as possible. Both cases, however, show a rational process at work.

The resource-based view

The resources that could be assigned to various operations largely conditioned the strategy of the Allies. The date of the invasion was delayed, in part, by the lack of suitable assault craft. Even after the invasion, Eisenhower found that he had to decide between Montgomery's and Patton's demands for priority because the logistic organisation could not support both. He gave first one, and then the other, the necessary supplies, but then reverted to a 'broad front' strategy which slowed the whole advance. Logistics proved the pacing factor because as the Allies raced across France, supplies were still being landed in Normandy, until Montgomery captured Antwerp. Although the total output of the economies of all contestants was given over to war, the strength of the American economy ultimately proved decisive. The Second World War was attritional in nature but the decisiveness of the economic factor in war has long been acknowledged. Garthoff (1966, p. 104) quoted a Soviet writer on war: 'under all circumstances, whether a war is swift moving or protracted, economic preparation for the repulse of the aggressor, and the competence of the economy to provide the armed forces with all requirements, will play a primary role in the course and the outcome of the war'. The availability of resources, particularly their distribution, had a direct effect on the selection of strategies and on their ultimate success.

Resources also affect Alenia Marconi Systems' strategy. The support of two large companies, the shareholders, is critical in assuring that adequate finance is available to support the aim of becoming the largest company in their market. The reason for the joint venture was, in part, to combine critical resources from two national companies. These resources included the skills of the employees, and the designs and knowledge that each company possessed. The joint venture is shaping the new company by divestments and acquisitions to make available the resources that are necessary to dominate the markets in which they trade.

Organisational politics

The Allies collaborated surprisingly well, but individual commanders tried to gain personal advantage by 'pulling strings'. The direct access by national commanders to their own Chiefs of Staff placed Eisenhower in a difficult situation. Montgomery used this access by keeping in close touch with General Sir Alan Brooke, the British CIGS, who, in turn, had the ear of Winston Churchill. Thus, operational matters could quickly become 'political', and complaints quickly reached a level above the Supreme Commander and caused many problems. Eisenhower, too, kept in close touch with General Marshall, and hence with President Roosevelt, in Washington. De Gaulle, also, caused problems because he had a political agenda and the capture of Paris was probably more important to him in the shorter term than the defeat of Germany.

Another way of viewing the combative nature of the alliance is to acknowledge what Janssens and Steyaert (1999, p. 126) called the cultural duality. They posed the question: 'To what extent can organizations transfer their human resources policies across cultures, or how far should they adapt to the local culture?' The Americans were committing more resources to the north-west Europe campaign than the other Allies, but Eisenhower was conscious that his preferences, arising from his country's culture, were constrained by the politics at work within the Alliance. In the main, Eisenhower proved to be better at politics than military strategy, but his will held the military alliance together.

Less evidence is available on the operation of organisational politics within Alenia Marconi Systems, but the presence of the different cultures of the two nations involved does affect the operations of the joint venture. At the strategic level, the British side is more ruthless in its dealings, whilst the Italians are softer in their dealings with people. The strategy selected will be a compromise that satisfies both cultures.

In these cases, organisational politics affect both the process and content of strategy. Their effects are difficult to determine, and even more difficult to predict.

Power

The strategy process was directly affected by the relative power of the nations and individuals concerned. In the early part of the war, the Americans felt it necessary to give in to many of the British proposals since the latter had greater experience of the war and, initially, deployed more military power in all three elements. The Americans were anxious to close with the enemy to gain this experience and to gain a stronger position in the Alliance. The American nation had superior wealth and resources and, when these were increasingly employed, they demanded a greater degree of control. Montgomery and his staff produced the strategic and the operational plans for D-Day but, as the campaign wore on, the large numbers of American troops and their equipment swamped the British contribution, and the UK became less significant. It can be argued that Eisenhower's broad-front strategy was based upon a 'fair shares for all' approach and that the British had more influence than their input of resources. The strategy process was directly affected by considerations of power.

Alenia Marconi Systems also has a disparity of power and resources in its shareholders, but the equal split of shares moderates this situation. If there are instances where power is used to gain influence, it is not evident to the outside observer.

The effect of power is a little easier to predict than that of organisational politics since a good negotiator in a strong bargaining position will achieve dominance.

Conflict amongst the dominant coalition

The relations between the generals forming the strategy for the conduct of the campaign in north-west Europe can be characterised as conflictual. There were marked disagreements on strategy, priorities, even aims, and the question arises as to whether this situation was unsatisfactory and unexpected. Eisenhardt *et al.* (1997) studied conflict among board members of twelve companies in the United States and concluded that it arose when:

(a) The team was heterogeneous in terms of age, gender and functional backgrounds;
(b) They frequently and intensely interacted;
(c) They cultivated distinct roles;
(d) They relied on multiple-lens heuristics.

This study by Eisenhardt *et al.* only imperfectly matches the northwest Europe case. The commanders were much of an age and were the same gender, but were of different nationality and came from varying arms (infantry, cavalry) and experience (Eisenhower had had no command experience in war at divisional or corps level). Some conflict could be expected among this heterogeneous group of dominating (even arrogant) commanders accustomed to having their own way. The face-to-face interactions, however, were not frequent and the communication was 'star-connected' (one to one) to Eisenhower. It is debatable, therefore, whether more numerous group meetings would have led to greater knowledge and understanding of the views of others or, as the Eisenhardt *et al.* work suggested, more heated arguments. The generals certainly displayed distinct roles and styles (Montgomery – cautious; Patton – bold; Bradley – steady; Eisenhower – pacifier) and these traits became more pronounced as the conflict between the generals became more intense. The tensions arising from the differing styles could be predicted to lead to conflict. Eisenhardt *et al.* (1997, p. 56) identified four heuristics which they found created conflict:

- Multiple alternatives – 'In high conflict teams, when a strategic issue arises, executives almost immediately begin to develop alternative paths.'
- Multiple scenarios – whereas the first was the generation of alternatives within a single scenario, multiple scenarios describe a variety of conditions that could conceivably occur.
- Competitor role-playing – one or more members of the team plays the role of a competitor.
- Overlapping subgroups – where the team is deliberately broken up into subgroups focusing on particular issues, such as strategic direction, alliance relationships, and so on.

The paper suggested that these methods were adopted deliberately to foster constructive conflict. There is no indication that Eisenhower used these heuristics, but multiple alternatives, multiple scenarios and overlapping subgroups certainly existed in the Allied camp and generated a good deal of argument, not all of which was constructive.

There is no evidence that the Alenia Marconi Systems board's relationships are conflictual, although the company is still in an early stage of development and has not faced a strategic crisis.

Collecting strong-willed, talented individuals who are accustomed to having their own way will lead to conflict. Disagreement, however, can be beneficial in that all proposals are tested by the rigour of controversy.

Vision and mission

The Allies shared a common vision of a world rid of Fascism and Japanese imperialism. In terms of the Ashridge Model (see p. 78), the Allies coupled this purpose with shared values and broadly common behaviour standards. When disagreements occurred on strategy (and they were frequent), it was often through contributory 'purposes'. So, there was unanimity on the strategy of defeating Germany first, but Admiral King retained the bulk of the available assault craft in the Pacific. The British agreed that an assault on north-west Europe was a priority, but showed more keenness on pursuing operations in the Mediterranean. The Allies agreed on the big aim, but found agreement of supporting missions more difficult to achieve. The visions of a postwar world were very much coloured by national factors, despite the agreement on the Atlantic Charter. The British were concerned about their views of the Soviet threat, de

Gaulle was intent in seizing power in France and restoring national pride and position, the Soviet Union wished to achieve communist domination of as much of Europe as possible, and so on. All were agreed, however, that Nazi Germany must be destroyed.

Alenia Marconi Systems has a clearly defined aim to become the largest company in their sector of the defence industry. What their vision of the company will be when that aim has been achieved (which is imminent) was not enunciated.

Vision is the definition of a desired future state, which may well take years to achieve. Along the way, there will be numerous aims and strategies, but the vision ensures that they cohere.

Conclusion

The strategic management concepts and theories are a relevant underpinning of an examination of the strategy process in these cases. The conflict between the use of rational thought, planning, intuition and muddling through pervades these cases, as it does in strategic management theory (*vide* the exchanges between Henry Mintzberg and Igor Ansoff in de Wit and Meyer, 1994). Strategy process, it seems, is not the clinical human endeavour that the practitioners would like it to be. The resource-based view, although mainly concerned with content and context, can be seen to be operating in these cases, because the superior resources of the Allies conferred upon them strategic advantage, and the power and resources of the participating nations influenced the strategy process. The equal split of shares in Alenia Marconi Systems is a guard against dominance by one party. The strategy process in 1944 was largely determined by the interplay of personalities within the dominant coalition, and the increasing power of the American leadership gave them a strengthened role in the decision-making. Political activity and conflict played their part in influencing the final selection of strategy. The shared aim and mission were vital precursors to victory in 1944, although each nation imposed its own slant on their vision. Alenia Marconi Systems have established their aim but this will have to be revised into a vision for the longer term as a guide to their strategy formation. Strategic management concepts shed light on the strategy formulation process for both Overlord and Alenia Marconi Systems, and show a number of similarities. Leadership has not been identified separately for analysis, but is a leitmotif of the case and will be discussed in Chapters 6 and 7. No major differences between strategy process in the military and business have emerged at this stage.

4

Strategy Formulation and Resources

4.1 Introduction

So far, the nature of business and military strategy has been considered and the underlying paradigms discussed. A general similarity has been observed between the process in both fields, and no differences have been observed. One conclusion that can be drawn is that in both military and business fields, strategy can be characterised as being about decision (Mintzberg, 1978; Pettigrew, 1977; Quinn, 1978). There is the problem that there does not seem to be a universally accepted definition of 'decision' (Groner et al., 1983), but the general view of it being a discontinuity or definable point in the development of human affairs at which a choice has to be made will suffice here. The strategy is intended to achieve the aims of the organisation or, put another way, to enable it to 'win', however that is defined. The value of the decision is the extent to which it satisfies the stated aims or objectives. A test of the process leading to the choice of the course of action is the extent to which it results in an optimal decision.

This chapter looks at the implications of decision for the study of the strategy process, and at some of the theories. The problem encountered by researchers in this field is to be able to make sustainable generalisations on process, given the variety of contexts, decision-makers, organisation structures, and other variables. This limitation must be borne in mind. The further factor in gauging the efficiency of the strategy process – its implementation – is deemed to be outside the scope of this study. The chapter concludes with two case studies that compare the strategy processes in two large organisations, one military (the British Ministry of Defence), and the other business (IBM).

Strategy as decision

The conceptual framework suggested here is, then, that within a given context, the strategy process leads to a decision nexus that results in strategy content and ends in implementation. The contention of the incrementalists that there is no separation of strategy decision and implementation still fits this sequence, if one regards the process as iterative. The decision, however, is seen here as being a part of the strategy process, a view shared by Scott (1967, p. 19), who identified the following ingredients common to all decision processes:

1   A search process to discover goals.
2   The formulation of objectives after search.
3   The selection of alternatives (strategies) to accomplish objectives.
4   The evaluation of outcomes.

Decisions, then, fit into the map of strategy developed in this thesis and can be categorised in the way suggested by Miller *et al.* (1996):

(a) *Rational choice*: This approach uses rational choice models from economics and modelling from mathematics and statistics.
(b) *Behavioural*: Organisational theorists, sociologists and social psychologists investigate decision-making in organisations.
(c) *Individual cognitive*: Psychologists concentrate on the behaviour of the individual in decision-making.

An alternative view of the process of decision (and thus of strategy formulation) is to generalise it into the model shown in Figure 4.1. The inclusion of 'judgement' further confuses the arguments on rationality. The decision-taker is now seen to be using experience, which may be rational, but is largely intuitive. Experience may be encapsulated in a series of heuristics (learning from mistakes, situations resonating with memory, general rules for decision-making acquired through experience, and so on) and, if fully developed, may take us back to rationality in the form of algorithms. Judgement is likely to distinguish the good decision-maker from the poor. If the process, in the extreme, were to be purely mechanistic and rational in a positivistic manner, it is unlikely that

Analysis → Identify options → Judgement → Decision

Figure 4.1   An illustrative model of the decision process.

there would be a variation in the outcome between one person and the next. This situation, in turn, would imply that there is no variation in the quality of decisions. Experience shows that this is not the case as there are good deciders and poor (and, in the military context, good generals and bad).

The nature of problems

Mason and Mitroff (1981) use Rittel's characterisation of strategic decisions as 'wicked'. The meaning of this term is that the situations requiring decision are highly complex and interconnected. They are intertwined and inseparable and, like Hydra's heads, tend to multiply as one is excised. Other types of problem may be complex, but they are 'disorganised' (de-integrated, perhaps) and so are more amenable to solution by the statistical methods for dealing with uncertainty. What is more, the solutions to these 'tame' problems can be tested, whereas those of wicked problems can be only good or bad in relation to other problems and decisions. 'Wicked' problems do not end with the 'solution' as tame ones do, but are indeterminate and always amenable to improvement. The very definition of what the problem is may, itself, prove to be extremely difficult, because of its connection with other problems, and 'wicked' ones have no definitive formulation. Mason and Mitroff (1981) go on to aver that most policy and strategy problems are wicked, and show the following characteristics, which affect the way in which they can be resolved:

(a) Interconnectedness
(b) Complicatedness
(c) Uncertainty
(d) Ambiguity
(e) Conflict
(f) Societal constraints

They conclude that, because of these factors, the process of decision must be widened to include all parties affected, and a wider spectrum of information must be gathered from a wide number of sources. Here, the premise is accepted that both managerial and military strategic problems are 'wicked'.

But, if strategic problems are 'wicked', the role of rational methods from mathematics is reduced, and the argument is simplified to considering whether the decision is taken individually or collectively. The emphasis in the discussion in this chapter is, therefore, away from the statistical, heuristic decision methods, which, though valuable in their place, are less suitable for strategic purposes.

Defining the problem

Clearly, the decision-maker must be sure that the problem before him or her is the proper one to solve. Ohmae (1982, p. 15) expressed this idea thus: 'The first stage in strategic thinking is to pinpoint the critical issue in the situation.' Analysis is required at this stage to strip away the superficial and look for the 'real' problem. It is too easy to treat symptoms rather than the disease. The danger of intuition is that the solutions can be imagined before the problem is properly understood. This idea is echoed by de Wit and Meyer (1999, p. 80), who illustrated their ideas with the diagram in Figure 4.2 and identify the four elements of strategic thinking as: *recognising, analysing, formulating* and *implementing.*

It is also important that the decision-maker is the person who 'owns' the problem. If it can be said, 'This is not my problem', then it is implied that the problem belongs to someone else. In most of the literature, the chief executive, who ultimately owns the problem, takes the strategic decisions. In truth, others may claim ownership and propose a fully developed strategy to the CEO, whose role then becomes one of an endorser, approver, or gatekeeper, rather than an originator. If the decision-maker is not the legitimate owner of the problem, their level of commitment may be insufficient and the subsequent decision could be open to rejection by those who *do* own the problem. In some cases, then, the decision on problem ownership may figure in the solution process.

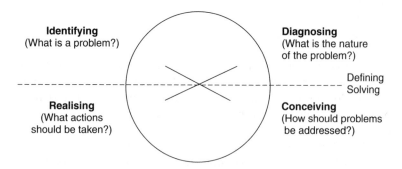

Figure 4.2　Elements of the strategic thought process.
Source: de Wit and Meyer (1999, p. 80).

Thinking about the problem

Cutting and Kouzmin (2000) developed an analysis of governance, which is based on the ideas of the neo-Platonists Plotinus and Proclus, who developed a trinitarian hierarchical structure to illustrate knowing and action. Figure 4.3 shows three levels of this analysis. Level 1 suggests that the individual will assess, reason or apply their will, dependent on their character. Level 2 relates these choices to personality and the way the individual reacts to social interaction. 'Heart-oriented people tend to move towards others to work together, head-oriented people prefer to move away and operate from a distance, while gut-orientated people hold ground and fight for their rights' (Cutting and Kouzmin, 2000, p. 484). Level 3 translates these styles to operations at group level, where the preferred governance of the 'gut' personalities is for a political mode, and so on.

Using this framework, the military commander would be likely to fit into the will–heart–leadership sequence in a war situation, but assess–gut–politics could be more appropriate in the routine formulation of defence policy. The business executive could fit into any of the sequences, and, in the view of psychologists, the orientation of these people is made early in life and developed into adulthood. In this context, Handy's (1980) view that corporate governance is essentially a political issue shows the difficulty for leaders in a bureaucracy.

De Wit and Meyer (1999, p. 67) also speculated on human cognition and identify the opposite ends of the spectrum of method which, for them, are *rational thinking* and *generative thinking*. The first assumes that problems can be solved by the application of logic but, as Simon (1965) has pointed out, the human brain can muster only limited rationality

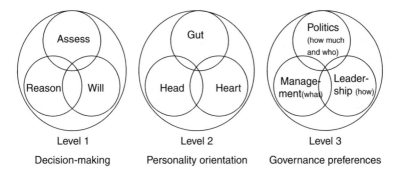

Level 1	Level 2	Level 3
Decision-making	Personality orientation	Governance preferences

Figure 4.3 Analysing individual approaches to decision.

because of factors such as limited information-sensing ability and limited information storage capacity. At the other end of the spectrum is the intuitive thinker who solves problems by instinct or experience alone. It is unlikely that either end of the rational–generative spectrum is practical in real life, so the strategic thinker is likely to tend to one end or the other dependent on personal predilection, or the nature of the problem. This point is developed in Hampden-Turner (1990) who argued that the strategic thinker must, as Scott Fitzgerald expressed it, 'hold . . . two opposed ideas in your mind at the same time'. Hampden-Turner stressed the dialectic nature of strategic thinking, which is the process of reconciling thesis and antithesis to produce the strategic synthesis. Hodgkinson and Bown (1998) described the two extremes of thinking as Type I (heuristic) – in which problems are addressed in a largely automated fashion – and Type II (elaborative) – which entails greater effort and conscious thought – and suggested that strategists do not use one to the exclusion of the other, but alternate between the two, depending on the nature of the problem that they face (familiar/unknown, simple/complex, and several other factors). Nutt (1990) investigated the influence of the manager's style on the strategic decision-making process. Initially, he used the Jungian classification, which asserted that individuals in acquiring information could be divided into two broad types: 'sensing' (preferring hard data), and 'intuitive' (qualitative and subjective). This categorisation was extended to those whose approaches to decision use 'thinking' and 'feeling'. The combination of these two ideas yields four personal styles:

ST   Sensation–thinking
NT   Intuition–thinking
SF   Sensation–feeling
NF   Intuition–feeling

Andersen (2000, pp. 46–7) further clarified the nature of these functions as defined by Jung:

> *Sensing.* The sensing type perceives things as they are. They show great respect for facts and information. Sensers have a great ability to register details and seldom fail when facts and details are part of the situation.

> *Intuition.* The intuitive person concentrates on the possibilities and is less concerned with details. He often finds the solutions directly without basing them on the facts.

Thinking. Thinkers are analytical, particular, precise and logical. They see things from an intellectual angle and often miss the emotional sides of the problem.

Feeling. The feeling types are interested in other people's feelings and dislike analysis. They stick to their own values and dislikes. They enjoy and prefer to work together with other people.

Andersen discovered from research on 200 managers that 32 per cent were intuitive and 23 per cent of the decision-makers had a 'creative–innovative' style. His aim of associating intuition with effectiveness could not be substantiated by his evidence.

Nutt (1990, p. 192) found from a series of experiments involving 79 top executives and 89 middle managers that:

> the decisions of top managers were *more* style dependent than those of middle managers. The judicial (SF) top executive was found to be action-orientated and the systematic (ST) top executive action-averse, with the speculative and heuristic (NT and NF) top executives taking nearly identical and neutral positions.

Since decision-making is essentially a human activity, the nature and outlook of those involved will have a marked effect on the process adopted. This factor is particularly relevant to a comparison of two fields of strategy-making, military and business, which, it can be argued, have a different ethos and a different context.

The nature of decisions

The end of the strategy process has to be a decision – 'we shall take this course of action, rather than another' – but strategy deals with the future and there are no facts beyond the past and present. Although the strategy process, up to this point, can be examined and listed, the actual decision-making activity is less easily understood. If one were to ask how a decision was taken, the decision-maker might find it difficult, if not impossible, to describe how it was done. Logical reasoning will have preceded the decision, but even the most obvious conclusion will contain an element of intuition. The process of turning data into information involves value judgements in differentiating facts and probabilities, and the assignment of 'meaning' to the knowledge acquired. Not all the 'facts' presented in the analysis phase will be true or unambiguous, the obvious conclusion may not be the most effective, and the decision-maker will not be free of bias. Furthermore, the facts and factors will have been prioritised and this process will affect the final choice, so even the most rational choice is to an extent judgemental. It might be argued that a computer algorithm will be free from human bias, but who constructed the program?

The decision situation is conceptualised by the decision-maker as a way of discovering meaning, and this ordering process will affect their attitude. They may, for instance, seek to reduce one large decision into subdecisions, which seem to be more amenable to a methodological approach, but the 'wicked' nature of true strategic problems may well make this simplification a delusion. Viewing the context of the decision as threatening or critical may well lead to a more draconian strategy than if the situation is seen to be normal and routine. This conceptual structure, this attempt to make sense of the vast external complexity, will also be affected by the decision-maker's past experience, education, gender, attitude to risk, and a range of other factors relating to the very being of the person involved. All will claim to be rational, impartial, logical, but there will always remain a large subjective element to any decision. Thus far, these generalisations about strategic decisions have been predicated on the assumption that the decision-maker is a singularity but seldom is it that an individual has sole control of the process. Mr Alan Hooper recalled (Interview, 8 December 1999) that Margaret Thatcher, Prime Minister at the time of the Falklands War, listened very carefully to, and questioned closely, the military briefings and advice she received from the Ministry of Defence staff. He said, 'The decision to sink the Belgrano was probably the most difficult decision she had to make, and she listened to the experts, took their advice, and acted on it.' In business and in the military, a decision is arrived at in the context of an organisation, and this complication introduces the elements of power and politics, bargaining, and disagreements. Often the final agreed solution is a compromise, which might be regarded by a sole, impartial observer as suboptimal. The introduction of other minds into the strategy process does not overcome those problems described by such as Simon (1965) and Cyert and March (1963), of bounded rationality, satisfying and the like.

Some decision parameters

The process adopted for the decision-making is influenced by the context and the culture of the organisation concerned. They are introduced at this stage but will be revisited in the light of the findings from the case studies and the interviews with strategy practitioners.

Formal or informal?

If the process is formal, the likelihood is that a greater degree of rationality will be demanded than in the informal mode. Informality may involve more people from the organisation who may feel freer to offer their opinions than in the formal setting. On the other hand, Papadakis *et al.* (1998) found that planning formality is positively associated with lateral communication higher'in the organisation. These views are not necessarily inconsistent in that there is a difference between seeking the views of middle management and involving them in the decision-making process. The military organisation is highly hierarchical, with rank being clearly indicated to all by various badges and insignia. The behaviour within the organisation is formal and the upper echelons do not expect to be contradicted publicly by those of lower rank. This situation should not be taken, however, to indicate that differences of opinion are not aired, or that the staff and decision-making processes are always positively top-down.

Routine or crisis?

Pettigrew (1977, p. 78) averred that 'the formation of strategy in organizations is a continuous process', which suggests that the process is routine (but not unimportant). Time to decision may not be important, so, widening the search for information, opening the discussion to be more inclusive, iterating around the problem-solving routine, and so on, may all be part of the normal process. Billings *et al.* (1980) constructed a model of decision in crisis that revised the earlier work of Hermann (1963), who had characterised crisis as being composed of a threat to valued goals, a restricted decision time, and surprise. Billings *et al.* (1980, p. 302) agreed with the literature existing at the time that held the view that 'the basic point is that a problem is perceived when a discrepancy or gap is perceived between the existing state...and a desired state'.

Three kinds of response are then identified: *inaction, routine solutions* and *original solutions*, and, if contingency plans exist, or the problem has been met before, the second option is the most likely to be adopted. Billings *et al.* (1980, p. 306) differed from Hermann in their view that 'crisis resides in the person as well as in the situation', so the identification of a crisis is perceptual. They end by considering the view of 'many' writers that crises produce a centralisation of authority:

First, increased time pressures will create a felt need to act quickly.

Second, the value of possible loss must be high for a crisis to be defined and 'the top' would intervene to reduce those losses.

Third, those lower in the organisation may feel unable to cope and may call in higher authority.

So, in a crisis, quick action is usually demanded, and so the decision can be limited to the CEO, or immediate high executives, at the cost of rationality and widespread discussion. Dutton (1993), Hermann (1963) and Papadakis *et al.* (1999) support this view. The latter described a crisis in the water industry in Greece, and discovered that the effects on the decision-making process were both positive and negative (summarised in Table 4.1 opposite). They observed on the positive side that:

(a) Managers were 'forced' to improve and create a large number of alternatives (some of them novel)' (Papadakis *et al.*, 1999, p. 30).
(b) 'Closer co-operation among various units within the organisation was the second positive outcome of the crisis' (ibid., p. 31).
(c) 'The third positive aspect was the speed of decision making . . . where similar investment processes could take years. In this case the whole process from the incubation period till the final decision . . . took less than four months' (ibid., pp. 31–2).
The negative aspects, however, were observed to be:
(d) 'The speed with which the decision had to be implemented resulted in short-termism.'
(e) 'Although much data was collected, these were never analysed in depth.'
(f) ' . . . managers *paid much less attention to the financial evaluation of the investment*'. (ibid., p. 32, emphasis in the original)

In their view, the managers involved in the decision responded differently depending on how they perceived the issues. An implication of this phenomenon is that the meaning of various situations might be manipulated to provoke a required response. For instance, classifying a situation as a 'crisis' might be used to close down political activity in the organisation and to permit a centralised decision from the top. A more benevolent view might be that more opportunistic, creative solutions might arise from a group of managers who have decided that they face a crisis. The results obtained by Papadakis *et al.* (1998) in their study of 70 strategic decisions in 38 Greek firms generally follow the pattern described above. They found it necessary, however, to differentiate the

Table 4.1 Comparing reactions to crisis versus opportunity

The characteristics of the decision-making process	Seen as a crisis	Seen as an opportunity
1 Comprehensiveness	• A broad range of alternatives was considered • Short-termism prevailed • Superficial examination of important aspects. Mindset to 'ease' the pain of the crisis	• In-depth evaluation of a small number of alternatives. Thorough data collection (procedural rationality) • Questioning attitude
2 Financial reporting	• Given the acute time pressure and the difficulty in data collection, strict financial evaluation of the project was somehow overlooked	• Thorough evaluation of the project • Effort to justify the project both inside and outside the organisation
3 Participation	• Close cooperation among departments	• More hierarchical decentralisation and middle-management participation
4 Politics	• No politics. Arguments centred on facts and ideas on how to ease the crisis	• Elements of political activity emerged. Various groups started questioning the appropriateness of the project
5 Duration and timing of	• Speedy process. Basic criterion was implementation speed	• Less time pressure
6 Short-term vs longer-term behaviour	• Short-term	• Longer-term

behaviour in 'mild crises' from that in more acute situations. In the former, the vital information often held by middle management can be exploited through hierarchical decentralisation of decision-making, but an acute crisis leads to centralisation. Nonetheless, the earlier observations made above apply: someone has to determine the acuteness of the crisis, and that process may be political.

Deliberate or emergent?

The process may be a regular cycle of events in which the strategy is revisited and reviewed. On the other hand, following Pettigrew (1977), the strategy can be constantly under consideration and emerge from a series of small steps, in contrast to the, say, annual review. The processes are quite different and will affect the types of participants. There is a correlation between deliberate/emergent and formal/informal, in that the deliberate process is more likely to be formal, and the emergent informal. A decision may be a discrete event, but it can also be a small step in a continuous, emergent strategy process, as illustrated in Figure 4.4.

Individual or collective?

In the small, entrepreneurial firm, it will often be the case that decisions are taken individually by the leader. The larger and more complex the organisation, the more one might expect the strategy process to involve more people from different parts of the organisation.

Bottom-up or top-down?

The ideas for strategy content may come from the top of the organisation down to the staff or from the lower management up to the top. Top-down can be conceptually driven, and the details are then worked out in the organisation, or bottom-up can be stimulus-driven from the environment to be approved by the executive. In some organisations, the actual strategy process can be a combination of these two in a repeating cycle.

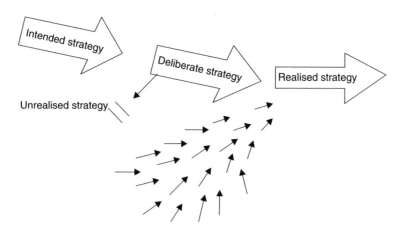

Figure 4.4   Forms of strategy.
Source: Mintzberg and Waters (1985).

Rational or intuitive?

Jungermann (1983, p. 64) concluded:

> Rationality is not a genuine term in scientific psychology but rather is a concept of philosophy and economics. The most common, and in this context most relevant, definition says that an action is rational if it is line with the values and beliefs of the individual concerned; or, more precisely, if it is 'logical' or 'consistent' as stated in a set of axioms. This specifies rational behaviour normatively.

He identified a school of criticism that views human judgement and decision-making as deficient because of: bias; the use of heuristics; inconsistencies arising from an imperfect representation of the problem; and defective searches for information. In contrast, an opposing school challenged the view that human judgement and decision are cognitively deficient because: judgements are seen as discrete events as opposed to forming part of a continuous process; the person- and context-dependencies are ignored; and the cost of rationality (that is searching for *all* possibilities, as opposed to satisficing) is not taken into account. Whereas Jungermann approached this issue from the psychology discipline, Isenberg (1984) studied twelve successful senior executives who were heads of company divisions to conclude that they relied heavily on a mix of intuition and disciplined analysis in their decision-making. He acknowledged the cognitive power of the brain, but drew attention to the following shortcomings (1984, p. 83):

(a) 'We (ie human beings) easily believe that salient events occur more frequently than they really do.'
(b) '...our overconfidence in our own expertise at making complex judgements'.
(c) '...we are not very good at assessing the degree of relationship among variables...Unless the relationships are obvious, we tend to rely on preconceptions and perceive illusory correlations.'

Even so, he believed that intuition is not the opposite of rationality, but is based upon the manager's experience and the heuristics that he or she has developed over years of combining gut feeling with systematic analysis, quantified data and thoughtfulness. Westley and Mintzberg (1989, p. 18) held a similar view: 'Like the craftsman, the strategic visionary would appear to develop strategic perception as much through practice and gut-level feel for the business, product, market and technology, as through conscious cognition.'

One can go further and assert that it is impossible to have intuition about a subject about which one knows little. In these circumstances, all one can do is guess, which is not the same as intuition.

Isenberg's (1984) solution to the phenomenon of the non-rational manager (he found all were so) was an increase in rationality of the organisation and its decision support systems. If, however, the decision-maker's paradigm is non-rational, it could not be changed merely by decree.

Mintzberg (in Campbell, 1991, p. 109) was convinced that strategic decision is essentially intuitive. He defines the spectrum as stretching from deliberate thought to emergent, intuitive thought:

> The difference is between the cerebral, which is based on words and numbers, and the insightful which is based on images and 'feel'... Intuition is a deeply held sense that something is going to work. It is grounded in the context in which it is relevant and based on experience of that context. I cannot be intuitive about something I know nothing about.

Lindbergh (1953) provided an example of such a decision process as he recalls sitting in his aircraft on Roosevelt Field, Long Island, before his record-breaking transatlantic flight:

> No, I can turn to no formula, the limits of logic are passed. Now the intangible elements of flight – experience, instinct, intuition – must make the final judgement, place their weight upon the scales. In the last analysis, when the margin is close, when all the known factors have been considered, after equations have produced their final life-less numbers, one measures a field with an eye, and checks the answer beyond the conscious mind.

High-velocity environments

Eisenhardt (1989b) studied the speed at which decisions are taken in fast-moving industries, the methods employed, and the effectiveness of the resulting decision. Her results are discussed below.

Those, then, are some parts of the vocabulary of strategy formulation that figure in the literature on the subject of strategic management.

These ideas are now revisited in the context of the influence they have on organisations in the strategy process.

Approaches to decision

There are a large number of decision methods proposed in the literature. Dean and Sharfman (1996) linked the decision-making process used to decision success achieved, and their work showed a positive relationship between procedural rationality and successful strategic decisions (and negatively to political behaviour which is discussed below, p. 138). Since strategic decisions are made under conditions of uncertainty (since they are future-orientated), attempts are made, in the rational approach, to enlist the aid of stochastic methods and, more recently, of game theory. There is a difference, however, between strategic decisions and strategy selection. The first may be an investment decision that could materially affect the profitability of the company, but does not alter significantly the selected strategy. Highly rational methods, like discounted cash-flow analysis, decision trees, minimax, minimax regret, and so on, can be highly relevant and helpful in these types of decision. Given the 'wicked' (that is, complex and integrated) nature of strategy decisions, however, statistical, probabilistic methods are too single-level to be of more than supportive value. Game theory, too, promises the opportunity to consider, in a structured way, the reactions of competitors to strategic moves, but Brandenburger and Nalebuff (1995, p. 57) observed that 'many people view games egocentrically – that is, they focus on their own position. The primary insight of game theory is the importance of focusing on others – namely allocentrism.'

On the other hand, games that are not zero-sum and involve multiple players (that is, are likely to be strategic) are beyond resolution by this technique. Camerer (1991, p. 137) observed: 'Its [game theory] greatest impact has been in economics, especially in the last 15 years in industrial organization.' The military have made considerable use of war-gaming, where one's own plans are played out against likely enemy reactions, and the probabilities of weapons' success, damage and so on are used to gauge the likely outcome. The use of Monte Carlo techniques to support these calculations can lead to success on one play, and failure on another. Although one might conclude that, in these circumstances, the plan is too brittle and needs amending, the method may lead to the selection of a strategy that is too pedestrian. Selection of a more daring plan, however, leads us back to the outlook of the decision-maker.

Highly rationalistic methods of this nature cannot be dismissed as worthless in the strategy process context for they may yield useful insights, but they are likely to be too simplistic to comprehend the complexities of truly strategic decisions, and may yield a cautious result that fails to exploit the true potentials of the situation. Chaos theory provides a justification for this view. Levy (1994) viewed business as a non-linear dynamic system, and Stacey (1993) saw it as a complex adaptive system. Thus, according to these views, we can expect chaotic (patterned, yet unpredictable) behaviour in business, where the initial state of play can strongly affect the future outcomes, where minute variations in input values can have a disproportionate effect, and where the actions of the various players can be synergistic: that is, the outcome is greater than the sum of the actions that produced them. Chaos theory can be seen as a warning against believing that the outcome of a linear/ rational analysis of the strategic business situation is 'true'. Chaos theory serves as a warning to strategists and as a demonstration of the need for flexibility and responsiveness, rather than providing a schema for the strategy process. Stochastic methods do, however, remind us all that luck plays a significant role in human affairs.

Models of the decision process

A number of attempts have been made to model the process of decision-making and some of these are now presented.

Morris

Morris (1969) suggested that the management decision process could be described as the sequence shown in Figure 4.5 (a diagram constructed by this author from the text referenced above). Morris's model of the process begins with some form of stimulus, a situation that indicates that a decision is required. The decision-maker searches their memory for similarities in their experience, and this process is selective and will affect what is perceived or recalled. Consideration of the problem and the memory will lead to a conceptualisation or a structuring of the

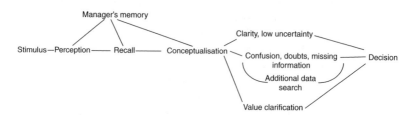

Figure 4.5   Morris's decision model.

situation requiring a decision. If the decision is deemed to be routine because of the clarity with which it can be conceptualised, and the associated uncertainty is low, the manager will proceed to decision. If, on the other hand, the initial view is one of confusion, doubts and uncertainty, the decision-maker may well search for more information or additional alternatives. A third response to the conceptualisation of the problem may be the need to clarify one's objectives, and how the outcomes of the alternatives relate to the achievement of them. A particular case is attitude to risk.

Mintzberg, Raisinghani and Théorét

The model proposed by Mintzberg *et al.* (1976) was the result of a field study of 25 strategic decision processes, which discovered a structure to 'unstructured' decisions. They referred to the earlier work of Simon (1965) who proposed the following phases of decision: *intelligence–design–choice*, but Mintzberg *et al.* preferred, as a result of their research, to use *identification, development and selection*. Their sequence of 'routines' was:

1 *Decision recognition routine* – is a decision required?
2 *Diagnosis routine* – reviewing existing information channels and opening new ones to clarify and define issues.
3 *Development phase* – comprises:
   - *Search* – for ready-made solutions
     - Memory search of existing information
     - Passive search waiting for unsolicited material to appear
     - Trap search by stimulating possible sources, such as suppliers
     - Active search by scanning sources
   - *Design* – develop custom-made solutions, which is a complex iterative process
4 *Selection phase* – can be more than a single choice and may require iteration back into the development phase
   - *Screen* – more concerned with eliminating unfeasible solutions
   - *Evaluation–choice* – can be seen as having three modes:
     - Judgement – by one individual, using procedures he cannot explain
     - Bargaining – selection by a group of decision-makers having conflicting goal systems
     - Analysis – factual evaluation by experts (that is, technocrats)
5 *Authorisation routine* – when the decision-maker does not have authority to commit the organisation to a course of action.

They commented, *inter alia*, that 'the evaluation–choice routine is in practice a crude one' (Mintzberg *et al.*, 1976, p. 259) and that many issues involving emotions, politics, power and personality must be considered. They later observed (ibid., p. 262) that 'political activities reflect the influence of individuals who seek to satisfy their personal and institutional needs by the decisions made in the organization' – usually manifested as bargaining.

Golub

Golub (1997, p. 2) offered the following definition: 'A good decision is the end result of carefully selecting a preferred course of action after studying what might happen were a variety of alternatives chosen.' His approach to decision-making is highly rational, although he includes the criticisms of this approach that (1) comprehensive analysis is overwhelmingly difficult, (2) the apolitical emphasis on the problem overlooks the people involved, and (3) the reliance on human reasoning is inherently flawed (ibid., p. 12). Nonetheless he offered a model of a sequence of ten steps comprising the 'Rational Model':

Decision analysis	Step 0	Agenda
	Step 1	Problem
	Step 2	Objectives
	Step 3	Alternatives
	Step 4	Forecast
	Step 5	Compare
	Step 6	Select
Administration	Step 7	Implement
	Step 8	Monitor
Evaluation	Step 9	Evaluate

Although this model suggests linearity, Golub points out that various steps can be revisited by looping back. For instance, the problem definition step might be reviewed as a result of identifying objectives. The methods described in the book emphasise mathematical methods, particularly in considering the problems of risk/uncertainty.

Chakravarthy and Lorange

Chakravarthy and Lorange (1991) described their conception of the strategy process as comprising the sequence: objective setting; strategic programming; budgeting; monitoring, control and learning; and, finally, incentives and staffing. The higher management of the firm should set the objectives, which should both incorporate the vision of the CEO and impart excitement and challenge to the firm's management. In a divisionalised company the supporting objectives are negotiated with the divisional leaders. Strategic programming was seen as involving the management of the firm in the process of achieving the objectives that have evolved in the first phase. This part of the process extends down into the functional areas of the management and will yield an estimate of the resources required. If, for instance, the first estimate of the resources required exceeds that which is practical, the planning sequence will have to be successively refined until a balance is reached between resources required and those available. The further steps, though important, are not relevant to the purposes of this study.

Chakravarthy and Lorange illustrated their ideas with the diagram in Figure 4.6, which shows the levels used in various steps and the iterative nature of the process.

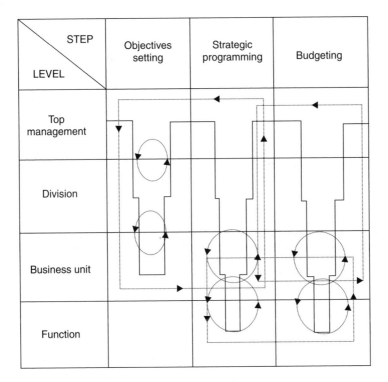

Figure 4.6   Interactions and iterations in the strategy process.
Source: Chakravarthy and Lorange (1991).

Cray, Mallory, Butler, Hickson and Wilson

Cray *et al.* (1991) based their findings on a study conducted in Bradford of 150 cases in 30 diverse organisations. Their results are summarised in Table 4.2. They found that *sporadic* decisions encountered more serious delay, took longer and were more informal. The process lurched from one impasse to the next with much debate. *Fluid* decisions moved more quickly and steadily, encountering fewer delays because of the greater use of formal committees. *Constricted* decisions were more concentrated around a single person or small group, and little effort was made to gather less accessible information.

Briefly, the explanatory variables of *complexity* are *rarity* (unfamiliar topics), *precursive* (novel, parameter-setting), *openness* (acceptability of some solutions), *seriousness* (effect on the organisation of a wrong decision), *diffusion of consequences* (how long it takes for consequences to emerge), *endurance* (how long consequences will last), *radicality of consequences* (departure from status quo), *involvements* (numbers involved), and

Table 4.2   Results from the Bradford study

Process type	Characterised by process variables	Modes of decision-making
Sporadic (informal, spasmodic and protracted)	More delays More impediments More sources of information More variability of information More informal interaction Some scope for negotiation More time to reach decision Decision taken at highest level	*Vortex* Diverse involvement Serious Non-precursive Contentious Externally influenced
Fluid (steadily paced, formally channelled and speedy)	Fewer delays Fewer impediments Fewer sources of information Less variability of information Some scope for negotiation More formal interaction Less time to reach decision Decision taken at highest level	*Tractable* Less diverse involvement Less serious Diffuse consequences Rare (novel) Precursive Non-contentious Evenly influenced
Constricted (narrowly channelled)	More sources of information Less effort to acquire information Little scope for negotiation Less formal interaction Decision taken below highest level	Familiar Non-novel Limited consequences Non-precursive Unevenly and internally influenced

Source: Cray *et al.* (1991).

diversity (functions involved). The variables of *politicality* are *contention* (how much disagreement), *pressure* (influence brought to bear), *imbalance* (powerful and weak groups), and *intervention* (outside influences).

It is difficult to simplify the results of this complex paper, but the political factor in decisions emerges as a clear factor and Cray *et al.* suggested (1991, p. 244) that the rationality in decision-making is 'a political rationality rooted in the calculus of control and influence rather than an abstract logical rationality'. The search for information is driven by the need for ammunition for the political battle, rather than being a drive towards greater rationality of decision. They conclude that the type of decision required tends to determine the method employed. Thus: 'Vortex kinds of decision most often generate sporadic types of process, tractable kinds of decision most often generate fluid types of process and familiar kinds of decision most often generate constricted types of process' (ibid, p. 246).

Eisenhardt

Eisenhardt (1989b) detailed the results of research into strategic decision-making in fast-moving industries, in which micro-computer firms were studied. Her propositions were as follows:

1 The greater the use of real-time information, the greater the speed of the strategic decision process. (p. 549)
2 The greater the number of alternatives considered simultaneously, the greater the speed of the strategic decision. (p. 556)
3 The greater the use of experienced counsellors, the greater the speed of the strategic decision process. (p. 559)
4 The greater the use of active conflict resolution, the greater the speed of the strategic decision process. (p. 562)
5 The greater the integration among decisions, the greater the speed of the strategic decision process. (p. 565)
6 The greater the speed of the strategic decision process, the greater the performance in high-velocity environments. (p. 567)

The conclusion that the more data considered, the speedier the decision, ran counter to earlier research. Eisenhardt found, however, that immersion in current real-time data improved the executives' grasp of the situation, particularly when several alternatives were considered simultaneously. Those executives who consulted experienced colleagues reached decisions quicker, but also used group consultation and teamwork in considering the many alternatives. Conflicts were best resolved by discussion within the group and such interactions are very frequent. Those who could integrate mentally the strategic decisions with the current realities facing the firm obtained the quickest results. By contrast, the slowest decisions were characterised by sequential consideration of alternatives (a different solution was not considered until the first had been rejected), and anxiety and irresolution by an isolated (perhaps autocratic) decision-maker, who would not act until a deadline approached. The time taken to reach a decision varied between one and a half months and twelve months. Eisenhardt (1989b, p. 570) quoted an executive of the firm Promise (a pseudonym): 'The only competitive advantage is in moving quickly.'

Image theory

Image theory is a unifying theory of decision-making for individuals making personal decisions, and decisions in the context of organisations. Beach, *et al.* (1992, p. 173) summarised the theory thus:

> The general idea is that the decision-maker is an individual agent working in the context of a group within an organization, be it a family, a club, or a job. Most decisions are made in concert with colleagues in the group, but the decision-maker has to make up his or her mind and then the diversity of opinions is resolved in some manner that depends upon the dynamics of the particular organization....
>
> The decision-maker has his or her own private principles, goals and plans, of course, but he or she also knows those of colleagues in the group and the transcendent values of the organization...the decision-maker differentiates between what is pertinent in one setting and what is pertinent in a different setting.
>
> The decision-maker possesses values, morals, ethics, and so on that define how things *should* be and how people *ought* to behave. [These principles] serve as the ultimate criteria for decision-making.

Image theory proposes the notion that decision-makers use schematic structures to organise their thinking about the past, present and future and these schemata are termed 'images'. The theory identifies three such images:

- *Organisational value image*: The organisation's norms, values, standards and ethics are regarded as imperative principles and the criteria against which any decision is judged.

- *Organisational trajectory image*: This image reflects the organisation's agenda for the future, its direction, goals and ends.
- *Organisational strategic image*: The plans that are in progress for attaining the goals and the forecasts on which they are based are the components of this image.

The theory suggested that potential decisions are tested against the fit between the option and the images. Decisions are adopted if they meet the value image and if the progress towards the trajectory and strategic images is satisfactory. Thus, this theory suggests that the values and culture of a company directly affect the acceptability of candidate solutions, which is an important conclusion for both the military and the business cases.

The vicarious decision

Although not described in the literature, there can be an attempt to solve a problem by applying a previously tried solution. So, it might be shown that, given a certain context or scenario, a particular solution led to success. Therefore, it might be argued that, if the given scenario is the same, the identical solution should be adopted in *this* case. How can one be sure, however, that the situations are identical, particularly since the problem is most likely to be 'wicked'? Perhaps some small, but vital, factor is different, which would invalidate an exact comparison. In which case, the whole rationale for the adoption of the solution could be destroyed. To a certain extent, this argument extends to *method* as well as the actual decision, and there is a danger that strategy textbooks can imply, 'use this methodology and the correct solution will emerge'. Such an approach might well overlook the contextual factors such as organisation (structure, power and politics), leadership (and competence), attitude to risk and all the variations possible between one scenario and another. Strategic thinking is not algorithmic. Machiavelli (1958, p. 27) observed: 'because men, walking almost always in paths beaten by others, and following by imitation their deeds, are yet unable to keep entirely to the ways of others or attain to the powers of those they imitate'.

Such an approach to decision-making is not the same as using one's favourite heuristic, but trying to hammer a previously used 'round' decision into a 'square' problem hole is unlikely to be successful in the vast majority of cases.

Tool sets

What has been attempted above is a description of business strategy decision theories in which there are some common factors, but which fail to settle the rational/intuitive dichotomy. Perhaps it is expecting too much to have a single, comprehensive theory for such a complex human activity where the context, the personality and the organisational environment are all so varied, and each has a marked effect on the process adopted. Commonly available to all is a series of techniques or approaches that can be seen as tools which can be applied to problems in search of a solution. These include: game theory, chaos theory, psychology, social science, and 'dominant logic' (Prahalad and Bettis, 1986). These do not qualify as *paradigms* using the definition in Chapter 3 above – 'an organising principle: a mindset' – although their acceptability will be affected by the beliefs of those considering content and process.

The effect of organisations on strategy process

'Each organization will need a different approach to strategy making and to the delivery of strategy' (Eden and Ackerman, 1998, p. 7). This view suggests that there are as many forms of strategy process as there are organisations. Even if that is so, some worthwhile generalisations have emerged on the effect of organisations on the strategy process.

The effect of structure

Fredrickson (1986) considered the effects that organisation structure imposes upon the strategy formulation process and considered them under the three dimensions: *centralisation, formalisation* and *complexity*. These he summarised as shown in Table 4.3. These results showed that as centralisation of decision is increased, fewer people would become involved, the goals would be more positive, the choice would be made using a rational approach and the greatest limitation would be that of the cognitive competence of the players. Formality in decision-making will make it more likely that strategic decisions will be made in response to crises, the goals will be remedial, the process will be a standardised routine, and the outcome may be lacking in attention to detail. Complexity will increasingly lead to a failure to recognise the need for strategic action, the process will be characterised by political bargaining and bias will be introduced by the parochial perceptions of the players.

Frederickson went on to relate these dimensions to three of the organisation types identified by Mintzberg, namely Simple, Machine Bureaucracy and Professional Bureaucracy. He combined the two as shown in Table 4.4.

Frederickson made the same point as Bailey and Johnson (1992) that these are not water-tight categories, and that the latter's research had shown that real organisations may well display elements of several of the identified traits. Bailey and Johnson (1992) also included an assessment

Table 4.3 Propositions regarding the effects of the three dimensions of structure

Centralisation	Formalisation	Complexity
Propositions 1 A–D. As the level level of centralisation increases, so does the probability that:	*Propositions 2 A–D*. As the level of formalisation increases, so does the probability that:	*Propositions 3 A–D.* As the level of complexity increases, so does the probability that:
1A The strategic decision process will be initiated only by the dominant few, and it will be the result of proactive, opportunity-seeking behaviour;	2A The strategic decision process will be initiated only in response to problems or crises that appear in variables that are monitored by the formal system;	3A Members initially exposed to the decision stimulus will not recognise it as being strategic, or will ignore it because of parochial preferences;
1B The decision process will be oriented toward achieving 'positive' goals (i.e. intended future domains) that will persist in spite of significant changes in means;	2B Decisions will be made to achieve precise, yet remedial goals, and that means will displace ends (goals);	3B A decision must satisfy a large constraint set, which decreases the likelihood that decisions will be made to achieve organisation-level goals;
1C Strategic action will be the result of intendedly rational 'strategic choice', and that moves will be major departures from the existing strategy; and	2C Strategic action will be the result of standardised organisational processes, and that moves will be incremental; and	3C Strategic action will be the result of an internal process of political bargaining, and that moves will be incremental; and
1D Top management's cognitive limitations will be the primary constraint on the comprehensiveness of the strategic process. The integration of decisions will be relatively high.	2D The level of detail that is achieved in the standardised organisational processes will be the primary constraint on the comprehensiveness of the strategic decision process. The integration of decisions will be intermediate.	3D Biases induced by members' parochial perceptions will be the primary constraint on the comprehensiveness of the strategic decision process. In general, the integration of decisions will be low.

Source: Frederickson (1986, p. 284).

Table 4.4   Mintzberg and the three dimensions of structure

Mintzberg	Centralisation	Formalisation	Complexity
Simple	Centralised	Informal	Simple
Machine Bureaucracy	Centralised	Formalised	Complex
Professional Bureaucracy	Decentralised	Informal	Complex

Source: Frederickson (1986).

of the possible effects of leadership on the strategy process, which is discussed below.

Eden and Ackerman (1998, p. 9) considered the characteristics of the strategy process in varying types of organisation. A conclusion that can be drawn from their work is that the bureaucratic organisation is more likely to favour ordered, linear/rational methods of strategy formulation, whereas the smaller, entrepreneurial body is likely to be individualistic and use 'emergent' processes. Furthermore, those using a deliberate, emergent strategy system work within a loose strategy framework, in contrast to the fully developed action plans used in the strategic planning regime.

Allison's (1971) analysis of the decisions taken during the Cuban Missile Crisis by the US government strategic decision-makers cast doubt on such a simplistic categorisation.

Janssens and Steyaert (1999, p. 124) proposed that organisations at the end of the second millennium would be having to learn to deal with instability and continual change, and that the hierarchical structures, whose principle is stability and order, are breaking down. This development may be true of business organisations, but is less so of the military, which require hierarchy for the exercise of command and control. The view of Moskos *et al.* (2000) was, however, that the military is becoming increasingly postmodern, and so some degree of deconstruction is to be expected. No evidence was gathered during the interviews for this study to shed light on these developments.

Politics in organisations

Allen *et al.* (1979, p. 77), saw politics as 'intentional acts of influence to enhance or protect the self-interest of individuals or groups'. There can be little argument that organisations are political, in the sense of the above definition, but for the purpose of this thesis, the role played by such activity and the effect on the strategy process are the focus of interest. Dean and Sharfman (1996) predicted 'that successful strategic decisions will be positively related to procedural rationality and negatively related to political behaviour' – a hypothesis confirmed by the findings of their study. Since the value of a strategic decision is related to the degree to which it achieves the aim of the organisation, an additional set of aims related to the interests of individuals or groups within the company must cause problems. Managers face the challenge of defending their own interests without undermining the effectiveness of the organisation. Papadakis *et al.* (1998) introduced a complication to the simple connection of rationality and politicking to the success of strategic decisions by their finding that formal planning systems for strategic decision-making *encouraged* political behaviour. They also found that uncertainty about some aspects of an issue (they instance problem definition) might introduce political activity in the formulation process, probably because factions can identify opportunities for the furtherance of their views, because of a lack of agreement within the organisation.

As with other forms of politics, that within organisations is concerned with the acquisition and wielding of power or, as Pfeffer (1981) had it, 'to overcome some resistance or opposition'. These individuals or groups can exercise negative power by excluding issues from the decision-making agenda, or positive power by seeking to determine to their own advantage the outcome of such an agenda. The usual connotation of such activity is dysfunctional or illegitimate but, as Hardy and Clegg (1996) pointed out, this view takes 'the organisation', or its elites, as the standard of legitimacy, perhaps because the organisation itself is a structure of dominance. A task for the dominant coalition is, then, to legitimise its own power: 'Politics concerns the creation of legitimacy for certain ideas, values and demands – not just action performed as a result of previously acquired legitimacy' (Pettigrew, 1977, p. 85).

Narayanan and Fahey (1982, p. 31) expressed a similar view:

> With respect to individual strategic decisions, the objectivity of the rational model must be couched within a political context: *the nature of alternative(s) sponsored and the extent to which they are accepted, modified, or rejected is dependent on the power/influence distribution within and across the relevant coalition(s).*

Handy (1990) concluded that there are three types of power in organisations:

(a) Resource power – power is gained from the control over money, property or the like. Physical and psychological intimidation are ways in which this power can be exercised.

(b) Position power – the title or role one has entitles them to take certain decisions.
(c) Expert power – knowledge or experience can be a source of influence and power.

Control of this power is attempted in organisations by the application of rules, so that, although authority may be delegated, control is maintained, or even increased. The rules, of course, must be policed.

Lee and Lawrence (1991, p. 79) offered the thought, 'A relationship is political if power operates between the parties and/or if the parties are relevant to each other's goal fulfilment'. In these circumstances, politics can be deemed to be operating in every organisation and there will be a multiplicity of goals to be satisfied, hence conflict is inevitable. Professor Ann Robinson commented (Interview, 5 September 1998) on the problem of fiefdoms within organisations, which could evolve aims of their own. She said:

> All organisations are highly political. It is the struggle for territory and power. So individuals' personal ambitions are tied up with their territory and power. Part of my strategy is to employ people who are on the way up and who will use this as a stepping-stone and make their mark by turning their bit round. The problem is, that when they get halfway through that process and they are ambitious, they start guarding their territory.

On the other hand, Mr Hooper had found (Interview, 8 December 1999) that politics did not exist in Honda (UK), which has a structure based upon openness, trust and communication. He went on:

> If an organisation doesn't have firm values and beliefs that are actually sewn into the culture of the organisation, then you are likely to have internal fighting and politicking. And, if you do that, all you do is waste time and effort ... There is no halfway ... it (that is, the organisation) is either completely open or it is not.

Sir John Harvey-Jones made some trenchant comments (Interview, 21 April 1998):

> Well, there is a lot of politicking, but it depends what the politicking is for. Politicking to achieve your business objectives is one thing. Politicking to enhance your 'brownie points' or shine up a few more

Table 4.5 Traps in decision-making

Trap	Defined	Reaction
Anchoring	Disproportionate weight to first information received	View problem from different perspectives Think independently before consulting others Be open-minded, think widely Beware anchoring advisers Beware anchors in negotiations
Status quo	Bias towards maintaining the status quo	Remind yourself of objectives Identify and evaluate other options Would status quo be chosen if it wasn't status quo ? Don't exaggerate switching costs away from status quo Will status quo be as good into the future? Don't default to status quo because choice is difficult
Sunk-cost	Justifying past choices	Seek views from those not involved in past Forget wounded self-esteem Are subordinates so biased? Driving out fear of failure
Confirming evidence	Seeking evidence confirming own views	Examine all evidence impartially Get a devil's advocate Be honest with yourself Don't ask other leading questions
Framing	Adding bias by the way the question is posed	Look for distortion from framing Pose questions in neutral way Rethink posing questions periodically during decision-making Check others' framing of questions
Estimating and forecasting	Bias introduced into forecasts	Always consider the extremes of possible range of values Challenge extreme values from advisers
Prudence	Over-caution	Estimate honestly Don't be unduly influenced by memory
Recallability	Using memorable, traumatic events from past	Get actual statistics whenever possible Be careful of 'impressions'

Source: Hammond *et al.* (1998).

apples, I think, is one thing that you have got to stop. You have got to make that bloody dangerous.

Thus 'politicians' can be acting principally in their own interests, rather than for the common weal. If individuals cannot gain the power of decision, they will have to adopt the role of influencers. Decision-makers have to acknowledge that politics in organisations are inevitable, but they need not be negative unless the individuals involved consider 'who said what?' rather than take the advice at face value. Bias can adversely affect the objectivity of those involved. If the power of the advisers is sufficiently strong, the strategy process will involve negotiation. The idea that decisions are taken by 'dominant coalitions' suggests that these groups are formed from common interest and subscribe to shared values.

Perhaps the best that can be hoped for is that those wielding power observe Thucydides' (1954, p. 55) criterion: 'Those who really deserve praise are the people who, while human enough to enjoy power, nevertheless pay more attention to justice than compelled to by their situation.'

Pitfalls in decision-making

Hammond, *et al.* (1998) produced a list of hidden traps that can adversely affect the quality of business decision-making. The pitfalls remind us of the complexity of the strategy decision process, but these are more likely to be part of the deciders' style rather than a checklist to be consulted on each occasion. Decision-makers need experience and common sense, both of which are costly to acquire. Table 4.5 is a summary of their findings.

Janis (1992) coined the term 'vigilant problem solving' to identify a systematic and rigorous decision-making process, but he had discovered that this system was rarely followed in full because of any or all of the following three major constraints:

(a) *Cognitive constraints*
- Limited time
- Perceived limitations of available resources for information search and appraisal
- Multiple tasks
- Perplexing complexity of issue
- Perceived lack of dependable knowledge
- Ideological commitments

(b) *Affiliative constraints*
  - Need to maintain:
  - power
  - status
  - compensation
  - social support
  - Need for acceptability of new policy within the organisation
(c) *Egocentric (self-serving and emotive) constraints*
  - Strong personal motive, for example, greed, desire for fame
  - Arousal of an emotional need, for example, anger, elation
  - Emotional stress of decisional conflict

Faced with constraints, Janis found that the decision-maker would adopt a simplistic approach, such as seeking an analogous situation from previous experience or 'satisfice'. The danger is that the 'rational actor' model, which was long held as typical of decision-makers in the past, and which was used as a 'straw man' in Allison (1971), will be replaced by the 'non-rational' actor as being the norm. Janis (1992) used, contrary to contemporary opinion, President Eisenhower as an example of a vigilant problem-solver. Attention is not drawn, however, to the fact that Eisenhower had been trained in military decision-making, particularly the Appreciation method (see pp. 145 ff. for a discussion of this technique). The leader's role, Janis asserted, is to remove or counteract the adverse influences, listed (a) to (c) above, which impede the application of rational analysis (as far as it is possible given contextual uncertainties), and to establish organisational norms and heuristics for problem-solving. For instance, the process is rarely linear, that is, following the top-down, hierarchical route, but is usually recursive where the various levels of the organisation interact repetitively.

Since decision-making is an attempt to realise the objectives (or aims, in military terms) set for the organisation, these must be clear, unambiguous and positive. Harrison (1996. p. 49) discussed the process of decision and observed: 'In the event that a given alternative once selected and implemented does not appear to produce the desired result, the decision maker may consider . . . corrective action, renewed search, or revised objectives.'

This last option of changing the objectives would suggest to the military that what was to be achieved had been given insufficient thought. Harrison later gave examples of successful strategic decisions: Philip Morris in 1984 'to reduce its dependency on profit from tobacco products' (p. 51), and Wells Fargo Bank 'to establish a major presence in the rapidly growing banking market in southern California' (p. 51). Both of these objectives were, no doubt, admirable but, to the military, would be too imprecise. Reduction on dependency for Philip Morris would be achieved if it fell by 5 per cent, but that would hardly be significant. But how much would be seen to be significant? In the event, the dependency fell from 92 per cent to 68 per cent, but there is no indication in the statement of objective that that achievement was what the strategy intended. Without a clear statement of aim, the strategy process can become confused and the final decision lacking in precision.

Personality and context

Strategy formulation is a process conducted by humans in a given situation which ends with a decision. The personality of the decision-maker affects the approach that is adopted and the context imposes constraints (or offers opportunities). A simplifying analysis could be conducted by forming a matrix in which the vertical axis contains the human types (sensing, intuition, thinking and feeling) and the horizontal axis the contextual situations (crisis, organisational politics, organisational structure – for example, bureaucratic). The matrix could then be used to indicate which type fits which situation. The reality is, however, that strategy formulation is too complex for such simplification. The human types are not exclusively, say, intuitive, but can be predominantly so, whilst showing evidence of, say, feeling. Constructing such a summarising matrix was abandoned.

Strategy is a human activity, and so it is affected by the personalities of those called upon to choose from the available options. Choosing is a decision, and the nature of problems and decisions in the business has been investigated. The context of the decision is also important and factors such as organisation structure, crisis, politics, can all have an effect on how the strategy is made. The argument now turns to the methods used by the military, before making a comparison of business and military practice.

4.2 Military methods

Introduction

The military have devised their own methodology for solving problems and reaching decisions. The first of these considered, the Appreciation, is an attempt to induce logical thinking and the second, the Principles of War, are tenets gained from years of experience, which act as a guide to military strategists. The military is a disciplined force, but not one repressed by martinets. Great store is placed on leadership in the armed forces, so its place in, and effect on, strategy needs to be considered.

The Appreciation

The military appreciation is a disciplined thought process designed to examine all relevant factors and produce the best reasoned solution. It can be used to solve both factual and technical problems to which there is often only one answer, and more complex Service problems, particularly in war, to which there may be no set or single answer. (JSP 101, [1992] p. 9–1)

The Appreciation is a logical sequence of reasoning leading to a solution of a problem, which in this context is a strategic one. Although the process can be used mentally for simpler problems, here the written Appreciation will be considered as more appropriate for the complex, strategic situation. The reference, JSP 101, stressed that problems should be approached critically, logically and with an open, unprejudiced mind. In particular, the set sequence *must* be followed rigidly to avoid jumping to premature conclusions. In this respect, the Appreciation format can be seen as a heuristic, which encapsulates the experience of generations of military decision-makers. The proponents of the process would claim that it is 'reliable' in that its findings, when applied by different people, are likely to be repeatable (an assertion not borne out by the author's personal experience in teaching the method at a staff college). There are five distinct steps in the process, which have been combined with the headings used in the Appreciation to form Table 4.6.

The sections of the Appreciation are now considered in more detail.

Table 4.6   The Appreciation process

Steps	Form of the Appreciation
1 Studying the existing situation	Review of the situation
2 Specifying the aim to be attained	Factors affecting selection of aim Aim
3 Examining and reasoning out all relevant factors	Factors Enemy courses Enemy's most probable course
4 Considering all practicable courses	Own courses
5 Deciding on the best course of action to attain the aim	Selection of best course Plan

Review of the situation

This section is an introduction and gives the essential background facts without being part of the argument. It provides contextual statements showing what has to be taken into account in the subsequent analysis. Any constraints, perhaps imposed by higher authority, are recorded in this section.

Factors affecting the selection of the aim

This section is only relevant when the commander has such freedom of action that he is able to determine his own aim. JSP 101 (pp. 9–4 and 9–5) showed five tests to apply to an aim:

(a) Will my aim secure a definite result in our favour?
(b) Does the wording express exactly what I want to bring about, without giving any indication of how to attain it?
(c) Is it in accordance with my instructions and responsibilities?
(d) Has it a reasonable chance of attainment in the situation?
(e) Is it the utmost I can do?

Aim

JSP 101 (para. 919) stated unequivocally: 'The aim is the crux of the appreciation. Unless the aim is right the whole appreciation may be worthless.' There must never be more than one aim, which is expressed in the infinitive. Negative verbs, such as 'prevent', 'stop', 'delay', should be avoided since they lack vigour and imply a negative, defensive frame of mind.

Factors

Factors are described as 'a circumstance, fact or influence contributing to a result' (JSP 101, para. 923) and the following are examples:

(a) Time and space
(b) Weather
(c) Surprise
(d) Comparison of forces
(e) Logistics
(f) Communications
(g) Morale
(h) Vital points

Each factor is discussed in relation to the aim and should lead to logical deductions bearing on the attainment of the aim. Differentiation of factors and deductions is most important and each should be tested by asking 'so what?' and if the answer is 'so nothing', the factor should be discarded. The factors are arranged so that the most important or overriding ones appear first and in an order such that each factor leads logically to the next. It is vital that, at this stage, temptations to draw conclusions on courses of action are resisted.

Enemy courses

The enemy's courses of action have to be considered impartially because they will impinge on our own courses. The only exception would be if we have the initiative, which confers a large measure of freedom of action, and there is a danger that we may sacrifice the ability to dictate what might happen. The enemy will be credited with acting logically and each possible course of action must be followed by the deductions:

(a) The likelihood of the enemy adopting the course.
(b) The effect of the enemy's adoption of the course on the attainment of the aim.

Enemy's most probable course

When the enemy's position has been analysed, their possible course of action should be summed up and, if possible, the most dangerous and threatening should be identified. If it is not possible to deduce which is the enemy's most likely course, the one most dangerous to us will be selected.

Own courses

What has gone before have been factors, whereas consideration of our own course is to review the options open to us. Our course of action is not to be seen as merely countering what has been deduced as the enemy's most likely course of action because we will wish to take the initiative and, possibly, use surprise. The acid test to be applied to each option considered is whether it will attain or contribute significantly to the achievement of the aim. Any superficially attractive but unprofitable course should be discussed and rejected. The courses are then described as main, combination or complementary and the merits of each are discussed logically and dispassionately (usually by appending the advantages and disadvantages of each).

Selection of the best course

At the culmination of the process, one course of action is weighed against the other, whereas previously the factors have all been discussed logically and without bias. Here the arguments leading to the final choice are discussed. Should a new idea emerge at this stage, the whole argument has to be repeated but including the new factor.

Plan

This final section of the Appreciation makes no contribution to the selection process but indicates the roles of the various forces involved and, if the Appreciation is accepted, forms the basis for the subsequent ordering of operations. The plan will usually include:

(a) Forces available and the command-and-control arrangements
(b) The roles of the forces
(c) Positions and timings
(d) An outline of administrative arrangements
(e) Communications and electronic warfare
(f) Security and defensive measures

Revision

JSP 101 (para. 954) went on to specify the following tests that should be made on completion of the appreciation:

(a) Is the reasoning valid?
(b) Is the sequence logical?
(c) Is everything in it relevant to the aim, and has anything been forgotten?
(d) Is it free from vagueness, ambiguity and prejudice?
(e) Is it accurate? Are positions, times and distances, and so on correct?
(f) Will the plan achieve the aim?

The Appreciation is a military problem-solving methodology, which is used mainly in the strategy formulation process. The sequence is designed to prevent consideration of later problems before the relevant factors have been considered and evaluated. In particular, the method seeks to prevent reaching conclusions that are not based upon facts, or, at least, logic. There is no reason why imaginative solutions should not be proposed, *as long as the logic of the appreciation process is maintained.* The Appreciation is similar to the formal, deliberate methods of strategy formulation described in the strategic management literature. In particular, Ansoff (1968) prescribed a method that Mintzberg and Lampel (1999, p. 22) described as follows: 'the process is not just cerebral but formal, decomposable into distinct steps, delineated by checklists, and supported by techniques (especially with regard to objectives, budgets, programs, and operating plans)'.

Principles of War

The study of war has led to the identification of broad precepts which experience has shown to be important in military operations. These principles are not a checklist, nor are they necessarily applied in every case, but are tenets, which are ignored at one's peril. Not all principles will apply to a particular operation. They are a part of the conceptual component of military doctrine, and different nations have compiled different lists to reflect their different cultures, geography, and so on. The list of ten principles below is that adopted by the United Kingdom.

Selection and maintenance of the aim

The definition of a clear aim for the military operation is seen as essential. The aim will lead first to the definition of mission and objectives, and then to the strategy that will achieve them. Once this aim has been carefully selected and defined, its maintenance by constant reference during operations will ensure that everything undertaken is in pursuit of achieving that aim. The importance attached to the aim is reflected in the paragraphs above on the Appreciation.

Maintenance of morale

It has long been acknowledged that wars are not won by material factors alone, and that moral factors have a great influence. Wars have been seen as being as much about a clash of wills of the two commanders as about weapons and armies. Similarly, smaller forces possessed of good morale have won conflicts over larger, uninspired armies. Thermopylae, the 1948 Arab/Israeli War and the Falklands War are only a few examples of this phenomenon. Leadership is a vital factor in inducing that mental state of trust, fighting spirit and cohesion that constitute high morale.

Security

Security is the package of measures seeking to lessen the effects of the enemy's interference with our operations. These measures can be physical protection of bases from infiltration by ground troops or attack from the air and passive protection of information being intercepted by the enemy. Wars are won by offensive action so, generally, the amount of effort devoted to security is the minimum to ensure that our own operations are not disrupted.

Surprise

Surprise can cause alarm and confusion amongst the enemy and yield results disproportionate to the means employed. Timing is an important factor whether the surprise is a ruse or a technological innovation. The Egyptian air attack in the Yom Kippur War, when the Israeli nation was occupied with a religious festival, is an example of a ruse that relied upon time as the crucial factor. Surprise, whether strategic, operational or tactical, is almost a precondition of success.

Offensive action

Success will usually follow from grasping the initiative, and offensive action is the chief means open to the commander to influence events in his own favour. The offensive spirit is not only an influence upon strategy but also permeates the whole thinking of the armed forces. If a defensive campaign is forced upon a commander by terrain, logistics, *matériel* imbalance, distance, and so on, it will be a second best and, whenever the situation allows, the offensive will be mounted.

Concentration of force

The art of generalship is the concentration of superior force at the decisive time and place. Dissipation of forces in a series of small attacks over a wide front is to invite being defeated in detail, and the essence of manoeuvre is to contrive a battle at a time and place of one's own choosing where overwhelming force can be applied to ensure victory.

Economy of effort

Economy of effort is the corollary of concentration of force in that the available resources must not be expended on operations that do not directly contribute to the achievement of the aim in the shortest time possible. All resources must be conserved for use in the decisive action.

Flexibility

Although maintenance of the aim suggests a dogged adherence to the plan, such an attitude is not likely to succeed if carried to extremes. The commander must exercise judgement and flexibility and there may well be occasions when success is best achieved in the longer term by a tactical withdrawal. The loss of General Paulus's army at Stalingrad through Hitler's rejection of plans to withdraw was a disaster brought about by intransigence and lack of flexibility.

Cooperation

Most modern military operations involve land, sea and air forces to some degree and cooperation between them in support of the common aim is clearly vital. In combating guerrilla warfare, the cooperation of the civil and political authorities is essential. Even before the introduction of air forces, the operations of the various arms (artillery, cavalry, infantry, engineers) all had to be coordinated to ensure success and avoid costly confusion.

Sustainability

This principle was, until recently, called 'administration' but the new term has been selected to reflect the need for forces to be supplied and mentally prepared for long-term operations. Thus, sound logistics is at the heart of every successful campaign, but the moral considerations will require such support as high-class medical facilities, good food, good postal services and chaplaincy services.

Organisational politics in the military

Earlier in this chapter there is a discussion of the part played by politics in strategy formulation in business organisations, so it is necessary now to consider the parallel situation in the military. Legitimacy is not a problem in the armed forces since the hierarchical system is manifested in the rank structure, which is backed up by the force of military law. Under these circumstances, some political activities in opposition to the leaders become a very dangerous undertaking since, in the extreme circumstance of active service, it is quite legal to have such opponents tried by court-martial for offences against good order and discipline. Despite this rigid structure, the higher ranks need the advice and support of their staffs to do the detailed work of strategy formulation (often by validation of an overall concept), and to provide clarification of the very complicated issues involved. Thus, the staff itself may be split into 'camps' favouring or opposing various solutions and it is the task of the chief of staff to resolve these conflicts in the best interests of achieving the aim. Promotion in the armed forces is competitive, so access to the commander may be seen as an aid to advancement, but overt political activity of this nature is generally frowned upon. The defence field is not devoid of political activity within the organisation, and long-running arguments, such as that of aircraft carriers versus land-based air power, have not always been conducted on the factual, rational basis that most military staff would consider desirable. Apportionment of limited funds will inevitably raise the need in some to secure the necessary money for their project, not necessarily on selfish grounds, but also from the basis that this solution is the best for the defence of the country. Thus, it would be wrong to believe that organisational politics do not exist in the military, even in war, but, within a particular staff, such activity is generally frowned upon as being disruptive of the cohesion so necessary in a disciplined force, and may well be self-policed by the staff itself.

An example of the process in action can be seen in the following mini-case, which is based on a radio interview given by Lieutenant General Short of the United States Air Force on the air operations in the former Yugoslavia.

General Short acknowledged that his involvement in the air operations in Vietnam had strongly influenced his views, which were that, when war becomes necessary, the operations should be conducted with overwhelming force directed at 'the head of the snake'. So, when he was called upon to propose the plan for the conduct of air operations against Serbia, he envisaged strikes to suppress the air defence system, and attacks against strategic targets, namely the power generation system, lines of communication and military command centres. His estimate was that the Serbian Third Army could be driven from the field in Kosovo in 60 days.

Political factors, however, soon impinged upon General Short's planning. The political advice was that NATO needed to demonstrate their resolve to bomb Serbia and, after three nights, the enemy would call for negotiations. This assessment proved, in practice, to be quite wrong, but had to be used initially as a basis for planning. Short's planning was further complicated by the involvement of 19 nations, each with an equal vote, all of whom expressed political views, often limiting, about the selection of the targets. In Short's view the professional airmen of these nations were in agreement with the general strategy, but could not always convince their national politicians.

The complex sequence of decision was as follows:

(a) SACEUR General Clark asked, through US national channels, 'What could we do in Kosovo?'. General Jumper's response, from a brief from General Short and the staff, was that, with forces immediately to hand, he could bomb a target-set south of the 44 degree line and establish a no-fly zone in that same area.

(b) In June 1998, NATO was tasked with producing a plan for the operations. The proposed plan, devised in Naples and Vicenza, was for massive effort on the first night against enemy defence assets and strategic targets in Belgrade.

(c) General Clark was briefed on the plan and he concluded that security would be compromised if further planning were to be conducted within NATO, so he ordered that further work was to be done in US-only channels. General Short kept American colleagues in NATO informed of developments.

(d) The broad, strategic plan was now taken down to tactical level, where individual targets were selected, force requirements determined and weapons selected.

(e) NATO, however, continued to plan and proposed a five-phase operation.

- Phase 1: Attacks on the air defence system and military forces south of 44 degrees
- Phase 2: Expanded target set, south of 44 degrees
- Phase 3: If these phases were unsuccessful, targets would be attacked north of 44 degrees, including Belgrade
- Phase 4: Intensification of Phase 3
- Phase 5: Redeployment of forces

General Short disagreed with this incremental plan and wished to use maximum, overwhelming force from the outset.

(f) Opinion in the United States was that the US contribution was disproportionate and General Short was ordered by General Clark to review the numbers. Short reported the results of the review to General Clark by video conference. Clark demanded a reconnaissance plan, to be delivered within an hour, to determine whether Milosevic was applying ethnic cleansing. Short complied.

(g) General Short was sent as member of a diplomatic team to negotiate with Milosevic and his generals.

(h) After Short's return, when he was convinced that Milosevic would not back down, a further attempt was made to have the US staff's 'massive offensive' plan accepted. The US senior airmen thought that they had had their plan accepted, but General Clark, SACEUR, could not convince the politicians. Short bitterly

---

Box (*Continued*)

complained that they had been prevented by the chain of command from presenting their solution to the political heads.

Note: I am most grateful to Air Vice-Marshal Professor Mason for passing on the transcript that is unpublished in text.

The illustration shows that the strategy process was iterative. The top gave broad indications as to what was required and the staff proposed a strategy. The process was adversely affected by the number of nations whose agreement had to be sought, so, in frustration, the USA, who were providing most of the resources, planned alone. In the event, their plan for a classic air operation was rejected in favour of an incremental increase in the application of force. General Short was convinced that this approach was wrong, but he could not address the decision-makers to apply the force of his arguments because the hierarchical military structure prevented it. This process affected the strategy that was finally selected.

Leadership

Slim (1957) made the following observations on leadership:

1.   Personal leadership exists only as long as the officers demonstrate it by superior courage, wider knowledge, quicker initiative, and a greater readiness to accept responsibility than those they lead.

2.   Military command is not just a matter of bawling orders that will be obeyed for fear of punishment. Any commander's success comes more from being trusted than from being feared – from leading rather than driving.

3.   Officers and men feel themselves on the same side only as long as the officers show integrity and unselfishness in all their dealing, and place the well-being of their men before their own.

4.   In war the general may not be haunted by finance, but his is the responsibility for good management and economy in matters more important than money – his men's lives.

Bailey and Johnson (1992) observed some effects of leaders in business who operated in their 'visionary perspective'. They found that leaders could bring a vision of a desired future state for the company but also could apply their frame of reference to strategy formulation. This frame of reference could have been formed in another organisation: 'For example some of the new chief executives appointed to newly privatise UK industries in the 1980s came from private sector companies' (ibid., p. 161). The effect of these leadership traits is likely to be more pronounced in the Simple and Machine Bureaucracy organisation types of Mintzberg (1991).

Conclusion

Strategy formulation is a process that ends in decision. The decision seeks ways of achieving the objectives or aims established for the organisation within the means available. The military stress the importance of defining a precise aim before the selection of a strategy can be made. The strategic management literature acknowledges that an aim is the starting point for strategy formulation. The process and the decision are influenced by the nature of the decision-maker and the context in which the decision is made. Decision-makers will have a preferred style that arises from their personality type, and no evidence has been found to suggest that one psychological type is more effective than another. The decision process in business has been shown in studies recorded in the literature and found to vary by degrees between the extremes of deliberateness and emergent. A similar spectrum has been observed that extends from rational to intuitive. The military methods appear, from an examination of the Appreciation method, to be more overtly rational. On the other hand, to declare a method is one thing, but to use it in real situations may be another. Inevitably, organisational politics has an influence in both fields on the strategy process and its outcome. Since the strategy process is an intensely human activity concentrated in the upper levels of both military and business organisations, leadership plays a crucial role. This topic is addressed in detail in Chapters 6 and 7.

4.3   Case study 1: military strategy formulation in Britain

Introduction

Military strategy formulation is a process that has to proceed year on year, so that advances in weaponry can be absorbed, account taken of the changing geopolitical environment, and the budget matched to the availability of funds. From time to time, however, the routine is punctuated by armed conflicts that need a strategy, and periodically by the need for a fundamental review of defence policy. This case study begins with an account of the development of the chiefs of staff system in the United Kingdom, is followed by a brief description of the strategy process within the Ministry of Defence in the late 1990s, and concludes with a consideration of the 1998 Strategic Defence Review.

The chiefs of staff

Beginnings

Jackson and Bramall (1992) recounted how, following the Glorious Revolution of 1688, responsibility for defence of the realm devolved from the monarch alone to become the joint concern of Crown and Parliament. The army's professional head was the Commander-in-Chief, whilst that of the navy was the Lord High Admiral and it seems that over the years they seldom conferred and never agreed. The principal reason for this situation was not necessarily the obduracy of the individuals concerned, but because of the continued (and continuing) disagreement over whether Great Britain was best served by a maritime or a continental strategy. In the eighteenth and nineteenth centuries, however, strategy was the responsibility of the man on the spot (the slowness of communications effectively prevented any alternative) and the result of pressures arising from: 'the imperatives of defeat, the pressure of public opinion and the ever present Parliamentary quest for economies in military expenditure.' (Jackson and Bramall, 1992, p. 7).

Reforms in the nineteenth century

In 1868, Edward Cardwell, who became Secretary of State for War and was supported by progressive soldiers, civil servants and politicians, embarked on a series of reforms that had been needed since the debacle of the Crimean War had exposed muddle and inefficiency in the armed forces. The Cardwell reforms were:

(a) The Commander-in-Chief was made subordinate to the Secretary of State for War (rather than to the monarch) and his small staff was co-located with that of the War Office.
(b) Infantry regiments were divided into battalions, a regular one serving overseas, whilst the other regular battalion remained in the UK depot for training and recruiting, and holding responsibility for two or more militia battalions.

(c) Long-service engagements were to be seven years with the colours plus seven years in the reserve.

(d) Purchase of commissions was abolished.

(e) Army garrisons were to be withdrawn from self-governing colonies.

The reforms, however, did not introduce a strategic and operational planning staff using the precedent set by Germany as described in Chapter 3. Furthermore, there was no mechanism for inter-service cooperation, or for coordination with other ministries in Whitehall.

A step towards such development and integration of strategic thinking was the establishment in 1879 of a Colonial Defence Committee, comprising officials from the Admiralty, War Office, Colonial Office and Treasury, 'to consider what steps should be taken at short notice to provide some measure of security of Colonial ports' (Jackson and Bramall, 1992, p. 12). This body only lasted for one year but the growing threats to Great Britain at this time prompted its re-establishment in 1885, when it examined plans made by colonial governments for the defence of overseas territories and made changes deemed necessary by Whitehall ministries. Although some sixty such plans were approved in the first seven years, there was no attempt at a comprehensive defence plan. The Royal Commission under Lord Hartington in 1888, which might have provided an opportunity for those seeking the formation of a general staff, was directed to enquire into the administration of the naval and military departments and their relation to each other and the Treasury. Members of the Commission were, however, to prove influential in the setting up of a general staff, and the Hartington Commission recommended the abolishing of the post of Commander-in-Chief and the creation of a Chief of General Staff. The opposition from, amongst others, the Queen was such, however, that this modest proposal was not implemented. The Commission's work did influence, however, thought on the mechanisms for the coordination of defence, which culminated in 1895 in the formation of a Cabinet Defence Committee, backed by the Naval and Military Committees at official level. This first step was not an immediate success and, as Jackson and Bramall (1992, p. 23) commented:

> What was not generally understood in the run up to the 20th Century was the impracticability of combining the roles of C-in-C and Chief of Staff. Decisive military command by one man could only be exercised, and, indeed, was only practicable in Army Commands and Fleets at sea. In Whitehall, the need was for careful development of

policies through informed debate, tapping all the best military, technological and financial advice, and assessing relevant information and intelligence from a wide variety of sources. That was the task of a Chief of Staff, supported by a highly trained and motivated General Staff such as von Moltke had created.

Developments, 1900–14

In 1902, the then Prime Minister, Balfour, reestablished the Cabinet Defence Committee to try to correct the deficiencies of the defence system exposed by the Boer War. He went on to establish a committee under Lord Esher to reorganise the War Office, but which also raised again the perennial dilemma of maritime versus continental strategy, because all three of its members subscribed to the former view. The result of the Esher Committee was the formation in 1904 of a Committee of Imperial Defence (CID) with its own secretariat; a solution somewhat short of the Ministry of Defence that the committee had favoured, but radical enough for the times. Within the War Office, a General Staff was created with Directorates in the Chief of General Staff's Department: Military Operations (including Intelligence), Staff Duties and Military Training. Despite the setting up of a Combined Operations Sub-Committee of the CID, the gulf that had grown between the navy and army increased and the fundamental arguments on strategy were not resolved. When Haldane took over the War Office, the balance swung a little away from the navy, under its forceful chief, Fisher (an indication that strategy formulation and selection are influenced by the personalities involved). Haldane created an expeditionary force of six regular infantry divisions and a cavalry division and, importantly, created a Territorial Army of fourteen divisions from the militia, yeomanry and volunteer units. When Churchill took charge of the Admiralty, he and Haldane cooperated such that war plans were developed at the 'official' level whereas the politicians had relied on war strategies being developed by the CID.

In March 1912, Maurice Hankey became Secretary of the CID, where he was to remain through the periods of office of seven prime ministers, which continuity, coupled with his acceptability to both services and his considerable talents, made him an influential figure in the military strategy process, although as a discreet facilitator rather than a leading force. One important contribution of his was the creation of a 'War Book' which laid down the actions that various ministries had to take at each stage of alert leading to war. Under Asquith, the CID membership had grown to the extent that the various factions within it obstructed its work of agreeing a strategy, such that a 'High Level Brigade' (a dominant coalition?) of five was formed to coordinate naval and military policy. In the secret talks held by the army staff with their French counterparts, strategy was already being decided (effectively from the bottom up) so that the CID's room for manoeuvre was restricted. On 1 August 1914 the French ordered mobilisation, and on that same day the British Cabinet reaffirmed that it had no commitment to give other than naval aid to the French. Later that same day, the newly formed War Council decided to despatch a four-division British Expeditionary Force to France!

The First World War (1914–18)

Although some reforms had been made to the decision-making organisation, Britain was still not ready for a large-scale continental war. Consideration of the higher-level command-and-control structure had been avoided, conscription was rejected, and industry was not mobilised to provide the required equipment for the army, whose scales were more relevant to the Boer War than a conflict with Germany. A part of the reason for this situation was the expectation that the war would be over quickly. Furthermore, Asquith, the Prime Minister, began to run the war from the Cabinet and bypassed the Committee of Imperial Defence, whilst Kitchener, as Secretary of State for War, did not use the General Staff and acted as a 'Supremo' making decisions without staff advice. It was not long before Asquith realised that the war could not be conducted by the whole Cabinet, so he formed a War Council of six (with Hankey as the Secretary), and the two chiefs were used as advisers, not Council members. The Council had the task of considering a strategy to break the deadlock on the Western Front but Kitchener wished to apply the principle of 'concentration of force' and focus all effort on the Western Front.

Now opinion was divided between Easterners and Westerners, who, in a sense, followed the enduring debate between maritime and continental advocates. Despite opposition from Fisher, the First Sea Lord, and Kitchener, the War Council approved Churchill's proposal for a landing in Gallipoli. There was no effective General Staff to plan the operation and the result is well-known.

The waves caused by the failure of the eastern strategy caused many changes of personality and much political manoeuvring, and, in 1916, Lloyd George became, first, Secretary of State for War, and then Prime Minister. When Prime Minister he created a War Cabinet of five members, which became, in effect, an oligarchy but it did provide unity of political direction, and central direction of the 'home front'. Lloyd George often sought advice from independents and junior service officers, but did not have a grasp of military and naval matters, a deficiency exacerbated by his mistrust of his Admiralty and War Office advisers. Although there were many changes of personality and much manoeuvring in this latter part of the war, two significant events impacted on the strategy process: the formation of an air arm in Britain, and the creation of a Supreme Allied War Council with a General Staff composed of permanent national military representatives. This last move led to the appointment of General Foch as the Allied Supreme Commander. The war eventually ended but its conduct in Britain had been characterised by suspicion between the politicians and the military, and little coordination between the fiefdoms of the Admiralty, the War Office and the Air Ministry.

Between the wars

The interwar years were a period of financial constraint (and thus a battle for resources), and inter-service rivalry centring round the role of air power and its control. The Committee of Imperial Defence was reformed, but the three services largely went their own way with little coordination. In 1922, the three ministries submitted contradictory plans for Britain's response to the Chanak crisis in Turkey, and the response was the formation of an *ad hoc* Chiefs of Staff Committee. A sub-committee of the CID under the Marquess of Salisbury, formed to study issues of national and imperial defence, stopped short of recommending the formation of a Ministry of Defence, as some had wanted, but it did confirm the existence of the Chiefs of Staff Committee, which met for the first time on 17 July 1923. The chairmanship of this committee was in the hands of the Prime Minister's nominee and did not necessarily rotate amongst the services. The coordination process was enhanced by the formation of the Joint Planning Sub-Committee, and, later, the Joint Intelligence Sub-Committee. Some harmony and collective voice was also evident when the publication of the Chiefs of Staff Annual Review was instituted, probably a precursor of the annual Defence White Paper.

In 1933, as the world situation was deteriorating, with the Germans and Japanese becoming increasingly belligerent, the Defence Requirements Sub-Committee was formed in Britain to try to reconcile the competition between the services and improve the defence posture. The British economy, however, remained weak and the government had to try to balance the need to counter the increasing threats from Germany, Italy and Japan with the imperative of remaining solvent. In addition, there was the need to divide the defence spending between the three arms and Chamberlain, then Prime Minister, not the Chiefs of Staff Committee, determined the defence priorities in favour of the air force in the late 1930s. In 1936, a further attempt at harmonising defence strategy was made with the appointment of a Minister for the Co-ordination of Defence, Sir Thomas Inskip. Inskip instituted a defence review within the strategic guidelines set by the Cabinet and the spending ceiling imposed by the Treasury. Although bitter arguments were still raging over the use of air power, battleships, and so on, the Chiefs of Staff were producing sound advice on the conduct of future military operations.

The Second World War (1939–45)

The Chiefs of Staff system was carried forward as the war began, with the advantage that the chiefs who decided what had to be done were also the leaders who had to carry out the requisite actions. The system reached its full effectiveness with the appointment of General Brooke as its chairman, and was subsequently adopted by the Americans and jointly as the Combined Chiefs of Staff of both nations. (Discussion of the formulation of Allied strategy can be found in Chapter 3, 'Case studies'.) Churchill soon took over the Prime Minister's post, and also became Minister of Defence, a situation which paralleled that of Lloyd George's 'dictatorship' in the First World War. Churchill's system provided unity of command, and a subordination of military to political strategy. Brooke was able to withstand the pressure of Churchill's strength of character and proffer military advice, which, often after much argument, was accepted. Lesser military commanders were sacked when their results seemed inadequate. Jackson and Bramall (1992, p. 215) summed up Brooke thus:

> Brooke was soon to prove himself a master of grand strategy, and a match for the Prime Minister in strategic thinking. His precise mind could filter essentials from complex detail, and he could discern the pattern of events as they unfolded with perceptive clarity. Paradoxically, his great strength of conviction and intellectual integrity were matched by a remarkable flexibility of mind. He would hammer his points home relentlessly in his clipped, staccato mode of speaking, but he was always prepared to accept valid opposing arguments and to modify his policies accordingly.

Churchill formed a Defence Committee with two panels, one for operations and one for supply, and formed sub-committees to solve particular problems as they arose. The interaction of the chiefs, led by Brooke, and Churchill proved crucial to the successful conduct of the war. The conflicting claims of the three services continued and affected the allocation of resources, although the bitter battles of the interwar years were largely set aside in the interests of beating the enemy. Nonetheless, there were serious differences of opinion, for instance, over the strategic bombing campaign. On a broader canvas, the Americans disagreed with the British Mediterranean strategy and favoured a direct blow through France.

Postwar

With peace came a wholesale change of personalities, and Attlee, the new Prime Minister, reverted to a Cabinet consensus approach now that the crisis of war was over. The Chiefs of Staff Committee system had worked well in war, and there was no pressure to change it in peacetime. The Defence Committee of the Cabinet was chaired by the Prime Minister who appointed a Minister of Defence, whose duties were non-executive and coordinative. His staff numbered 50 and they occupied offices in Storey's Gate. The Chiefs of Staff Committee, Joint Planning Staff and Joint Intelligence Committee were deemed to be part of the Ministry of Defence, but the service ministries remained powerful and autonomous. After Field Marshal Montgomery's tenure of the chair of the Chiefs of Staff Committee, it became evident that the system would only work well in the absence of personality clashes, and there was a lack of a coordinated tri-service view. Repeated attempts were made to take a coordinated view, starting with a 'Global Strategy' paper produced by the chiefs in 1952, and followed by government-conducted 'Radical Reviews' in 1953 and 1954. In 1955, the new Prime Minister, Eden, wished to make the Minister of Defence responsible for strategic policy with the assistance of his own Chief of Staff. The then Chairman of COSC, General Templer, however, threatened to resign if this diminution of the service ministries and corporate responsibility was enforced. Eden watered down his proposals.

Nevertheless, the trend towards the formation of a central body for defence continued, particularly as increasingly stringent financial measures had to be taken to reduce the defence budget, and the services responded by searching for savings through increased efficiency and elimination of duplication of effort. Although the first Chief of Defence Staff was Marshal of the Royal Air Force Sir William Dickson (appointed in 1957), pressures for radical change became evident when Earl Mountbatten assumed that post in 1959. Mountbatten, having been associated with Joint Operations in Europe and, later, as Supreme Commander South East Asia during the last war, was convinced that the corporate responsibility of the individual service chiefs had to give way to a 'Supremo' who would formulate defence policy with the Cabinet.

The process of centralisation, begun at this time, has continued and now the strategy formulation is in the hands of a central staff that has taken on much of what had been done in the single-service staffs. The central machinery, however, takes account of single-service inputs and the three service chiefs sit on the highest MOD bodies – the Defence Council, the Chiefs of Staff Committee and the Finance, Planning and Management Group. These developments have not made the differences of opinion disappear, but have made it possible to take balanced decisions, taking into account the many confusing political, military, financial and technological factors. The principle that the staff that makes the plans is also responsible for their execution is still maintained, but the solution adopted by the Canadian government (the formation of a single service wearing a green uniform) was rejected in Britain.

Little has been written about the Defence Secretariat in the above account, but although the civil servants under the Permanent Under-Secretary provide the continuity in policy formation that would be a difficulty for the military who tend to serve tours of two to three years in the Ministry, these officials are less likely to take a parochial single-service view of problems. Cynics observe that this situation confers the real power on the civil service staff, which is in a unique position to manipulate the system with such tactics as divide and rule. Furthermore, the members of the civilian staff, themselves, are moved from post to post, so the continuity argument may not hold. Opponents also question the ability of civilians to form valid judgements on military matters (although some do attend Staff Colleges). Essentially, though, the British system is strategy formulation by committee with all the consequent advantages and disadvantages, but the final responsibility rests with the Prime Minister, not least for carrying the opinion of Parliament in support of the military.

Comment

As the demands on defence increased, not least through technological developments, the method of determining strategy had to become more complex and broadly based. The responsibility for deciding strategy moved from the monarch to a single commander-in-chief and then progressively to responsibility shared by leading military and political figures, supported by a trained staff. The progress was hampered by the innate suspicion of the military by the politicians (arising from Cromwell's use of military force to sustain political power), the power and influence of the Treasury, and also by the military 'tribes', first two and then a third as the Royal Air Force was formed, which vied for supremacy and for the acceptance of *their* strategic solution.

In business terms, the evolution of the idea of 'grand' strategy was analogous to the concept of 'corporate' strategy, as determining at the highest level the business the country was in (that is, its place in the world) and the ways to succeed there. The 'CEO' responsibility for deciding strategy progressively moved to a dominant coalition, although the Prime Minister still has the final decision The nexus of power within that coalition moved according to changes in the personalities involved and their competence. In crisis, that is, in effect, during the two World Wars, power rested with the chief executive, but was influenced by military advice, depending on the strength of the principal military leaders. Public opinion exerted a 'stakeholder' influence, not least because of electoral considerations of the politicians.

For many years the process of strategy formulation was hampered by the independence of the three arms of defence, who each determined their own strategy. This situation is analogous to the 'primacy of the SBU' (Strategic Business Unit) (Prahalad and Hamel, 1990). Increasingly, the decisions on defence have been centralised into the Defence Ministry and greater power has accrued to the officials at the expense of the single-service departments. The politics of the organisation are a potent factor in the strategy formulation process. It is noteworthy that, when the nation was faced with the enormous problems of two World Wars, the system adopted became a virtual dictatorship with decision vested in one person, albeit after discussion and advice. These events are supportive of the notion that crisis leads to centralisation of decision.

Strategy formulation in the late 1990s

(*Note: The following description does not necessarily reflect in detail the current state of the continuously developing organisation and methods for strategy formulation in the Ministry of Defence.*)

Defence strategy formulation

The responsibility for the determination of defence policy to fulfil the political aims of the government is, in the period of the late 1990s, the responsibility of the Secretary of State for Defence, and he is assisted in this task by the staff of the Ministry of Defence. Although defence policy has to reflect the aims of the nation's foreign policy, it also has to

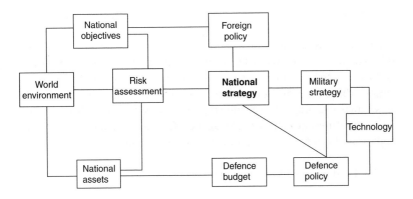

Figure 4.7 An idealised model of the national strategy formulation process.

work within the financial constraints imposed by the government's Public Expenditure Survey (PES), and frequently these two forces are countervailing.

Figure 4.7 shows an idealised schematic (suggested by the author) of the national strategy formulation indicating links between national objectives (what do we want to achieve?), national assets (are these appropriate for the objectives?) and the world environment (what forces are likely to act for and against us?). From these factors, tempered by an assessment of the risks involved, the national strategy is selected. This national strategy (the country's 'corporate strategy') is then supported by, amongst others, foreign and defence policies ('business strategies'). Within the constraints of budgets and defence policies, military strategy is formed, with due account being taken of the advantages and disadvantages of available technology. At times in the past, however, the defence strategy process has often been driven by financial arguments rather than considerations of grand strategy. The factors in Figure 4.7 are acting all the time but the consideration of them is considered, to the degree thought necessary at the time, within the Ministry of Defence in an annual process, which, in 1997, was still called the Long Term Costing cycle.

The long term costings

The aim of the Long Term Costing (LTC) was 'to construct the most coherent and effective defence programme which is affordable within the forecast resources available (Director of Air Force Plans and Programmes, 1997, p. 1). Since the LTC was essentially a budgetary process, it is necessary to consider, without delving too deeply into the sequence of steps used, that it was also strategic.

The main assumptions on which the whole of the defence programme is based are issued by the MOD Central Staffs in the spring of each year, and the top level of these assumptions is the Departmental Plan, which defines the targets and outputs of the MOD, and has an annex which lays down the major front-line strengths of each of the three services. The Departmental Plan sets the agenda for the next four years for the department (air force, navy, and so on) concerned.

The Central Staffs have two main sections:

a   The staff under the Chief of Defence Staff and the Permanent Under-Secretary are responsible for formulating defence policy, crisis management and planning the Defence Programme...

b   The staff under the 2nd Permanent Under-Secretary form the second section. The Resources, Programmes and Finance divisions provide the civilian input into the LTC process under the Principal Finance Officer...(Director of Air Force Plans and Programmes, 1997, p. 1)

Much of the work in the Ministry's Central Staff is conducted in or under the authority of committees such as:

* Finance, Planning and Management Group
* Defence Programme Steering Group
* Senior Executive Committee
* Policy and Programmes Steering Group (PPSG)
* Internal Study Group

Much of the work of these committees is very much tied to the LTC process, which began each spring and was implemented in the following winter, but the PPSG is concerned with longer-term balance of investment issues. The problem faced in this planning process was the matching of equipment and departmental programmes to the needs of the Defence Policy (which is issued for Parliament each year as the Defence Estimates White Paper) and to the estimates of the money likely to be allocated by the Treasury, whilst achieving the correct priorities for each of the single-service departments. The Directorate of Air Plans (1997, p. 1) acknowledged the problems:

The Defence Programme is a juggernaut which (barring major Defence Reviews and exercises such as Options for Change) alters course slowly. New ideas can be and are introduced in the medium or longer term, but the momentum of the machine is such that sudden, large changes in direction are difficult to achieve. They can be very disruptive because so much of the short to medium term programme is already contractually committed.

The planning horizon extended to ten years ahead, although the equipment cycle to complete a programme for a new aircraft or ship is more like twenty years. The operating budget, however, was for the next four years.

Development of the system

Hopkinson (2000) provided an insider view of the workings of Whitehall and how the system has progressed in recent years. He observed that a fundamental characteristic of the defence policy system was that resource-balancing through weapons programmes was frequently the main shaper of strategy, rather than the staffs charged with that responsibility. Perhaps for this reason, the governments in the 1980s tried to avoid defence reviews and relied on a continuing process of assessment and reassessment: emergent strategy in business strategy terms. Hopkinson went on to give a summary of strategy formulation in Whitehall:

> Policy evolves from a subtle interplay of individuals; officials, often fairly junior players, sharing particular concerns with colleagues and with ministers ... The art of Whitehall is knowing what to put to ministers and when. Thus, there is, and can be, no simple guide to policy formulation. There are certain grand issues at the highest level ... which must be decided by ministers collectively ... Other major policy issues ... are likely to be decided in the light of preparatory work by officials and put to ministers collectively, or at least to a committee of senior ministerial players. (Hopkinson, 2000, pp. 26–7)

Some policy changes, such as Options for Change and the Defence Costs Study, were conducted by a handful of key actors, but much of the work in the past was conducted through a complex system of committees. In more recent times, however, the number of committees has been much reduced and the barriers erected by the single services are being broken down. Hopkinson's (2000) criticism, however, is that the various organisational factors impinging on the strategy process lead to a lack of radicalism: 'Given a concrete task to perform, the machine does very well; left to answer the question of what is the right question, it is rather less impressive' (p. 91). Thus, although individuals may foresee the need for change, they may not have the power to institute remedial action. On the whole, such vision has been lacking. The LTC system, now abandoned, restricted thinking to resource considerations, and the long-term nature of defence projects militated against ever starting with a clean sheet of paper.

Comment

The system described is that which pertained in 1997 and was reconsidered during the 1998 Strategic Defence Review. The system was a quintessential, planning-style strategy formulation process, and the broad assumptions were hammered out by the Central Staffs in committees, so one can assume that they were subject to horse-trading and politics, as each protagonist tried to have his or her point of view accepted.

The resulting strategy was likely to be a compromise, lacking radicalism, because the system was likely to dampen any attempt at forcing through a point of view by the exercise of power (although it has been tried). The process was largely built up from the bottom from the previous plan, but a top-down view frequently had to be imposed when it came to adjusting priorities, whether for affordability reasons, or because a major imbalance of investment choice had been identified. The resulting strategy was likely to be conservative and incremental, although events like the collapse of the former Soviet Union provoked more fundamental reappraisals. The incremental approach carries with it a risk of strategic drift, which eventually necessitates a radical review. Such a realisation or maybe the election of a different political party into government can trigger a defence review, in which sacred cows can be sacrificed in an exercise of a process which may resemble that depicted in Figure 4.8 (see p. 171).

The Strategic Defence Review

The reasons for the Review

The publication in July 1998 of Command 3999, *The Strategic Defence Review* (SDR), fulfilled a manifesto commitment by the incoming government of 1997 to conduct a foreign policy-led defence review. The process by which this Review was carried out has been documented in the first supporting essay attached to the White Paper, and in the BBC2 television programme, *A Paper War*.

Background

The Joint Warfare Publication (JWP) 0–01 *British Defence Doctrine* (1997) was issued under the previous administration and sought to underpin development of defence policy by stating the doctrinal practices adopted by British armed forces. Doctrine was defined as 'that which is taught' (Portillo, 1997, p. 1.2) and (quoting Sir Julian Corbett) 'a common vehicle for expression and a common plane of thought'. Doctrinal statements affect the strategy content because they are 'the way we do things'. There is, for instance, an air power doctrine, which will generally dictate the way in which the air war is to be fought (see 'Military methods' above (p. 144) for an example). Doctrine is ideological and thus has a normative effect on strategy formation, somewhat akin to the Principles of War.

JWP 0-01 (Portillo, 1997, pp. 1.8 and 1.9) identified four levels of strategy:

Grand strategy is the application of national resources to achieve national policy objectives (including alliance of coalition objectives)...

Military strategy is the application of military resources to help achieve grand strategic objectives...

The operational level is concerned with the direction of military resources to achieve military strategic objectives...

The tactical level involves the direction of military resources to achieve operational objectives...

JWP 0-01 quoted Field Marshal Viscount Alanbrooke's description of the art of strategy:

to determine the aim, which should be political: to derive from that aim a series of military objectives to be achieved: to assess these objectives as to the military requirements they create, and the pre-conditions which the achievement of each is likely to necessitate: to measure available and potential resources against the requirements and to chart from this process a coherent pattern of priorities and a rational course of action. (Portillo, 1997, p. 4.2)

The JWP (on the same page) went on to echo Mintzberg (1987b) by stating that: 'Strategy seeks to create a desired pattern of events where the ends, the ways and the means are brought into balance, despite the efforts of the enemy to create an entirely different pattern.'

Responsibility for the development of strategy and proposals for the size and shape of the forces to meet the requirements of defence policy, within the resources allocated, is vested in the central staff of the Ministry of Defence Headquarters. The Departmental Plan (Portillo, 1997, p. 5.16) is the vehicle for setting out the aims, objectives, priorities and plans of the department, within the limits set by the Government's Public Expenditure Survey. A joint command-and-control structure centred on a Permanent Joint Headquarters plans and executes operations. This headquarters is permanently established, which means it not only runs operations on a continuous basis, but also has a role in monitoring and planning for crises. The command-and-control principles adopted require direction at the highest level necessary to achieve unity of purpose, combined with the delegation of authority for achieving objectives to the lowest level for the most effective use of forces.

Thus the strategy process in the United Kingdom can be seen as taking its rhythm from the necessity for devising the Departmental Plan (which is based upon grand strategy) but is punctuated by occasional operations that require a specific military strategy to be generated, within the resources available. From time to time, the government will deem it necessary to conduct a more fundamental review of defence policy, in the context of foreign and fiscal policies, reflecting the current view of Britain's place in the world.

The context of the Strategic Defence Review (SDR)

First, SDR was conducted under the doctrinal umbrella of JWP 0-01. The government's manifesto commitment was the second contextual factor. Defence is reconsidered annually before the publication of the Defence White Paper, and in preparation for the debate in the Houses of Parliament on the Defence Estimates, but as a budgetary exercise rather than a strategic one. The estimates have to be agreed by the Public Expenditure Survey. The priority accorded to defence is a governmental decision and SDR was preceded by a series of exercises (Front Line First, Options for Change, and so on) which cynics saw as studying what could be achieved given the Treasury limits on defence expenditure.

SDR claimed to be a study of defence as the servant of foreign and security policy and its stated aims were (Command 3999, 1998, p. 6):'to provide the country with modern, effective and affordable Armed Forces which meet today's challenges but are also flexible enough to

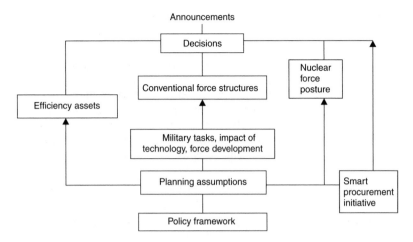

Figure 4.8 The SDR process illustrated.
Source: *Strategic Defence Review* (1998, p. 2).

adapt to change. It provides a vision for the modernisation of Britain's defence into the 21st century.'

The aim of the Review

At a press conference on 28 May 1997, the Defence Secretary, the Right Honourable George Robertson, MP, said of the Review 'Its aim is clear cut; to build on the developing consensus on defence and to establish the widest possible shared vision about Britain's future security needs and the tasks of its Armed Forces . . . to provide Britain's Armed Forces with a new sense of clarity, coherence and consensus' (*Strategic Defence Review* (1998) Essay 1, p. 1). This aim had been the subject of a battle between the Treasury and the Ministry of Defence on the leadership of the Review, and it took the combined efforts of the MOD and the Foreign and Commonwealth Office to prevent the exercise being savings-led.

The process of SDR

The following principles were adopted as guidance during the process:

- Openness
- The maximum use of existing structures
- The widest possible involvement within the Ministry of Defence, the government as a whole and more widely

Table 4.7 A broad summary of the SDR sequence

Event	Activity	Participants
First stage	Assess national interests, commitments and responsibilities, potential risks and challenges. Draft Policy Framework	Ministry of Defence, Foreign and Commonwealth Office
Seminars	Two open seminars in London and Coventry (3 and 11 July 1997)	MPs, academics, media, ministers, officials, non-governmental bodies
Endorsement	The Policy Framework endorsed by ministers	Ministers of Defence and Foreign Office
Planning assumptions	Converting policy into detailed guidance for defence planning	Working groups
Third seminar	Discuss external submissions held in MOD	MOD staff, outside experts and public
Develop missions	Eight missions identified by planning assumptions divided into 28 military tasks	Working groups
Second phase	Assess forces, capabilities, equipment, and support for missions and military tasks	Working groups
High-level discussions	Early 1998, consider costed options and discuss issues	Defence Secretary, chiefs of staff, senior officials
Decision	Approve coherent package of measures	Defence Secretary and senior advisers

The process was illustrated in the diagram in Essay 1, page 2, reproduced here as Figure 4.8.

The actual sequence adopted is summarised in Table 4.7, but the various stages were often characterised by iterations before moving on to the next event. Nuclear forces were the subject of a separate assessment and so the sequence in Table 4.7 refers to conventional forces after the third seminar. The process set out to involve a wide range of individuals from inside and outside the Ministry of Defence, so the working groups comprised military and civilian personnel and representatives of other government departments. The work of these groups was managed under the aegis of the Vice-Chief of Defence Staff and the Second Permanent Secretary, but in detail by the existing bodies, the Policy and

Programmes Steering Group and the Internal Study Group. Senior committees, up to and including the Defence Council, discussed their output. Thus the Review was conducted by a mixture of the existing staff of Defence Headquarters and outside influences.

The *Strategic Defence Review*, Essay 1, suggested that SDR was a unique exercise in consultation on defence. 'Over five hundred submissions were received, from MPs and peers, local authorities, academics, industry, interest groups, journalists and members of the public' (*Strategic Defence Review*, 1998, Essay 1, p. 4). Additional outside advice was gained through a panel of 18 'outsiders' with interests and experience in defence whose role was to comment on and evaluate the conclusions emerging from the working groups. A further team sought the frank views of the rank and file in the three services. Finally the views of the trade unions were also sought.

In Figure 4.9 is a reproduction of a diagram in Essay 1 (p. 5) which summarises the sources consulted in the *Strategic Defence Review*.

'A Paper War'

BBC2 screened a 50-minute documentary programme on the Strategic Defence Review, which showed aspects of the process within the Ministry of Defence and other government offices. The programme revealed that forty different groups had been working on elements of the strategy review and the expert panel had been used as a sounding board for the ideas generated.

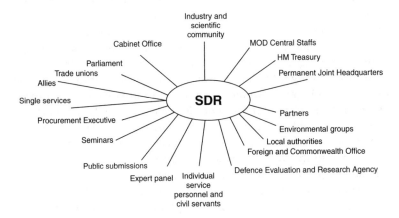

Figure 4.9 Inputs to the Strategic Defence Review.
Source: *Strategic Defence Review* (1998, p. 5).

Key to the results that emerged from the Review were the assumptions on which the subsequent calculations were based, and it was quickly established that these had to be subjected to sensitivity analysis to identify critical choices. Scenarios were developed based on these assumptions and operational analysis techniques were used to evaluate the suggested responses. Defence priorities were agreed with the Foreign Office.

The Treasury were alert to the possibilities for financial savings and they demanded a range of options from which choices could be made. A difficulty arose that the number of options and combinations available quickly became too numerous to handle. The Treasury staff wished to track major policy ideas through to their detailed implications in terms of force levels and equipment.

The organisation structure of the Ministry of Defence is hierarchical, and proved an impediment to the open discussions adopted in the review process. The television programme revealed evidence of resistance to change and special pleading from groups within the staff, although this approach is only to be expected and, it can be argued, is their role. It must have been evident that there was an element of competition between forces that might be seen as alternatives. The long-standing arguments between the Royal Air Force, as proponents of land-based air power, and the Royal Navy, arguing the case for sea-based air power, were likely to reappear since these principles would be mutually exclusive, given the absence of increased spending on defence. Despite the efforts at impartiality and rationality, it was evident that the decisions were judgemental and good advocacy of the case presented could be an advantage. That the senior participants were aware of these factors was evidenced by the Secretary of State's jocular comments about 'party political broadcasts' following one presentation. Nonetheless, the Chief of Naval Staff and the Chief of Air Staff cooperated to put such arguments in the past and reached agreement on Joint Force 2000 (a comment made during interview by Admiral of the Fleet Sir Julian Oswald, 4 February 1999) and a whole range of joint initiatives emerged naturally from the analysis of defence needs as a whole. Efforts were made to consult 'stakeholders' from the existing armed forces, but a gulf was evident between those engaged in the review discussions and the men and women in the front line who viewed the whole exercise with cynicism and suspicion. These reactions, however, would be evident in such a fundamental review in any large organisation, although the previous and recent defence reviews had an effect in this case. It was not clear what effect these inputs had, other than to be interpreted in terms of morale.

Comment

The consensus of opinion suggests that the Strategic Defence Review was an honest attempt at an objective appraisal of defence strategy similar to that shown in Figure 4.7. In contrast to other recent 'reviews', the exercise was not Treasury-led, although clearly this body had a major input into the deliberations. The process drew in opinion from many sources, a number of which were outside the normal planning and decision-making machinery. Inevitably, the 'professionals' had the greater knowledge on which to base their judgements and advice so the outcome could not be expected to be a fundamental shift of defence strategy, particularly since the historical dichotomy of maritime versus continental was still present together with arguments about naval, land and air power. The pack may have been shuffled, but it contained much the same cards. The constituents of the dominant coalition at the centre of the decision-making nexus have changed following the developments described in the 'Chiefs of staff' section above and officials play a greater part than would have been the case earlier in the twentieth century. The SDR was designed to be both bottom-up and top-down, but the top is always going to hold better, more powerful cards than the lower echelons. Nonetheless, the opinions of many were sought and were considered. A review is necessary periodically to check that strategic thinking has not drifted away from national aims during the time that the incremental, year-on-year process has held sway. SDR, given the enormity of the task and the deadweight of history and prejudice surrounding the subject, fulfilled that requirement.

4.4 Case study 2: strategy formulation in IBM

Introduction

This thesis is comparative in nature, so a case subject is needed that provides a business parallel with the military example above. Inevitably, the business in question will be large-scale and bureaucratic so that like can be compared with like. The company chosen is IBM, which was the largest company in the world in terms of turnover, profit and number of people employed.

The early days

The Computing–Tabulating–Recording Company was established in 1911 and, in 1914, Thomas J. Watson, Senior joined the company. He changed the name of the company to International Business Machines in 1924 and remained the CEO until 1956, when he handed over to his son, Thomas Watson, Junior. During the formative years of the company, the strategy was largely in the hands of the entrepreneurial CEO who adopted an international perspective from the outset, but national companies within IBM were 'run by locals and given leeway in deciding product mix and pricing policies' (Yoffie and Pearson, 1990, p. 1). During the Watson era, the principle was established that people were the most important of IBM's assets and a 'contention' management style was adopted to develop and air conflicting views on key issues. Management, however, made the final choice.

Computing

IBM was well-placed to participate in the development of digital computing and their 7000 and 1400 series were successful products in what became known as the 'mainframe' range. The System 360, however, introduced in 1964, established IBM's technical leadership in this field. The growth of the company can be illustrated by comparing data from the start of three decades, and is shown in Table 4.8.

By the late 1980s, IBM was selling 10 000 computer hardware, software and peripheral products in more than 130 countries, but was also strong in other office products. IBM dominated the mainframe computing market and was a company that was held to be a shining example of a well-run company.

The technology of computing was developing, however, and new integrated circuits were conferring greater power on smaller computers: minis, personal computers (PCs), and workstations. These changes threatened IBM's market position because the smaller units were reducing the demand for mainframes, especially as networking of PCs became possible. This latter development led to distributed computing architectures, the power of which could be increased by the addition of further

Table 4.8   The growth of IBM

	1970	1980	1990
Total revenues*	7504	26 213	69 018
Net income*	1018	3562	6020
Total employees	269 291	341 279	373 816

*Figures in $ millions.
Source: Yoffie and Pearson (1990, p. 16).

PCs, and, eventually, to client/server solutions where several databases could be included instead of the monolithic mainframe solution.

Paradoxically, IBM pioneered 'open systems integration', which set an industry standard, permitting a wide choice of peripherals and software from many suppliers on a standardised PC, the design of which was eventually released into the public domain. This 'IBM' PC standardised the operating system (MSDOS) and most applications from all companies were made compatible (other operating systems, such as cpm, eventually died out, with the exception of MACDOS for the rival Apple computers). This standardising move was beneficial to the development of PCs, and the whole industry could move forward with new developments at an increasing pace, but IBM, although a major supplier of PCs, did not reap the financial rewards. IBM subsequently tried to break free of MSDOS by introducing the OS2 operating system, which had the additional agenda of facilitating operating PCs into mainframes. Despite heavy investment and initial help from Microsoft, OS2 failed to make the progress expected. Even when Microsoft 'Windows' was dominating the market, IBM continued to spend heavily on OS2. IBM continued to view computing and their market as being principally the mainframe from which the company was deriving 70–80 per cent of its profits (Yoffie and Pearson, 1990, p. 3).

Decline and stumble

In 1985, profits began to decrease. IBM's market share in PCs fell from 27 per cent to 16.5 per cent. Product overpricing, enforced by central management, impeded its entry into workstations and laptops (Verity *et al.*, 1991), but the problem went deeper than mere price. Fundamentally, IBM failed to understand the requirements of workstation users, and concentrated on introducing AIX as an attempt to improve upon the existing software standard, UNIX. In addition, IBM was not keeping abreast of the required technology, and their workstations were poorly supported by software developers. The first IBM laptop also lacked quality and innovation, and a costly recall was necessary. An attempt to solve the problem by subcontracting to vendors in the Far East also failed. Eventually, the problems were resolved by the introduction of the 'Thinkpad' range, but, by that time, Toshiba had become the market leaders in this field, and IBM had to concentrate upon the high end of the market. A massive software development aimed at supporting mainframe sales failed. IBM's share of the world computer market dropped from 36 per cent to 23 per cent in the 1980s. The initial management reaction was the standard one of reducing staff but, owing to the long-standing IBM policy of 'no lay-offs', a costly early retirement programme was the method adopted. Unfortunately, economic recession reduced demand, and turnover declined at the same time. Eventually, the thick skin of complacency was pierced and the Chairman, John Akers since 1985, realised that more drastic measures were required. His assessment was:

> In the mid-1980s we asked ourselves 'How well are we positioned?' Our answer, 'Not well at all!' Our market strength was in large hardware, whereas the market growth was taking place in software, services and smaller machines (ie PCs and workstations). Furthermore, we were organised around hardware, not markets, so we weren't well set up to solve customer problems. It was clear that we needed to change IBM and find ways to facilitate constant transformation. (Yoffie and Pearson, 1990, p. 6)

But Akers, although a long-time IBM man, did not last. As the stock market valuation of the company continued to fall (the share price fell from nearly $160 in 1985 to $48 in 1992), investors called for the Chairman's replacement. On 1 April 1993, Louis V. Gerstner became the first outsider to head IBM. Some concern was expressed as to his lack of technological knowledge, but he came to IBM with a record of success at American Express and RJR Nabisco. Morris (1997, p. 42) described the situation: 'IBM had been flattened by the desktop revolution, and nearly everyone – including much of IBM's own management — had written off the mainframe. The stock had collapsed; John Akers was actually splitting the organization 13 ways and contemplating spinning off some parts.'

Gerstner recognised that the changes instituted by Akers had not changed the culture of IBM, and the bureaucracy, the endless meetings, the contention, and the slowness of decision remained. Morris (1997, p. 43) described the new CEO's approach:

> Heedless of criticism inside and outside the company, Gerstner began to cut costs, restructure, weed out disbelievers. He jolted the culture with shock therapy. He cheer-led the overhaul and revival of the mainframe, stoked the services business and brought IBM back to the party in PCs. He slashed long-term debt from $14.6 billion to $9.9 billion, managed nonetheless to buy back $10.7 billion in stock.

In 1994 Gerstner, in his Chairman's Letter, reported, 'I think it's fair to say that the question about IBM is no longer one of survival', which would indicate that failure of the company had been seen earlier as a distinct possibility.

Hammer and Stanton (1999) described how IBM at this time, in a reaction to the increasing globalisation of their customers' businesses, changed its organisational processes to reduce the power of their country and product managers. Standardisation was adjudged to be required in the company, and a member of the Corporate Executive Committee was made responsible for the development of processes, which were then assigned to a business process executive for its implementation by all business units in the company.

IBM in the United Kingdom

As might be expected, IBM in the UK was very similar to the company in the USA and it was:

> built on a strong centralised planning and control system combined with a highly effective sales branch structure. The company was largely product and technology driven, and product strategies were primarily developed at corporate headquarters. Countries were responsible for short and medium term targets and for managing their resources and skills to achieve these targets. (Lloyd and Phillips, 1994, p. 53)

The hierarchy had seven layers of management in 1991 with an average span of control of eight, which was changed to four layers and a span of twenty by 1994 as the organisation structure was changed to a federation of 25 businesses. In the early, high-growth years, the company employed a number of ex-service people who would have been comfortable in the rigid hierarchy and the quarterly planning cycle, which aimed to update the annual rolling plan. Some of the conclusions reached in the UK filtered up to Europe and thence to the USA, but the board in the USA viewed the world as homogeneous and thus an extension of America. The problem still remained that IBM was product- rather than customer-focused and the mainframe group dominated the rest.

In the Gerstner era, the drawing of decision-making to the centre (because of the need for increased speed of reaction and greater coordination in the crisis) removed autonomy from regions like the UK, where the result was a loss of motivation. The regions were useful in gathering masses of information, but were largely denied the decision-making powers that they had enjoyed in the past. The crisis had introduced an element of short-termism, because the stock market was demanding results, and the future was sacrificed for the present. Fear and poor results undermined the confidence of IBM: a company that had been arrogant in its self-belief.

Strategy process

Whilst the overall strategy for IBM was decided by the CEO and the Management Committee (Weston, 1991), its working out in detail was a lengthy bureaucratic process which had first been introduced in principle in the 1930s. Although the process resulted in a sales plan, the steps were fleshing out the objectives set by the Management Committee (see Table 4.9).

The activity in the autumn included the development of the 'October Rolling Plan'. In response to a guidance document from the area headquarters, business units converted the product assumptions into a business plan, with profit-and-loss projections. This activity absorbed a great deal of staff effort in a number of iterations before the plan was agreed with area HQ.

This planning routine resulted in a company-wide behaviour pattern amongst the sales force that meant that January was a period of inactivity

Table 4.9   The planning cycle in IBM in the United States

Step	Month	Action
1	January	Management Committee, advised by planning staff and a six-year business model, creates objectives and passes them to US operating units
2	January to June	US operating units establish their own objectives, investment patterns and targeted returns for the current year, plus two more
3	June	US operating managers present plans to the Management Committee. CEO and Committee give specific quantitative objectives, including revenues, profits and return on assets
4	July	Sales plan development staff calculate the money to be allocated to commissions
5	Autumn	Sales plan development activity. Consulting branch offices. Defined quotas by product category
6	November	Sales plan development staff present final draft plan to area managers
7	December	Area plans agreed and region managers allocate their quotas to branches

awaiting the issue of the plan. Then, when the sales plan was issued, the sales force would study it carefully to see how *they* could make money. Often, salesmen would change territory at the start of the year, so they would aim to make their targets before moving on by heavy discounting at the end of the year. The problem was then passed on to the new salesman for the area who had a glut of uninstalled product waiting for his attention with the customer. This culture rolled over into the PC business, and the customer exploited the need for salesmen to make their quotas at year-end by negotiating high discounts. This practice cost IBM a fortune: perhaps acceptable when the business was successful, but disastrous when the downturn came. So embedded in the IBM culture was this practice that it was not eliminated until about 1998.

The executive, comprising the CEO and the rest of the Management Committee (three more people), determined the strategy and the vision. Their staff assisted in defining objectives and sales targets, but the process was top-down. For many years, given the stability in customer demand, the overall strategy did not need to be changed often, but, when change was necessary, IBM was slow to react. Miller (1992, p. 455) could almost have had IBM in mind when he describes his 'decoupling' trajectory of decline: 'transforms *salesmen* – organizations with unparalleled marketing skills, prominent brand names, and broad markets, ...into aimless, bureaucratic *drifters* whose sales fetish obscures design issues, and who produce a stale and disjointed line of "me too" offerings'.

In 1987, the Chairman and CEO, John Akers, declared the 'Year of the Customer' which was meant to signal the change from a product-driven to a customer-driven company. IBM, however, proved to be like a super-tanker that travels many miles before it responds to the helm. The sales commission was based on a complicated points system, which used the list price of hardware – the higher the price, the greater the commission. Sales of a mainframe system would generate a large commission, whereas the lower unit price of PCs meant that much more work was required to reach the same commission. Increasingly, too, as the 1980s ended and the 1990s began, less profit was in hardware and more in software and facilities management. The culture of the company was slow to change.

In 1991, further changes became necessary, as the business was not recovering quickly enough. Now, Akers decided to split the monolithic giant IBM into a number of autonomous businesses, effectively decentralising authority and decision-making from the Management Committee. The Sales Team, however, was not to be split and the recovery in the share price was reversed when the market analysts learned that the changes were to be evolutionary rather than a sudden overhaul. The dilemma of all very large companies – how to be at the same time entrepreneurial and controlled – was evident in IBM, and the endless meetings within the bureaucracy before a decision was made slowed down the introduction of new products and lost the premium of being the first into the market with innovation: this at a time when technology was developing rapidly and products were quickly made obsolescent. In reality, few moves were possible without the approval of the management at Armonk, which was the bastion of the mainframe computer division. One by-product of the decentralisation process was the increase in the number of cooperative ventures with prominent industry companies such as Digital, Apple and Microsoft.

Akers used three 'Rounds' to implement his strategy of better customer relations, improve product competitiveness and strengthen structural efficiency:

- *Round One.* Round One was begun in 1987 and, as part of this process 10 000 US employees left on early retirement. An in-depth study concluded that IBM was largely responsible for its own downturn and the senior management interpreted this problem as arising from ineffective execution and the inability to offer complete business solutions to customers.
- *Round Two.* In 1988, Akers enacted a sweeping reorganisation of the company as part of Round Two. Three product development Lines of Business (LOBs) were created, namely: Personal Systems; Application Business Systems; and Enterprise Systems. In addition three software and components LOBs were created, namely: Communication Systems; Programming Systems; and Technology Products. The Management Committee now intervened less in operational decisions and more responsibility was delegated to the senior LOB executives.
- *Round Three.* Round Three, begun in 1989, executed these changes to make IBM more market-responsive. Emphasis was placed on improving quality and a corporate priority was to win the Malcolm Baldridge National Quality Award.

During this period the strategic planning process was streamlined. According to Peter Schavoir, IBM's Director of Strategy (Yoffie and Pearson, 1990, p. 10):

the strategic planning process was too long, involved too many people (sometimes into the thousands) and inevitably involved too much trivia. Starting in 1990, we cut the cycle time almost in half and dramatically reduced the number of staff and line participants. We also moved away from a rigid numerical planning system to one where we offered alternative scenarios, which each geographical region had to respond to.

At the same time, Akers abolished the contention system to speed the decision-making process: there simply was not time for protracted debate. He met twice a year with his entire top management team in Strategic Planning Conferences at which new initiatives were communicated, priorities were reset and the company's performance was discussed.

Despite the best efforts of Akers, the company continued to decline, and Gerstner was appointed to replace him as Chairman and CEO. The new man came from outside the company and adopted shock tactics to bring about change. He was abrupt, abrasive, dominating and self-important, but he finally began to penetrate the traditional IBM culture and bring about changes. Although he retained a number of IBM veterans in top operational jobs, he imported key people from his past: David B. Kalis as Senior Public Relations Officer (from Amex and RJR); Lawrence R. Ricciardi as General Counsel (from Amex and RJR); Abby Kohnstamm as Head of Marketing (from Amex); G. Richard Thoman as Chief Finance Officer (from McKinsey, Amex and RJR); and Isabelle Cummins as Executive Assistant (from Amex and RJR).

What is more, Gerstner reduced the size of the board from 19 to 11 and, at the same time, introduced a number of new members, most of them new to IBM. Hausman and Burke (1995) quoted Bob Djurdjevic (president of a market research firm): 'The old board had no relationship whatsoever to IBM's business. They didn't know enough to question the strategies [ex-IBM Chairman] John Akers was implementing.'

So, Gerstner surrounded himself with people whom he knew and could trust. They would carry out the measures that Gerstner dictated; and it was a top-down dictatorship in the early crisis period. He brought focus, toughness and discipline to an organisation that had become flabby and introspective. His moves to standardise business process gave a greater degree of control of how the business was run. Gerstner had no respect for the comfortable policy of never firing anyone: now, it was perform or out. He sized up his people and used his own judgement to differentiate bad advice from good. He said, 'There's no question that, during the first year, there were some attempts to feed me intellectual arsenic – some bad ideas, some pet projects'

(Morris, 1997, p. 45). By 1996, he could articulate a strategic vision for the company:

> a networked world that transforms the way people work, interact, learn and do business. I said our vision wasn't some slogan or a flashy-but-improbable dream. Rather it was our view, grounded in decades of experience, of where technology and commerce around the world were headed, and that we would help our customers use networking computing to improve what they do and how they do it. (Gerstner, 1996, p.1)

Gerstner, then, had exercised strong leadership at a time of crisis. He had taken difficult decisions and had them successfully implemented. He had created a vision and had made progress in changing the culture of the company, in particular reducing the bureaucracy and speeding its reaction time. His style was not democratic, although he did listen to advice and opinion from the organisation. He standardised and thus reduced the autonomy of IBM executives in countries around the world. For instance, he abolished the 'October Rolling Plan' by developing plans centrally. Now, business units could comment but, effectively, the 'draft' plan became a mandate.

4.5   A commentary on the cases

Introduction

Both of the cases in Chapter 4 are written on large, bureaucratic organisations. IBM was faced with a crisis, which affected their strategy formulation process, and the Ministry of Defence similarly had to cope with interruptions by wars to their year-by-year strategy development.

Organisational effects

Mintzberg (1991) proposed a pentagon of forces acting in organisations, and related them to five configurations in which each of the forces predominated. Thus, when the primary need in a company is for *direction*, the configuration is *entrepreneurial*. The force of *efficiency*, however, is related to a configuration which he calls *machine* (that is, bureaucratic). This latter description seems to be appropriate to IBM. In its early years, the company was directed, top-down, by the entrepreneurial Thomas J. Watson, Senior and, although discussion was increasingly encouraged, he remained the strategist. As the company grew, so did the rules, regulations and processes deemed necessary for the control of a giant organisation. The problems became more complex and, although over-all strategy was set from the top, the machine ground out the detailed solutions in a planning cycle that generated a detailed plan, which, in effect, informed people what they had to do. Such a system worked well until the pace of change increased and, as Mintzberg (1990b) points out, some form of 'emergent' process is needed when the environment is turbulent (a conclusion rejected by Ansoff (1991)). Under these circum-stances, companies are under the force of *concentration* and the appro-priate configuration is *diversified* (diversification and divisionalisation). It can be argued, however, that IBM was already divisionalised. What was lacking, though, from Mintzberg's theoretical standpoint, was the divisional autonomy that is necessary if companies are to concentrate on their many lines of business. IBM, then, found it difficult to respond quickly to their market when, after years of relative stability when IBM made most of the innovations, it became very turbulent and much of the innovation was coming from companies other than IBM. These developments are similar to those in defence, where the autocratic leader form gave way to a more inclusive style of strategy process. The armed forces have long been divided into 'arms' as a means of pursuing efficiency, and these two cases together confirm the theory that large, bureaucratic organisations use linear/rational processes, which involve much of the organisation.

It is evident that, in Mason and Mitroff's (1981) terms, defence strat-egy problems are 'wicked' in that they are highly interconnected with issues in many other fields. If that is so, defence strategy demands the broad participation of all parties affected and the collection of a wide spectrum of information from diverse sources. So, strategic choice will be based upon staff advice, and will only be controversial if consensus has not been reached at lower levels. In the early years of IBM, their strat-egy process followed a similar pattern, but responded to the increasing complexity of the market environment by the introduction of a bureau-cratic system.

Societal effects

Military strategy formulation in the United Kingdom has evolved under the pressures of changes in society, developments in technology and the shifts of power in the country. The monarch, although still Cap-tain-General of the armed forces, plays little or no real part in the decision-making. The individual armed forces have lost much of their power as the process has become more centralised and bureaucratic, and officials are more prominent now in the strategy process. The 'system' will find ways of stifling the individual who propounds an unconventional view (as it did with Field Marshal Montgomery after the war) but powerful and adroit individuals can nudge the strategy to lasting effect (as in the case of Earl Mountbatten's pressure for a powerful Chief of Defence Staff). IBM similarly became a conformist society (despite the apparent encouragement of dissent), which could not produce the radical solution needed to reverse their decline.

Resource effects

The routine defence strategy process is driven by economic factors, particularly in seeking to achieve efficiency and flexibility through thorough training and wise equipment procurement. So, the resource-based view is a valid lens through which to view the formulation of defence policy. The resources afforded to defence are both a determinant and a limiter of the strategy options that are available. For instance, contemporary society in Britain is less tolerant of casualties in battle than in the past. Technology continues to influence the tactical use of military power, but it also has a strategic effect, particularly on arguments for the choice of either a maritime or a continental focus, the place of air power, and also the enormous cost of modern weapons systems. All contingencies cannot be foreseen, and the armed forces in war will have to operate with the resources provided by the routine strategy process. IBM had a strong resource base, but encountered problems because they based their strategy on a misapprehension. The company failed to identify the significant change in the market and so nurtured the wrong resource.

The strategy process

The Ministry of Defence is a very large organisation and handles issues of great importance, so it is unsurprising that its methods are bureaucratic, consensus-driven and subject to internal politics. The case study of strategy formulation in the British MOD reveals a bureaucratic process that seeks to reconcile many different opinions and departmental aims. Decisions are expected to emerge from discussions and negotiations between the parties involved, but always the Treasury has to be satisfied, or at least appeased. Radical change in the shorter term is unlikely from such a system, nor would it be welcome. The parallel with a divisionalised corporation (such as IBM) is evident in that often policies are proposed that benefit a sectional interest, rather than the body as a whole. The 'mainframe' clique distorted the strategy of IBM to the company's disadvantage. In recent years, the individualism of each of the services has been largely given up to produce a more integrated system, which should lead to a wider, more coherent strategic vision. Entrepreneurial activity in defence, in which one service exploits a given situation to secure growth and greater power, had been the underlying mode of operation, particularly since the formation of the separate air force. The move toward a greater integration in defence, however, can be seen in business terms as an attempt to realise the synergies, and thus efficiencies, in the armed forces. Strategy decisions have been largely withdrawn from the 'divisions' (that is, individual service departments) and concentrated in corporate headquarters (Defence Staff), although, at the same time, delegation of operational or tactical authority was introduced in the 1980s with the New Management Strategy. Under this regime, commanders at all levels were given discretionary spending powers, albeit within very close limits. IBM also used linear rational methods routinely to determine their strategy, but, as discussed below, crisis brought them onto a 'war' footing when, again, they reacted to crisis in a similar way to the military in war.

The formation of strategy in defence is evolutionary and incremental, reacting to the changes in the environment and the resources available. This approach can lead to strategic drift over time and a mismatch with the aspirations and requirements of the nation. At these points, fundamental reviews of strategy are required (even if no change results) and SDR was an attempt at just such an objective look at aims, missions, tasks and forces. In business terms, these exercises would be viewed as ascribing to a 'market-led' (external) approach, whereas earlier cost-cutting moves purporting to be strategic (Options for Change, and so on) arise from a 'resource-based' (internal) view. IBM, too, drifted away from competitive advantage because they failed to spot that their previously successful strategy had become inappropriate. The inertia of success had masked the need for change.

The effect of crisis

In a crisis, there is a distinct tendency for defence decisions to lie in the hands of the central few, or even solely with the Prime Minister. IBM in trouble appointed a single, powerful leader, even though they had always previously used a consensus approach. In crisis, the military strategy method is synoptic and linear/rational, with a strong emphasis on the importance of goals. In war, the military expect the declaration of a clear aim from the politicians for their operations and the maintenance of this aim is a prime principle to be observed. The military solution is directly related to the achievement of the stated aim *and no other*. The Falklands War required an assault against a defended territory thousands of miles away from Britain, and was undertaken even though such operations had been forsworn in earlier Defence White Papers. Some might quote this operation as vindication of Hamel and Prahalad's (1993) theory of strategy as stretch and leverage.

Style

Both the British Armed Forces and IBM have a style that influences their approach to tasks. Both value integrity and both conduct their business with a degree of formality. The ordered, hierarchical culture affects their strategy processes, and there is a danger that an authoritarian approach may dampen the expression of different, critical opinions. The cultural context materially affects the strategy process adopted, and, when considered in detail, there is a different process for every organisation. The theories of strategic management are generalisations that encompass many variations in detail.

Conclusion

Defence strategy formulation, then, is analogous to that used in very large, bureaucratic companies, such as IBM. Crisis has a similar effect in both defence and business, in that it centralises decision, reduces organisational politics, stresses leadership and, perhaps, releases extra resources. Military strategy can be described as being formulated in two distinct modes:

(a) The year-on-year development and maintenance of military capacity in support of national goals in general, and foreign policy in particular;
(b) The formulation of strategy for the successful achievement of a particular objective in a campaign or operation.

The second process is conducted within the constraints and resources imposed by the first. A single commander is chosen to bear the responsibility for a successful outcome in war, and risk is more likely to be countenanced than in the routine days of peace. IBM adopted a similar, centralising course of action when faced with a threat to their survival. The bureaucratic context is mirrored in IBM, until crisis occurred. It can be argued that, if Gerstner, the ruthless, decisive leader, had not been appointed, IBM would have continued its decline to mediocrity.

5
Making Strategic Decisions

5.1 Introduction

The thesis so far has been largely concerned with what has been written on the subject of strategy formulation. The argument now turns to focus on the evidence collected through interviews with practitioners in the strategy field, combined with that from the four case studies written around strategy process. The evidence is only a sample from a vast field of human experience, but there is enough to compare with the theory. From this comparison, not only can a view be formed on the comparability of the evidence and the theory, but also the findings on the strategy process in the military and business fields can themselves be compared.

5.2 The findings so far

From the literature, strategy process can be seen as identifying the winning formula for the organisation, but the certain determination of an infallible and optimum course of action is too complex for the human brain to accomplish. Strategy has been seen to be concerned with the longer term, although the turbulence in, and complexity of, the environment limits the distance of the horizon of future planning. The solution to this problem is that the strategist(s) will work through the complexity until a satisfactory solution is found, which is then likely to be adopted. The chosen strategy must take account of the environmental situation and the capabilities of the organisation itself.

The relative importance of these two domains is situation-dependent, but a modern tendency is to place more importance on the resources, competences and capabilities of the organisation than on the environment.

This has led to a body of opinion that suggests that the knowledge and the experience 'intangible assets' possessed by the organisation are the ultimate source of competitive advantage. The strategy process is likely to be controlled by a dominant coalition in the organisation, who will probably take some advice from the staff, although the degree of acceptance of differing views is dependent on the autocratic or democratic nature of the controlling few. Although the intention is that the process will be rational, the outcome will be influenced by the personalities involved, organisational politics and the methods adopted. It is accepted by many that the final choice will be influenced by non-rational factors such as intuition, tradition (organisational culture), ideology and political necessity. Some organisations use a programmed sequence of actions leading to a choice of strategy, whereas others are less formal and consider strategic issues continually. The military stress the importance of the aim, but business seems less certain of its ability to formulate its intentions with the same degree of precision. Business is more likely to express its intentions in terms of mission or vision, with the underlying intention of profitability.

The determination of a vision for the future (a feature also valued by the military) is seen to be the principal task of the leader. Since strategy is ultimately a matter of decision, the role of the leader is crucial in this process. The leader must take the final decision, even though this action may be no more than endorsement of the preferred solution arrived at by an iterative, bargaining process. A parallel is drawn with 'statecraft' which is taken to mean the ability to take an objective and comprehensive view of the aims and direction of the enterprise, to isolate the essence of the problem without submerging in a morass of detail, and to reach wise, humane decisions.

5.3   The interviewees

A number of interviews were conducted on people who had experience of the strategy process in either the military or business, or, in a few cases, both. They are categorised in Table 5.1.

One academic, Mr Alan Hooper, has been classified as 'business' since he directs the Centre for Leadership Studies, but he is also a retired Colonel of the Royal Marines and frequently used military examples and perspectives. Air Chief Marshal Sir Patrick Hine is classified as a 'military' board member, but at the time of the interview he was on the board of British Aerospace as Military Adviser. The military board members comprise one naval, two army and two air force officers.

Table 5.1 The interviewees categorised

	Military	Business
Board Level	5	8
Top management	1	3
Middle management	1	0
Consultancy	0	1
Academe	4	1
Total	11	13

5.4   The framework for analysis

In Chapter 1, the research question was treated as a phylum and the sub-questions derived from the central question. This analysis suggested dimensions into which the study could be subdivided, and these can also be viewed as drivers of the strategy process:

1   Organisational factors
2   Leadership factors
3   The attitude to risk
4   The theory and practice of strategy formulation
5   The influence of context

This framework will now be used to consider the findings.

The interviewees were not specifically asked for their definition of 'strategy', but Professor Freedman posited the view that 'strategy', in Schelling's (1980, p. 16) words, 'is "interdependent decision making where you know that the outcomes taken from your decisions depend on how they affect other persons' decisions"'.

5.5   Organisational factors

Top-down or bottom-up?

The principal organisational issue is where and how the strategy is formulated. The assumption in the military seems to be that strategy is the prerogative of the commander in war, but, in peace, the staff more often handled the issues, with guidance from the top. General Maxwell Thurman (1991, p. 17) held the view that: 'Half the people believe that the G-3 ought to write it [the concept of operations] and give it to the general. The general can edit it and ship it downward. That is not what you are trying to do. The general has to set the tone for what the organization is going to do in the campaign plan.'

On the other hand, Mr John D. Rittenhouse (1991, p. 62) at the same conference in 1991 recounted his experience as head of General Electric Aerospace: 'One of the things that I found difficult to believe when I entered GE was that when people in GE say "CEO" they mean this box of three people. They *don't* mean Jack Welsh.' Collective leadership of this nature would not be attractive to the military, but having a single commander does not necessarily imply an autocratic, top-down process.

The interviewees were asked whether the strategy process was top-down or bottom-up, and the answers were inconclusive. For instance, Sir Ian Pedder's experience was that 'strategy should really be developed quite near the top and signed off by all the Directors' (Interview, 16 September 1999). No one interviewed thought that strategy was formulated wholly top-down or bottom-up, but the majority view was that the process was iterative around levels in the organisation. The military favoured the top-down direction, but the difficulty of determining a clear answer is illustrated by Schwarzkopf's (1993) account of the sequence adopted in the Gulf War of 1991:

> Not satisfied that we were thinking creatively enough, I sent a message in early September to the Army requesting a fresh team of planners. A four-man team of graduates from the School of Advanced Military Studies...I instructed: 'Assume a ground attack will follow an air campaign. I want you to study the enemy dispositions and the terrain and tell me the best way to drive Iraq out of Kuwait given the forces we have available'...On October 6, the planning wizards delivered their proposed battle plan. It turned out to be exactly what I'd sketched on scrap paper almost two months before...[the General then took action to acquire more forces]. The textbook way to defeat such a force would have been to hold it in place with a frontal attack while sending an even bigger army to outflank it, to envelop it, and crush it against the sea. But Washington now appeared willing to consider sending more divisions, and that changed everything...On October 15, I told Central Command's planners to assume another armoured corps and to develop a flanking attack. (pp. 439–49)

Sir Christopher Benson provided a clue when he observed, 'in every firm and company that I have been involved in, we have all approached strategy in a totally different way' (Interview, 8 July 1999). Sir Ian Pedder made a somewhat similar point when he said that 'the strategies you adopt depend on where you are sitting' (Interview, 16 September 1999). Sir Christopher went on to express the views that strategy formulation is 'a muddle as a rule', and was complicated by the 'baronies' that formed in companies. Nonetheless, he believed that the board was responsible for setting company objectives, whilst subordinate executives were tasked to devise the strategy. Often, he observed, strategies were hit upon by accident, but the important organisational factor was two-way communications, or, as he put it, 'a two-way stream with no traffic lights'.

Sir John Harvey-Jones described the system he introduced into ICI:

we required every business every territory . . . to produce a strategy against, usually, three different scenarios we drew for them. One was, what would they do if they were totally untrammelled, totally free, and had access to all the money, all the people they needed; another one was, if they had to live within their own cash flow: and, usually, an intermediate one. We then took all of those ['we' being the board], then used to go away and spend two or three days together. First of all saying what we thought the group as a whole needed to do, what we needed to go for and getting all the intelligence we could as well, where our competitors were going – in broad terms. And then we iterated round and round and round with the individual businesses until the pattern of all the individual businesses lined up – roughly – with what we wanted. (Interview, 21 April 1998)

This system had the advantage that the constant iteration resulted in the final strategy being owned by everyone. For that reason the strategy had to be simple, or in Harvey-Jones's terms, 'a one-liner'.

GKN had taken a similar stance during Mr George's tenure as Company Secretary, when the board had decided to disband their planning body. Their divisional heads were charged with setting their own strategies, but, since the board was the prime investment centre, the final decision and endorsement (or modification) were made by the board, which operated in a collegiate manner. Colonel Gooderson described a similar process in LoadLok Ltd where proposals were made to the board and the process iterated between middle managers and executives until agreement was reached. The board of LoadLok were open to proposals at any time but met twice a year formally to review their company strategy.

Sir Peter Walters recalled (Interview, 2 June 1999) that when he was chairman of BP, the various subsidiary companies largely pursued their own strategies. He instituted a matrix structure with two axes; one was exploration, production, marketing and shipping, whilst the other was country coordination. He told the company, 'Look, this is the strategy straight down the line', which was a clear top-down approach.

Mr Kevin Bounds, a consultant, is a user of the Balanced Scorecard concept, and has discussed its use with the originators, Kaplan and Norton. He described the process: 'you have a vision, it is an analytical process, you get it down to critical success factors, you define your key force indicators, you identify the strategic action programmes you need to implement it. Now that is a very top-down process' (Interview, 28 June 2000).

On the other hand, he acknowledged that those driving this process do not do it alone. He said, 'to improve the quality of your decision-making and your strategy formulation, you have to go down the organisation and find out what really happens'. There is a danger that decisions will be taken by executives who are ignorant of the true situation. A principle adopted by the American armed forces is always to take decisions at the highest possible level, thus ensuring a synoptic view, but there is a danger that the conditions at the tactical level will be misunderstood.

Entrepreneurs often adopt the top-down approach, because they usually take the strategic decisions themselves. Sir Ian Pedder recalled his experience as a Director of Davis and Newman and DanAir: 'But it was a company that was totally dominated by one man [that is, Mr Fred Davis], who indicated what the annual plan should be and, as the plan hit the table, he immediately started modifying it to his own wishes' (Interview, 16 September 1999).

Lord Bramall's view was that, in the British military, the commander gave guidance to his staff, which worked out the detail, whereas, in the American military, the staff produced a number of options from which the commander selected his preference. Sir Patrick Hine, too, thought that the broad ideas emerged from the commander. Sir John Harvey-Jones took a different view: 'I always thought during the war the great men looked to move into Africa or whatever, but, of course, it didn't work that way at all. Quite junior staff officers would feed the information and campaign for a strategy to the top, who would then reject or change it.'

Professor Mason's evidence showed that the planning of the air campaign for Kosovo was done at mid-level in the staff and modified by the strategic leaders, whose views were strongly affected by political considerations and the views of other nations in the coalition. He stressed that the nations, although in NATO, were operating as a coalition, not an alliance, and, therefore, the links were not formal and binding. This difference affected the strategy process, which had to be more consensual than would have been the case in an integrated, alliance staff.

Conclusion

Strategy, in practice, is unlikely to be formed wholly top-down, or bottom-up, in either of the contexts studied. Decisions are usually taken at the top, but the wise executive will ensure that essential facts are not overlooked. The choice of method is influenced if there is deemed to be a need to satisfy the humans involved, or if, by contrast, the organisation's leader acts autocratically. The military have become less top-down as the concept of the general staff gathered acceptance, and as society in general has become more democratic. Strategy process is currently more consensual and negotiated than in the past, except in the few cases where autocrats persist.

Organisational politics

All interviewees saw organisational politics as a fact of life. Organisations have a tendency to spawn baronies, which may be divisions or lesser groups, and the danger becomes that the aims of these lesser groups may not accord totally with the company strategy. The baronies may attempt to modify the company strategy to benefit themselves, and, even if they believe that they are acting in the best interests of the company, the dominant coalition cannot allow separatism. General Eisenhower (Case study 1 in Chapter 3) was faced with this problem and his strategy of advancing on a broad front could well have been forced upon him by the need to avoid having to choose between the cries for priority from Montgomery, Bradley and Patton. In the MOD, the internecine struggles of the past were bitterly fought (particularly those involving the new Royal Air Force) which, in the 1920s and 1930s, reached Cabinet level. The military, then, are not immune from the manoeuvrings of organisational politics and their concentration on generating doctrine is an ideological attempt to further cooperation and conformance, and to avoid dissonance. In war, however, political activities below the strategic level would probably be viewed as disloyalty.

Mr Bounds, whilst acknowledging the existence of organisational politics, pointed out that they could arise from shortcomings in the strategy process: 'I think it comes back to the articulation of strategies, because quite often the young turks are very focussed and very goal-oriented. If there isn't a set of corporate goals they can latch onto, they will create their own' (Interview, 28 June 2000). Power is the main-spring of politics and the bottom-up approach can lead to ambitious groups within the organisation trying to modify the company strategy to favour their ideas. The board, which receives these ideas, need to bear this factor in mind. Sir John Harvey-Jones's view that 'Politicking to achieve your business objectives, is one thing – politicking to enhance your "brownie points"...is one thing I think you have to stop' (Interview, 21 April 1998) shows that the perceptive leaders are aware of the problem. McNulty and Pettigrew (1999, p. 50) endorsed this view: 'The purpose of a board of directors is to monitor top management and resist the opportunism and self-interested behaviour of managers.'

Conclusion

Organisational politics is endemic, and the strategy process must identify and isolate those groups and individuals whose activities run counter to the greater good. The politician will seek personal power for its own ends, whereas the statesman will use power more selflessly and perceptively. There is little difference, in this respect, between military and business organisations.

Organisational structure

The entrepreneurs interviewed (Dr King, Ms Bradley and Mr Mayers) all tended to criticise large bureaucratic organisations for the negative effect they have upon the generation of new ideas. Thus, Dr King said:

> The bureaucratic structure of these very large companies are an impediment since their divisionalised structure will lead to partial, blinkered vision of the company problem...Big companies, in the main, do not have really good bright ideas because the bureaucracy makes it difficult for budding entrepreneurs to get past the gatekeepers. It would seem better for those with bright ideas to leave and start up their own firm. (Interview, 1 November 1999)

The large organisation has the problem of allowing autonomy to foster entrepreneurial activity, whilst keeping control. A balance has to be struck between rigidity and chaos, but it seems to be inevitable that the large organisation will form its strategy in a more controlled, struc-tured way. The alternative is the centralised autocracy more often found in small, entrepreneurial firms. The three levels of business strategy (corporate, business and functional) must be nested like *matrioshki*, the Russian dolls, and a greater involvement of management is more likely as the strategy being considered nears the tactical and operational level. The strategy process has to encompass, simultaneously, alignment and involvement. Clearly, a positive and precise aim is an essential lodestar for the strategy process in large organisations. The military will tolerate maverick tactical commanders, provided the aim is not threatened, but their strategy must align with the 'grand' strategy.

Several interviewees (for example, Dr Robinson, Dr King, Sir John Harvey-Jones) commented that 'away days' were often an effective technique for large companies since, given an open debate, the restrictive structure could be broken down, if only temporarily, and some staff involvement in the strategy process can be gained. Sir Ian Pedder suggested that 'decisions must be made by a team of people' (Interview, 16 September 1999).

5.6   Leadership factors

Leadership was seen by all those interviewed to be a potent factor in the strategy formulation process, so this study was extended to include a more detailed consideration of the place of leadership in strategy formulation and how leaders were chosen and trained.

Many saw the leader's role as that of creating vision and meaning. The latter task is illustrated in the following extract from the interview (24 February 1999) with Lord Bramall:

> the British system like to feel that the top men give the staff some guidance about what to do. I remember there was a silly story about Patton, who was a brilliant general, and his staff were doing something and there was a British liaison officer with them in the Planning Staff and he said we should get some guidance, we don't even know if we are going forwards or backwards – we must get some steer, even if it is a one-liner. So in fear and trepidation, they went up to Patton and he puffed on his cigar and said 'I guess we'll bite 'em in the ass!' And with those very clear directions they went off and made the plan.

The vision, meaning and strategy were clear.

Sir John Harvey-Jones strongly endorsed the need for leadership in both the military and industry and defined it as 'the ability to get extraordinary results from ordinary people'. He did go on to warn, however, that the extraordinary results could be helpful or unhelpful. He had found the work of Warren Bennis useful in analysing leadership and supported the view that there are three basic characteristics of a leader:

(a) He/she must have vision.
(b) He/she must communicate.
(c) He/she is robust, both physically and mentally.

Sir Christopher Benson saw leadership as injecting energy and determination into the organisation. He felt that company boards should comprise *line* directors because, in addition to leadership, they brought competence and direct experience to the discussions.

During the interviews and background reading, it became evident that leadership held a central place in the strategy process. Not surprisingly, the military emphasised the need for strategic leadership, but the business executives interviewed also stressed the need for those at the top of organisations to be leaders, not just managers. As a result of the importance assigned to this topic by those interviewed, the next two chapters in this book are given over to consideration of strategic leadership and how these leaders are identified and trained. Conclusions, therefore, will not be drawn at this stage.

5.7   The attitude to risk

Risk did not figure much in the interviews. Most interviewees were risk-averse, and even the entrepreneurs were not seeking bold and risky courses of action. The military commander has the burden of the lives of the men and women under command, and, ethics and humanitarianism aside, modern society will not tolerate a high casualty rate. The Defence Committee of the House of Commons recognised (Defence Committee, 2000, p. xxix) the minimising of casualties as an important factor in military operations:

> **This risk-averse mentality is one, which it is widely recognized, is going to have to be factored in to any future operation of a similar nature. Political, humanitarian, legal and public relations considerations had a profound effect on the nature of the strategy adopted by the Alliance.** (Text **emboldened** in the original)

The businessman is responsible to the various stakeholders involved in the enterprise (variously, shareholders, employees, customers, suppliers, government), who, in the main, do not wish to gamble with their liveli-hood or their assets. The fundamental equation that risk should be commensurate with expected return applies in both cases, and risk is generally avoided unless a favourable outcome would significantly leverage competitive advantage. Attempts are made by many to quan-tify the risk by a careful consideration of the expected outcomes of a strategy. The military use computer war-gaming, but the results are dependent upon the accuracy of the forecast of the probabilities, and also the roll of the dice. Luck is an ever-present factor, and only by sensitivity analysis can action be taken to avoid a brittle plan where the avoidance of disaster is down to luck. Identifying dangerous courses of action needs experience and common sense.

Conclusion

Risk is ever present, and the prudent strategist will seek to minimise its effect. Risks are only taken by the military and the businessman when the likely return is high, and the probability of success acceptable. The uncertainty of the future is often risky enough.

5.8 The theory and practice of strategy formulation

In the field of strategy, much thought has been given to whether the process is rational, intuitive, or some combination of both.

Rationality is related to the positivistic, evidential approach to thought. Sir Christopher Benson reflected the problem of choosing one mode:

> people who have engineering degrees ... are people who are actually analytical, they will spend time looking. They don't take anything at face value. [Later, instancing a particularly effective executive] ... He will want to ensure that his intuition, in fact, is not just intuition but it's *informed* intuition ... but he would proceed from an intuitive base.

Mr George, perhaps reflecting views of one from an engineering company, thought that intuition was not as useful as detailed planning. His experience was in a large company, but the view of Dr King, who had started two companies in the past, was:

> Now (that is, in small companies), the strategy process is much more intuitive than in the big company case, but the entrepreneur will still use as many facts as possible, although they may be more difficult to acquire The CEO has to take all the decisions, and the

firm's staff expect that this should be the case. (Interview, 1 November 1999)

Contrast those views with Sir John Harvey-Jones's opinion:

the effect of poor Lord Kelvin (whom I curse every day) entirely is to put value on the things you can measure. So the whole business is involved in maximising the things that are measurable, particularly measurable in money. In fact, everything is measurable, but an awful lot of it is subjective. Because subjective judgements are mistrusted, they tend to be ignored altogether, and people will only measure what they can actually touch, and those are usually the least important, and the most obvious of the lot. At the end of the day, it is the fighting spirit of the troops and what can be done about the fighting spirit of the troops, together with the qualitative character of the leadership. A really determined guy will achieve a strategy which logic tells you is unachievable.

Mr Bounds's experience was that 'working with some quite senior people is that a lot of them work intuitively and only use analysis to back up their hunch'.

Professor Freedman took the Clausewitzian view that strategy is an art, not a science: 'because my view of strategy is that it brings together interests and resources and that's an art, it's not a science a lot of it is judgement, because good strategy involves a grasp of what somebody else is likely to do' (Interview 12 March 1997). The professor, however, went on to point out the limitation of the intuitive approach in that it can be 'very, very wrong or very, very right. Like MacArthur . . . who was very right about Inchon, but very wrong about going up to the Yalu'.

Colonel Gooderson, whilst acknowledging the usefulness of intuition, needed to have any solutions thus identified to be checked against a rational process: in his case, the military appreciation format. He did acknowledge, however, that the plan was not the strategy, just its implementation. Brigadier Hooper said that in his experience the commander would first turn to his Chief of Staff and say, 'Have a look at this problem. Do me an appreciation.' But the Brigadier felt that only a few problems were truly strategic and many could be more properly classified as tactical, and thus in the domain of the Managing Director. He did, however, agree that there was an intuitive element to military problem solving and said, 'I believe that the Napoleons of this world who are those who have that element of common sense, and they can see that kernel of truth in the middle'. Sir Patrick Hine took the same view, and said that the fundamental requirement for a strategist was 'nous'.

There was some divergence of opinion amongst the military inter-viewees as to the value and use of the appreciation method of strategic decision-making. Most acknowledged that it was a logical pattern that conditioned the approach to solving problems, but only a few had had occasion to use it in practice. Mr Hooper recalled his service in the Royal Marines when he had had to assist in preparing a plan for an amphibious operation during the Falklands War. On this occasion an amphibious appreciation was conducted, and the 'air' one was prepared by the air staff. Colonel Gooderson said that he frequently used the appreciation format in approaching business problems. The purpose of this formalised procedure is to prevent jumping to conclusions before a proper consideration of all the factors had been made (in the service jargon: 'situating the appreciation'). General Sir Hugh Beach (Interview, 16 October 1997) thought that the appreciation method was 'absolutely indispensable', but observed that the military strategy process is cre-ative as opposed to merely rational. Despite this rationality, strategy was still, on occasions, devised intuitively, but the military would always have such ideas examined in detail by the staff to ensure their feasibility and to identify any shortcomings.

Sir Peter Walters (Interview, 2 June 1999) outlined the yearly review of strategy in SmithKline Beecham which the company called '10–3–1'. Looking ten years ahead was feasible for a pharmaceutical company, three years brought the long-term strategy into sharper focus, and one year was, in effect, the operating plan. Information for the ten-year horizon was collected and processed by the corporate planning staff, and passed to the divisions for the preparation of their three-year plans. The plans were then subjected to the scrutiny of the 20-strong Corporate Management Team, comprising members of the executive, before being placed before the board for decision.

A further concern of theorists has been to debate whether the strategy process is deliberate or emergent. The military process, in addition to being mainly rational, is also deliberate when directed at a particular campaign. The routine, marginal process of strategy as practised in the Ministry of Defence has an element of the emergent, but the yearly rou-tine and the bureaucratic organisation limit the speedy responsiveness to emergent issues. Alenia Marconi Systems recognised the benefits of a combination of deliberate and emergent methods (Interview with Mr Terry Soame, 24 January 2001) and is trying to evolve such methods in their large, complex organisation.

Conclusion

There is a tendency in both the military and business for large organisations to use deliberate, rational methods, although intuition is not entirely absent. The smaller organisations are better able to act emergently, and to include wide opinion from their members. The entrepreneur is more likely to be intuitive, although they will still use facts whenever possible. Some organisations are trying to evolve methods that combine the best of both approaches.

5.9   Contextual factors

The strategy process can be affected by the context within which this activity is conducted.

Routine or crisis?

One contrasting set of conditions is whether the organisation is formulating strategy as a routine, or whether a crisis has occurred.

The British Ministry of Defence reviews yearly its expenditure plans for the future, and much of this process is focused upon equipment procurement, some of which has to be planned ten years, or more, ahead of the in-service date. This annual, staff planning exercise involves the injection of views and opinion from the lowest reaches of the organisation, and it may be difficult for the Defence Council to comprehend the totality in strategic terms. Mr Hatfield described this Long Term Costing process as being essentially marginal, and which only became strategic in its consideration of the longer term. Thus, although this approach appears to be firmly in the 'Design School' (Mintzberg, 1990b) category, it does have some elements of the emergent approach to strategy as identified in the strategic management literature. Professor Freedman identified with the emergent view: 'it is not simply that it is reactive, events clarify and, when you don't have the events, things tend to be very bureaucratically routinised'.

There is, however, the problem of strategic drift in both business and military, where small changes on the margin accumulate into a change of strategic direction, which may or not be appropriate. Although Lord Bramall identified the Chiefs of Staff as those who must identify strategic drift, reviews have to be conducted from time to time to reconsider the fundamentals of strategy. Hopefully, the approach is via foreign policy, but more often it is a Treasury-driven move to save money. The conduct of the latest review, the Strategic Defence Review (detailed in the case study in Chapter 4 above, 'Military strategy formulation in Britain') was characterised by an attempt to return to fundamentals with no preconceptions. A wide range of opinions was sought, including those of industrialists, politicians, retired servicemen and academics. The final, compromise solution emerged after rounds of bargaining and negotiating, which were influenced by intra- and interdepartmental politics. From the evidence, many companies, too, have a regular round of review, leading to a budgetary exercise, and the problem in both cases is recognising when previously held assumptions have become invalid. The existing strategy has inertia, a built-in resistance to change, that can prejudice adoption of a needed new direction which can seem radical and risky.

The particular problems in defence strategy are:

(a) The armed forces may be called upon to perform a wide range of duties, not all of which can be foreseen. On the other hand, over-insurance is not an option because of the high cost. The last 5 per cent of insurance against risks is the most expensive.

(b) The 'output' of armed forces cannot easily be measured in peacetime, in the way that a company can show its success in profits or shareholder value or market share, or some other metric. This factor can be a disadvantage when the Treasury challenges the defence budget, since the arguments for a particular policy tend to be qualitative: not a good defence against fiscal departments. When operations become necessary, the armed forces have to fight with what has been provided by the routine strategy process.

Because, in Mr Hatfield's view, probably only the United States is strong enough in the defence area to have the choice of a completely independent strategy, Britain must exercise its defence role principally through alliances. These may be formal and long-standing such as the North Atlantic Treaty Organisation (NATO) or in a more *ad hoc* coalition as in Britain's assistance to the Australian forces, who were acting for the United Nations in East Timor. So, year on year, the criteria for a creating a British defence policy (a 'wicked' problem) is, in Mr Hatfield's words: 'Have you got a programme which looks sensible, which goes into the long term, is affordable, which doesn't create any political problems, and which everybody is happy with?' (Mr Richard Hatfield, Interview 12 January 98).

All those interviewed agreed that the effect of a crisis was a tendency to centralise the strategy process and decision-making. Thus, in war, a commander is appointed with the task of achieving the aims set by the statesmen and politicians, but, even then, unless time is impossibly short, the consultation of and iteration through the staff continues. Sir John Harvey-Jones deprecated the centralising reaction to crisis:

> I believe the reaction of most of British industry is dead wrong in a crisis. What tends to happen is they centralise everything back to the middle and they try to run things in a monolithic way. The outstanding example of this is the banks. [When crisis occurred], the banks removed all the discretion from the bank managers. Everything went to risk management departments, which is a computer anyway, and yet people who managed the risks were the managers. The managers knew on the ground what was happening to people they were lending to when business goes bad you have to push the responsibility right down the line, and let the boys get on with it.

Crisis can also be used as a tool. Mr Bounds, the consultant, illustrated the use of crisis: 'A lot of our job is to create the case for change, which is persuading people there is a crisis, because unless they believe it, they are not going to move. So I think, in many ways, major corporate changes are easier to do when you are in a crisis.'

Lord Bramall, on the other hand, reflecting the military mind, thought, 'crisis cries out for top down'. Professor Freedman's view was that crisis limits time, and limited time restricts iteration. A slightly different view, however, is that the perception that time is short creates tension, but this stress can be the origin of new ideas in the mind of the strategist who should, therefore, endure the tension by waiting. In this situation, providing personal emotions can be controlled, the tension of crisis can become creative. The Duke of Wellington is reported (Longford, 1967, p. 208) to have said, 'I will get upon my horse and have a look; and then I will tell you.' Brigadier Hooper also stressed the importance of time and timing in military operations, and contrasted this preoccupation with that of business, which was money. Sir Patrick Hine observed that crisis in the military could release more resources, but in companies the effect could be quite the opposite.

The IBM case in Chapter 4 shows how the new CEO, Gerstner, took firm control of the company when it was in crisis. The iterative, bureaucratic process became top-down from a decisive, autocratic leader. Dr King's view was that, from his experience as a consultant, large companies 'seldom review their strategy if the business is going well . . . they seldom seem to listen to ideas emanating from their staff, who are not encouraged by the system to propose strategies' (Interview, 1 November 1999). In his view, the reaction to a crisis in these large companies was to call in outside consultants, and the board would reach a collective decision on the basis of the report they received.

The military try to arm themselves for conflict but, in Britain, the Ministry of Defence has tried to identify the roles that its armed forces should perform. Contingency plans are drawn up, and in some cases war-gamed, so that more time can be gained in the event of a crisis. Intelligence is vital in securing as much warning as possible of impending conflict, but when operations become inevitable, a single commander is appointed.

Conclusion

The evidence shows that crisis leads to a centralising of decision, which also applies to strategy formulation. Some deprecate this tendency, but vesting power in a single individual, or a small number of executives, speeds decision and reduces opposition, such as political activity. The necessary stability is provided by the control system, which can be adjusted to meet the circumstances.

Networking

Mr Hooper introduced the added factor of the value of networking to leaders. He gave the example of General Sir Michael Rose in Bosnia who kept in close contact (he speaks fluent French) with allies and military, diplomatic and political contacts. In this way he knew to whom to turn for advice, and could discuss issues on a personal level. Although this attribute is valuable, it has to be seen against the background of organisational politics discussed in p. 195.

Aims and objectives

Strategy is the method that an organisation has chosen in order to reach its aims.

Professor Mason sought to compare the setting of aims in business and the military:

> In the military, the aim is set by politicians, not the commander, whereas in business, those who devise the strategy also set the aims of their enterprise. So, the fundamental problem facing the construction of military strategy is to identify the political circumstances and the political objectives for which it will be an instrument. Clausewitz recognised this problem in the final version of his famous dictum,

'War is the continuation of politics *with the addition* of other means' [that is, diplomacy continues during wartime]. (Emphasis added)

Large companies often seem to live with much less precise aims than would be tolerated by the military. Although Ms Bradley (Interview, 9 December 2000) stated the aims of her enterprise with a military clarity, the necessity for precision in setting company objectives was not an issue for most of those businessmen interviewed. This imprecision raises the problem of how an effective, incisive strategy can be formulated if what is to be achieved is indistinct.

Mr Bounds spoke from the experience of consultancy projects in, mainly, financial companies:

A lot of companies will set down financial targets and the actual target is derived from the strategy, but they don't articulate the strategic goals they want the different units to work towards. So you end up with a strategic vacuum.

...Lots of organisations I have worked in, you go in and ask relatively senior management what the company's vision is, and they don't know. It is extraordinary how often you find that.

Conclusion

The definition of precise aims must be the opening of the strategy process, because strategy must have a purpose. The military set great store by the selection and maintenance of the aim, whilst a number of businesses are less disciplined.

5.10   Emergent issues

Some issues emerged from the interviews that did not fit into the framework for analysis adopted for this study, but they are of sufficient interest to be included here.

The use of history

Interviewees were asked their views as to the value of books on strategy, biographies and histories, and, in the main, they were seen as interesting, but peripheral. Sir John Harvey-Jones, in his early days in management, had read avidly the books on business and management. Professor Mason, of course, valued accounts of warfare since they provided subjects for his analysis, but, he warned, 'The task of the analyst is to identify the temporary from the recurring.' He went on that lessons from history have to be treated with caution. He gave as an example that analysis of the military lessons of the First World War resulted in the Maginot Line from the French, and *Blitzkrieg* from German (and some English) thinking. He said, 'You can learn all the lessons in the world [but] you [need] to know the next examiner', which is similar to the comment that the military always start to operate in a new war in the way that they had fought the last. Business, too, needs to examine critically the lessons from history, because the effective strategy is one that breaks the mould. Merely copying successful formulas from the past is unlikely to succeed in a changed context.

Societal change

Both businesses and the military are caught up in the process of societal change, and the emergence of new ideas and mores. It has been seen in the study that the rejection of the concept of the divine right of kings, and the adoption of the ideas from the eighteenth-century French Revolution, affected the military strategy process by changing it from authoritarian and top-down to one allowing the acceptance of expert advice. The ending of the practice of the purchase of commissions in Britain began the transition to a meritocracy, particularly in the arms using high technology. Now, military strategy is formed by an iterative process that prefers consensus. The process of change will not cease, and, as the role of the armed forces moves from conducting global nuclear warfare to peacekeeping and humanitarian missions, the idea of postmodern armed forces could gather pace. So the comment (quoted by Professor Mason) made by a US general that the US armed forces do not do operations other than war seems very dated. The armed forces, in contrast to businesses, cannot choose their territory or mode of operations, and cannot say, 'we don't do mountains, we don't do jungles, we only do deserts' (A jocular comment made by Professor Mason but one containing a real truth). They have to move into new business areas as dictated by the new roles to which they are assigned. The point here is that changes in role will probably force changes in strategy process, which, in turn, will require different training, or even different types of leader. Business strategy, too, is changing with, for instance, the growth of environmental issues, and strategy process may have to be modified to ensure that companies are in tune with the new gestalt. Society changes, and the more successful military and business cultures adapt, however reluctantly.

People

'People' issues recurred throughout the interviews, but then strategy is a process conducted by humans. Much of what was said on this topic was peripheral to the main issue of strategy process but people, their skills, motivation, training, efforts and value, constantly arose during these discussions. People at all levels could make a contribution to strategy formulation, but even if they could not, their involvement could gain their tacit support for what was decided. People in an organisation must know what the company strategy is if they are to work for the achievement of the strategy.

The effect of individuals, and their personalities, on the strategy process and its outcome proved to be too complex and varied to be analysed in this study. An illustration of some effects of individual style on strategy process, however, can be found in a case on Honda Motors (Mair, 1997, pp. 898–9):

> The collective process was symbolized in the physical layout of the Honda headquarters 'board room', in which none of the executives had their own offices, but instead shared an open space where there were not only individual desks but also various areas for them to meet, sit and talk together...The joint board room had actually been set up in the mid 1960s by Takeo Fujisawa, who saw it as an adjunct structure to Soichiro Honda's highly individualistic style, a means of encouraging executives to talk about problems and solutions with each other, and to prepare younger managers for the day the founders would retire...When Honda and Fujisawa retired in 1973, new president Kiyoshi Kawashima shifted Honda further towards a collective decision-making mode with the wide-ranging committee structure that he set up. When Tadashi Kume in turn succeeded Kawashima as president in 1983, he too instituted his own changes...As company president in 1991, Nobuhiko Kawamoto introduced significant reforms to the top management structure. He established a clear hierarchy at executive level, with two leading executives joining him to form an innermost leadership circle. He also announced that executives could have private offices if they so wished.

If there are useful generalisations to be made on this topic, beyond the leadership issues discussed later, they will have to be studied separately.

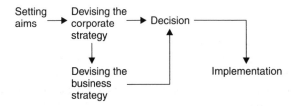

Figure 5.1   The strategy formulation process simplified.

5.11   Discussion

The strategy process begins with setting aims and leads to a decision. These two steps are usually taken at the top of the organisation, whilst the devising and implementing will involve subordinate layers in the organisation. Corporate strategy defines the business that the company will be in, and so is most likely to be formed at high level. (see Figure 5.1.)

Proposals for business strategies often arise from divisions, strategic business units, or smaller groups within the organisation, but the aims and corporate strategy must be in place to avoid dissipation of energy on diversionary moves. Such a process is followed in the military where 'grand strategy' is formed at the very top, and subordinate units are given some freedom to devise their own strategies to meet the aim given the constraints of the environmental conditions they face. Harmony of purpose is achieved by stating aims at every level, and coordinating the planning of the implementation.

The first task of the strategist is the setting of the aims and objectives of the enterprise, and then using them constantly as a lodestar and the criteria against which decisions are made. The border between the setting of aims and the actual strategy process (which seeks a means of achieving these aims) is important. The prime principle of war – selection and maintenance of the aim – is equally relevant to businesses, but the latter do not seem to be always as punctilious as the military in articulating and disseminating their precise aims. A company may wish to increase market share and profits, but the strategy for the first might require reducing prices, which, in the shorter term, might reduce profit. Winning strategies cannot be devised unless the aim is precisely defined. Setting aims in the military is much more likely to be top-down than the strategy formulation process, which iterates around commanders and staff. Similarly, in business, setting aims is the task of the Chief Executive Officer and the board of directors (the dominant coalition), whilst the evolution of strategy is a process that varies from one organisation to another, but generally seems to be iterative. A difference between military and business is that the military have their aims set for them, whereas in business, those who set the aims are usually those who decide the strategy. Such a process has the added virtue of encouraging ownership of the chosen strategy by the lower levels of the organisation. (In retrospect, the separation of aim-setting and strategy process could have been more clearly investigated with interviewees. Further work in this field could investigate these two activities.)

The border between strategy and tactics is important. The leaders of the company or armed force need to be free of the routine of implementing decisions so that they can focus upon the strategic issues. There is a danger that leaders of enterprises will interfere with the work at the lower levels through which they have risen on the way to the top. It may be comforting to perform skills in which one has excelled, but, for instance, leading a squadron is not the job of the Chief of Air Staff. The results of tactical operations can have a strategic effect, and leaders must be alert to the cumulative effects of day-to-day business in relation to the achievement of strategic aims. Knowledge of detail may be needed in reaching a decision, but the evidence from this study suggests that common sense and judgements are more important in strategy formulation than expert knowledge.

5.12   The case studies

The case studies, in the main, show the strategy process as being mainly top-down. On the other hand, the routine process in the Ministry of Defence has strong bottom-up emphasis and Alenia Marconi Systems are trying to increase the input from the lower reaches of their organisation. The thought process in all those organisations illustrated in the cases is rational, and the intuitive thinking occurs mainly at the tactical level with gifted commanders like General Patton. Crisis centralises decision, which, in turn, leads to a top-down approach. Organisational politics is evident in all the case studies and, in the case of the campaign in north-west Europe in 1944–5, affected the choice of strategy. The introduction of alliances complicates and slows the strategy process, but the addition of the extra resources more than compensates for these disadvantages. Leadership is a positive factor in the north-west Europe and IBM cases, but is less evident in the routine and bureaucratic strategy processes in the British Ministry of Defence and Alenia Marconi Systems. This does not mean that leadership is *not* being exercised but that it is not so evident a factor. The organisations studied all had aims,

	Mainly top-down	Mainly bottom-up
Rational	Military in war Autocratic business Crisis	Military in peace Democratic business
Intuitive	Entrepreneurs	Creative business

Figure 5.2   Summarising the strategy process.

but the businesses seem to have a shorter-term view. IBM concentrated on reversing the adverse trend in their business and Alenia Marconi Systems were concentrating on becoming the biggest company in their sector (which they have now achieved).

In sum, the cases show a similarity between military and business strategy process, where the greatest difference is in their approach to the setting of aims.

5.13   Summarising the strategy process

Figure 5.2 is an attempt to summarise what has been found out from the interviews and case studies about strategy process in the business and military.

The strategy process is top-down and rational when some form of crisis occurs, and in those companies with a dominating, autocratic leader. In peacetime for the military, and in democratic businesses the process is more bottom-up, although still rational in approach. The entrepreneur will take the decisions in a top-down direction, and is more likely to use an intuitive style, even though facts will be considered if available. The bottom-up/intuitive combination is unusual, and may only be used in creative businesses. It is most unlikely that this combination will occur in the military.

Figure 5.3 combines the rational/intuitive dimension with the deliberate/emergent. The military employ rational methods, probably because intuitive thought is more risky than conclusions drawn from factual data. In peacetime, the process can be more emergent, but there is the danger that strategic drift will lead ultimately to undesirable strategies. If this is thought to be happening, a strategic review will be ordered to reestablish a better direction. Larger businesses seem less willing to draw

	Deliberate	Emergent
Rational	Military in war Large businesses	Military in peace Small businesses
Intuitive	Entrepreneurs	Creative businesses

Figure 5.3   Comparing modes of strategy formulation.

ideas from the lower reaches of the organisation, but care has to be taken in making such generalisations because many companies do involve staff in strategy formulation. In any event, all the evidence collected here suggests that the strategy process is iterative around the layers of the organisation. Small businesses have the advantage of having fewer layers in their organisation and are sufficiently responsive as to be capable of handling emergent modes of strategy formulation. The entrepreneur may be intuitive and deliberate, although, again, the evidence suggests that facts are still used, if available, and an emergent style may suit many. Again, the fourth quadrant will not include the military and is not likely to be heavily populated.

A further summary is shown in Table 5.2, which compares the military and business under various heads. This analysis has the advantage

Table 5.2   A military–business comparison

Factors	Military	Business
Process	Iterative	Iterative
Direction	Mainly top-down	Mainly top-down
Crisis	Centralises decision	Centralises decision
Risk	Risk-averse	Mainly risk-averse
Aims	Strong emphasis	Weaker emphasis
Organisational politics	In peace, but not in war	Active
Leadership	Positive effect	Positive effect
Implementation planning	Always used	Some use, more in larger companies
Rational/intuitive	Rational, occasional intuition	Rational, but more use of intuition
Deliberate/emergent	Deliberate, but some emersion in peace	Varies widely, but large companies more likely to use deliberate methods

of being a little more flexible, and reflects some of the uncertainties in drawing generalisations from the complexity of differing organisations, cultures and contexts. There is the problem of judging what can reasonably be concluded from the evidence assembled. On the one hand, there is the accumulated theory of strategy process and the extra evidence adduced here, which, on the other, must be set against the great complexity of the realities of military and business life. The pessimistic view is that no safe general conclusions can be drawn, but no progress will be made in understanding unless careful attempts are made at conclusions from the evidence. Ezra Pound's (1934, p. 1) view was: 'Any general statement is like a checque [*sic*] drawn on a bank. Its value depends on what is there to meet it.'

What have emerged here are *tendencies* rather than firm generalisations. These results are summarised in Table 5.2, where it can be seen that there is a lot of similarity between the process of strategy in the military and business fields, but the attention to the statement of aims is the largest area of divergence.

6

Strategic Leaders' Perceptions of the Strategy Formulation Process

6.1 Introduction

Strategy formation is the responsibility of those at the top of an organisation. These executives are in a leadership position, so strategy decision is vested in those who lead. This chapter delves deeper into the topic of leadership by considering the relevant literature, and how it relates to the evidence previously discussed in Chapter 5. Leadership is itself a process and has various attributes that can be investigated, but here consideration will be limited to those aspects that bear upon the research question. First, though, the nature of the phenomenon is considered.

6.2 The nature of leadership

The term 'leadership' is in everyday usage and yet it has proved to be difficult to define. Stogdill (1950) in Bryman (1996, p. 276) offered:

> Leadership may be considered as the process (act) of influencing the activities of an organized group in its efforts toward goal setting and goal achievement.

In the view of Dixon (1976, p. 214):

> leadership is no more than exercising such an influence upon others that they tend to act in concert towards achieving a goal which they might not have achieved so readily had they been left to their own devices.

The US Army's definition (Elton, 1987, p. 2) was:

> To achieve understanding and commitment of subordinates for the accomplishment of purposes, goals and objectives envisioned by the leader, beyond that which is possible through the use of authority alone.

Lenz (1993, p. 172) particularised his definition to executive leadership:

> Executive leadership is described as the exercise of influence by senior-level managers within inter and intraorganizational decision-making processes with the intent of effecting strategic change.

Essentially, leadership is practised through the consent of those being led, and seeks to influence the behaviour of the group towards a particular end.

Studies of leadership have tried to determine whether effectiveness in leadership is attributable to the traits of the individual, the style of the individual, situational factors (that is, contingencies), or how well the leader articulates a vision of the organisation's mission and its values. The obvious conclusion is that all of these are important in differing proportions that are case-dependent. Zaleznik's (1970, p. 59) view was that: it is...their [that is, business executives'] ability to define problems worthy of thought and action and to use their organisation to evolve solutions which characterise their style'.

One limitation of the 'trait' approach is the possible implication that leaders are born, not made, which may have been a view held in earlier times when tenure of positions of authority was largely the domain of the upper classes in society, but which now has been shown to be, at the very least, dubious. Considerable efforts are made by the armed forces to train leaders and to improve their performance (discussed further in Chapter 7) and selection for this training is not done predominantly on a class basis, although some vestiges remain. On the other hand, it is likely that not everyone has the special attributes necessary to become a 'great' leader. Whether these special traits are inborn or developed through upbringing, education or special application by the individual is uncertain.

Leadership is not practised in the same manner at all levels of the organisation because the task becomes more complex as the individual reaches higher levels of authority and responsibility. Thus the CEO is less concerned with 'managerial' issues and the 'here and now' than broader questions of organisational identity and purpose and 'chang[ing] the way people think about what is desirable, possible and necessary' (Zaleznik 1977, p. 71). Jacobs (1991, p. 187) offered a different view of leaders:

> Leaders make logical sense out of situations that may be too complex, or too loaded with intangibles, for their subordinates to figure out. It also implies knowing where the levers that can activate those systems with a minimum input of energy are, in order to make something happen at a macro level.

Magee (1998, p. 16) asserted, 'Strategic leaders develop and communicate a compelling, understandable strategic vision for the organisation. That strategic vision is a means of focusing effort and progressing toward a desired future – what ought to be.' The strategic leader's task is the creation of that vision, which he need not create alone but collaboratively with others, as the focal point of the process. The idea of collaboration is also found in Westley and Mintzberg (1989, p. 18), who wrote: 'we assume that visionary leadership is a dynamic, interactive phenomenon, as opposed to a unidirectional process'.

Mr Hooper expressed his view of the guiding power of vision:

> people need to have a broad idea of where they are going. That comes from a vision; that comes from a sense of direction; but within that to allow more flexibility, so that new factors come in and people within the organisation have the confidence to be able to pick up a new idea, to run with it and know that it is generally in the right direction. (Interview, 8 December 1999)

Harrison and Pelletier (1997) concluded that 'strategic decision success signifies intended ends accomplished within designated means' and that the decision is accomplished through successful strategic leadership. In their study of 61 Chief Executive Officers from the San Francisco Bay area, they considered which of two perspectives best fitted their evidence:

- Perspective 1:   That strategic leadership at the CEO level is relatively unimportant. They consider three variations:
  - Variation 1: Strategic leadership is unimportant at any level in the organisation.

– Variation 2: The CEO's unilateral role is less important than shared strategic leadership.

– Variation 3: Strategic leadership is participative with all levels of the organisation.

- Perspective 2: The role of the CEO is exalted. They consider two variations:

  – Variation 1: The strategic leadership role of the CEO is inherent in the position.

  – Variation 2: The degree of strategic leadership applied is discretionary, largely dependent on the external environment, the internal organisation, and the CEO's level of competence and personal attributes.

The results gained showed that their sample were operating in Perspective 2, Variation 2, and the primary determinants of the discretion are the stakeholders, the internal power structure and the employees. In their view, 'the commitment of middle managers is essential to ensure that the results of strategy correspond with its objectives' (Harrison and Pelletier, 1997).

Strategic leadership, then, is likely to be found, or at least required, at the top of the organisation. The personality of the leader will influence, or more likely determine, how this leadership is applied. The leadership is likely to be visionary and must secure the commitment of those being led.

6.3   Issues of personality

The personality of the leader must be the starting point for consideration of the nature of leadership and, although this subject is the concern of psychologists, some lay observations taken from their works may help to shed light on the operation of leaders in strategy formulation. Since leaders are also required to be decision-makers, the discussion of the process of decision in Chapter 4 above needs to be borne in mind.

Jung

Since leaders are human beings, personal style is bound to have an effect. Jung addressed the issue of personality types through describing how people of varying types perceive and judge data. He proposed that the two dominant, but opposed, forms of perceiving information are: sensing and intuition. Figure 6.1 (taken from Stumpf and Mullen, 1991)

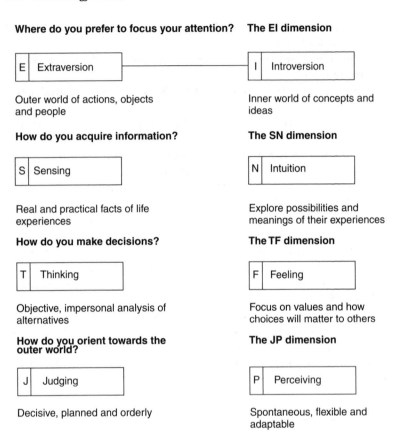

Where do you prefer to focus your attention?   **The EI dimension**

| E | Extraversion |

| I | Introversion |

Outer world of actions, objects and people

Inner world of concepts and ideas

How do you acquire information?   **The SN dimension**

| S | Sensing |

| N | Intuition |

Real and practical facts of life experiences

Explore possibilities and meanings of their experiences

How do you make decisions?   **The TF dimension**

| T | Thinking |

| F | Feeling |

Objective, impersonal analysis of alternatives

Focus on values and how choices will matter to others

How do you orient towards the outer world?   **The JP dimension**

| J | Judging |

| P | Perceiving |

Decisive, planned and orderly

Spontaneous, flexible and adaptable

Figure 6.1   Dimensions of personal style.
Source: Stumpf and Mullen (1991).

illustrates Jung's classification of these dominant forms as a continuum between two extremes, each of which defines a dimension.

These dimensions will affect not only the approach to decision, but also the style that the executive will bring to the task of leading. There is no value judgement here, and individuals are not being encouraged to attempt to modify their personalities.

Myers–Briggs

The Myers–Briggs Type Indicator (MBTI) is a development of the Jungian theory described above, and has been widely, and successfully, used in studies to classify psychological types. In this system, as in the Jungian one, four dimensions of psychological preference are measured:

(a) 'Introversion–Extraversion' is concerned with how an individual acquires his or her energy internally or externally. Furthermore, is the person interested in the inner world of concepts and ideas or the outer world of people and things?

(b) The 'Sensing–Intuition' dimension is concerned with perception and data-gathering. Sensing individuals use their five senses to concentrate upon what is concrete, practical and existing in the present. Intuitive people, however, rely more on hunches and concentrate upon the abstract, the possible, the theoretical and what is in the future.

(c) Individuals who favour 'Thinking' prefer to make judgements logically, remaining impersonal and objective. Individuals with a 'Feeling' preference tend to make personal and subjective judgements and may not rely upon the facts alone.

(d) The 'Judging' and 'Perceiving' dimensions relate to the way the individual deals with the outside world. Judging individuals desire closure of the decision process and reach conclusions with little hesitation. The Perceivers prefer to gather more information before making the decision and are thus liable to remain open, flexible and adaptive.

MBTI seeks to extend Jungian theory into the practical realm of discovering and classifying the personalities of leaders.

Kiersey and Bates

Kiersey and Bates (1978) clustered the sixteen possible types derived from Myers-Briggs into four groups to form 'temperaments'. For example, SPs (Sensing Perceivers) are resourceful hands-on problem-solvers, SJs (Sensing Judgers) are task-orientated, practical and realistic individuals who quickly reach decisions through established policy or procedures, NTs (Intuitive Thinkers) are conceptualisers who see the big picture and can often discern underlying principles, and NFs (Intuitive Feelers) can also see possibilities but focus more on people than on ideas and concepts. In their work, Kiersey and Bates provided further tools to aid the search for knowledge of individual personalities.

Hersey and Blanchard

Some theorists hold that leadership style comprises a mixture of task-related and relationship-related behaviour. As regards task behaviour, the leader concentrates on achievement of the task set for the group using behaviour that is directive, *telling* in style. Relationship behaviour on the other hand, is more concerned with cooperation, communication and *selling* to the people in the group. The two-by-two matrix in

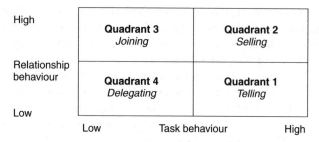

Figure 6.2   The Hersey–Blanchard approach.
Source: Hersey and Blanchard (1969, p. 262).

Figure 6.2, which is taken from Hersey and Blanchard (1969, p. 262), illustrates the mixture of the two styles, which are the ends of a spectrum of behaviour.

Hersey and Blanchard proposed that the leader should diagnose the maturity of the group being led and then choose the appropriate behaviour indicated by the quadrants shown above. Thus an immature team will need more direction (quadrant 1) than when the team is fully accustomed to the task and to working in this group, when quadrant 4 becomes more appropriate.

The implication of this work is that leadership styles are to be chosen by the individual manager and, to be successful, a style that matches a pre-given situation must be chosen (Stacey, 2000, p. 111).

Dixon

Dixon's (1976) work approached the personality traits of leaders from a negative angle since he investigated the psychology of incompetence in military leaders. A logical conclusion would be that a competent leader would tend to have the reverse of the traits he identified:

> we have argued that the psychology of authoritarianism lies at the heart of much military incompetence ... Such people will tend to be conformist, conventional and over-controlled. They will also tend to seek approval, enjoy occupying a position in a dominance–submission hierarchy, and derive satisfaction from the provision of *legitimate* outlets for their normally repressed aggression. They are, in short, authoritarian. But because the roots of authoritarianism lie far back in childhood such people also tend to manifest those other residues of early socialization: orderliness, parsimony and obstinacy – the so-called anal-obsessive triad. Finally, because such people are

threatened by the possible breakthrough of instinctual impulses they tend to be over-controlled, rigid and possessed of 'closed' as opposed to 'open' minds. They like to be governed by rules and abhor what is spontaneous, flexible or unusual. (Dixon, 1976, p. 285)

The opinions of these psychologists would seem to support the notion that leaders are made, not born. Of course, the talents with which the individual is blessed may make them potentially a great, or indifferent, leader as the case may be. Although the personality will basically have some particular traits, these can be modified by upbringing, particularly in early childhood, and by training and application of the individual in later life. Furthermore, the skilled and knowledgeable leader can adapt his or her style to the needs of the task and the team.

Conclusions on personality

Although the work described above can measure aspects of personality, conclusions on leadership and strategic decision-making are not immediately obvious. Volkema and Gorman (1998) studied the effects of cognitive-based group composition on the decision-making process and concluded that multi-temperament groups generally outperform uni-temperament groups, because the mix of approaches produces more ideas and sounder conclusions. Nutt (1990, p. 192) conducted a study of the decision style of 79 top executives and concluded:

The judicial (SF) top executive was found to be action-oriented and the systematic (ST) top executive action-averse, with the speculative and heuristic (NT and NF) top executives taking nearly identical and neutral positions ... Top executives with a pure ST style were much more conservative than the traditional STs and the pure SFs far more action-oriented than the traditionally defined SF.

Heller (1992), in his introduction, associated leadership and decision-making and questioned the view from traditional psychological literature that personality is a major determinant of leadership behaviour. The social science approach stresses contextual influences as bearing strongly on a successful outcome in decision-making. Nonetheless, personality traits will be important in the identification, selection and development of leaders, who do much more than merely make decisions. The social science view might temper the judgement of psychologists such as Dixon on the incompetence of some military commanders in the past, although the effects of personality will have played a part in the disasters. The acid test would be, however, whether a competent decision-maker in possession of the same facts as the incompetent would have made a better decision.

These works, however, do not tell us that these various styles are ineffective, and so one cannot conclude that any temperament is 'wrong' in a leader, but 'action-oriented' personalities would seem to be more appropriate for the military setting. If this is indeed so, there are implications for the selection of strategic leaders in both the business and military fields.

6.4   Leadership traits

Many writers have listed their views on the characteristics needed for those who would be a leader. These lists, particularly the comprehensive, can be dauntingly hagiographical to the ordinary mortal. The list in Roberts (1989, pp. 17–21) is fairly typical:

(a) Loyalty
(b) Courage (physical and moral)
(c) Desire (a strong wish to be a leader)
(d) Emotional stamina
(e) Physical stamina
(f) Empathy (sensitivity to others)
(g) Decisiveness
(h) Anticipation (actions and their consequences)
(i) Timing
(j) Competitiveness
(k) Self-confidence
(l) Accountability
(m) Responsibility
(n) Credibility
(o) Tenacity
(p) Dependability
(q) Stewardship (responsibility for subordinates)

One is reminded of the prescription of St Paul (Philippians 4:8): 'whatsoever things are true, whatsoever things are honest, whatsoever things are just, whatsoever things are pure, whatsoever things are lovely, whatsoever things are of good report; if there be any virtue, and if there be any praise, think on these things'.

General Sir Peter Inge (1993, p. 43) had a somewhat shorter list:

Personality and Character. Great leaders have the strength of character and personality to inspire confidence and to gain the trust of others ... I would emphasise that leaders do not have to be roaring extroverts to be successful. Some very charismatic leaders have been just quietly confident, although they had the ability to communicate.

Courage. Field Marshal Slim said, 'Courage is the greatest of all virtues.' Although he was talking about both physical and moral courage, it was moral courage on which he laid the greatest emphasis ... It is the courage to do what you believe is right without bothering about the consequences for yourself.

Willpower. A leader has to learn to dominate events and never allow these events to get the better of him and this determination or willpower concerns not only rival organisations or, in the case of the armed forces, the enemy, but equally colleagues and allies.

Knowledge. This means knowledge not only of your profession but equally knowledge of the men under your command ...

Initiative. This is, of course, a fundamentally important quality in any walk of life but nowhere more so than on the battlefield ... Field Marshal Slim [said]: 'Here one comes up against a conflict between determination, fixity of purpose and flexibility. There is always the danger that determination becomes plain obstinacy and flexibility, mere vacillation. If you can hold within yourself the balance between these two – strength of will and flexibility of mind – you will be well on the road to becoming a leader in a big way.'

Dixon's (1976, p. 67) observations are valuable in pointing out what leaders should *not* be. He lists (p. 67) the characteristics of the incompetence he observed in the leaders he studied:

1 An underestimation, sometimes bordering on arrogance, of the enemy.
2 An equating of war with sport.
3 An inability to profit from past experience.
4 A resistance to adopting and exploiting available technology and novel tactics.

5 An aversion to reconnaissance, coupled with a dislike of intelligence (in both senses of the word).

6 Great physical bravery but little moral courage.

7 An apparent imperviousness by commanders to loss of life and human suffering amongst their rank and file, or (its converse) an irrational and incapacitating state of compassion.

8 Passivity and indecisiveness in senior commanders.

9 A tendency to lay the blame on others.

10 A love of the frontal assault.

11 A love of 'bull', smartness, precision and strict preservation of 'the military pecking order'.

12 A high regard for tradition and other aspects of conservatism.

13 A lack of creativity, improvisation, inventiveness and open-mindedness.

14 A tendency to eschew moderate risks for tasks so difficult that failure might seem to be excusable.

15 Procrastination.

A damning list but one that was compiled from campaigns that are often quoted as outstanding examples of incompetence, such as the Crimean and Boer wars. They should not, then, be read as a commentary on current military practice but as a commentary on the pitfalls of leadership in general.

Professor Mason had occasion to ponder leadership qualities when he held the post of Air Secretary in the Royal Air Force. He concluded (Interview, 14 November 2000) that the following traits should be especially considered for those officers approaching air rank:

(a) *Inspiration*. Inspiring trust and confidence in others.

(b) *Integrity*. Setting an example of moral and physical courage.

(c) *Intelligence*. Identifying problems, marshalling facts, analysing problems, developing arguments, identifying possible solutions, and decision-making.

(d) *Determination*. Determination supported by sound judgement and consideration for other points of view. Determined but not dogmatic; flexible but not vacillatory.

(e) *Independence of thought*. Intellectual power and the confidence to seek new solutions. Making sound judgements.

(f) *Discrimination*. Identifying matters not appropriate for attention at his or her level.

(g) *Motivation*. Does personal ambition cloud judgement?

(h) *Spare capacity*. Is there spare capacity for extra responsibility?
(i) *Breadth of interests*. Awareness of issues beyond the immediate horizons. Possessing a sense of humour.
(j) *Resilience*. Physical and mental stamina.
(k) *Courage*. The courage to express his or her point of view when it is counter to superiors' views.

These can be seen to be a positive view (in contrast to Dixon's negative list), which suggests qualities that are needed in business executives, too.

Mr Hooper had interviewed leaders from industry, trade unions and the services and had found that 'the crucial thing that drives all of them is values and beliefs . . . What is important about the way you do your business? Everybody said, "Integrity, Honesty, Truth, being able to look people in the eye without blinking"' (Interview, 8 December 1999). He went on to say that he had identified five areas:

(a) Create understanding within the organisation.
(b) Communication, particularly communicating the reason for change.
(c) Developing potential in people.
(d) Effective management of one's time.
(e) Concentrate on listening and clarifying inputs from others.

The conclusion drawn here is that lists of virtues are not totally useful in determining the qualities required of a leader. Each person who reflects on either their own experience or that of others is likely to produce a different list. Not all the requirements are ever present and the example of Hitler has shown that a person can be a moral reprobate and still command the allegiance of millions. A better approach is deemed to be that it is better to investigate the roles and duties of leaders: the virtues required can be deduced from this investigation.

6.5 Influences on leaders

Hellegren and Melin (1993) found the main influences on business leaders' ways of thinking were their individual personalities, their core beliefs and their early industrial experience. Harris and Ghauri (2000, p. 127) added, from various sources, organisational culture, functional experience and professional background. These influences must also affect leaders in the military. Generals Patton and Montgomery in the case study 'Struggle for Europe, 1944–5' in Chapter 3 above were very

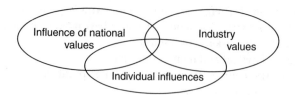

Figure 6.3   Influences on business leaders' 'ways of thinking' .
Source: Harris and Ghauri (2000, p. 128).

much influenced by their personalities, their early experience, the organisational culture, functional experience and professional background. Military leaders in general are moulded by the culture of honour, discipline, loyalty, integrity and *esprit de corps* which is impressed upon them in their earliest training and throughout their service life. Thus, the armed forces also have an 'industry recipe' which will tend to be manifested as a normative influence on their behaviour as leaders. Harris and Ghauri also drew attention to the influence of national values, to which we are all subject, and suggested the way of illustrating these relationships shown in Figure 6.3.

6.6   Leadership functions

Leaders have the responsibility of gaining the willing support of others in the accomplishment of a task. As we have seen, there is implied in that statement a task of balancing the needs of the task and the needs of the people. Adair (1988, p. 33) illustrated this idea in a Venn diagram, shown in Figure 6.4.

Figure 6.4   The functional approach.
Source: Adair (1988, p. 33).

Here we should acknowledge the different requirements for leaders in different levels of the organisation. Leaders have to be managers (although not all managers are leaders) because the role is task-related. As the position in the hierarchy changes (a process described in the *situational* theory of leadership), the style and requirements of the leader also alter. The leadership style of a foreman in business or a non-commissioned officer in the military is different from that of the chief executive or military commander because the task differs. Barber (1992, p. 6) identified three levels of leadership practice:

1. *Direct Leadership....* when the leader has face-to-face contact with all subordinate members of his/her work group and where the leaders are coaching and teaching technical and tactical proficiency, motivating, fostering cohesion, focused internally, task-oriented, and dealing at a relatively low level of complexity.

2. *Senior Leadership* predominates at the level of the organization where the leader cannot physically meet with all members of the group and therefore must indirectly influence them through other subordinate leaders and other communication channels...At this level of the organization leaders focus on building teamwork among subordinate elements, tailoring organizations to maximize productivity, setting organizational climate and, in general, dealing with more complex issues and problems.

3. *Strategic Leadership....* The leader more remotely influences the members of the organization but also has the responsibility for structuring the organization, making policy, interacting with the external environment, and setting the strategic vision for the organization ...Leaders at this level provide an interface between the organization and the external environment, garner resources, build or modify the organization to meet future needs, create policy, establish or maintain organizational culture, and work in a highly complex and ambiguous environment.

This study considers leadership in the third of the above categories and will not consider the issues surrounding the first two, although issues of transfer from one level to another and leadership development will be considered in Chapter 7.

The competencies required at different levels in a military organisation as used by Jacobs (1991), and attributed by him to Lawrence and

Lorsch, were that, in company-level grades, technical skills predominated. Field grades needed a nearly equal mixture of technical communication and conceptual skills. In general officers, conceptual skills predominated, with communication skills coming a close second.

These views were confirmed by the results of interviews conducted by Jacobs on general officers in the United States Army. The views of the interviewees were summed up in the following Table:

Nature of leadership (Jacobs, 1991, p. 194)
Changes across levels

Top level	Executive	Culture/values, External world
Mid level	Senior	Policies/climate, Internal world
Lower levels	Direct	Action team work

The functions of strategic leaders are summed up in Finlay (2000, p. 95) (albeit in terms of their required attributes):

Research findings suggest that successful leaders in complex organisations must have the following three attributes:

- they must have a strongly held vision;
- they must be able to communicate that vision;
- they must be able to convert the vision into reality.

The leader's role as a creator of vision is a view also held by McAlpine (2000) who proposed that the 'Prince' creates an 'Idea' which is the philosophy on which he will base all his actions and defines how he will compete with other leaders.

Magee (1998) drew attention to the need for leaders to be builders of consensus. Even in an authoritarian, top-down organisation the best results will not be obtained unless those who are to act out the strategy have accepted it willingly. Thus, the leader needs first to listen, so that the various views or participants are heard, and then to communicate once the decision has been made. Part of this process is influenced by the leader's ability to 'network' contacts, which can contribute to an understanding of the complexities of the external and internal environments (a point also made by Mr Hooper, Interview, 8 December 1999). In a non-authoritarian situation, the acceptance of the strategy may have to be negotiated and this is a further skill required of the leader. The head of an organisation who is unable to take advice from and to engage the full support of subordinates is no leader.

Leaders personify the organisational values which are held or aspired to by the majority of the group. These norms typify the organisation, and dissonant behaviour is opposed, not only by the leaders, but also by the rank and file. General Patton, the archetypal cavalry officer, cultivated a swashbuckling, unconventional style. He wore two pearl-handled revolvers and swore, literally, like a trooper. His career was very nearly ended by an incident during which he slapped a soldier who was in hospital with a psychological disorder. Patton viewed the man's complaint as cowardice: behaviour antithetical to all that the general held to and wished to portray. Patton encouraged his junior commanders to be bold, courageous and decisive: traits he personified. His personality was a symbol. The character and values of Sir Richard Branson are central to the diverse, and rather ramshackle, Virgin Group. His personality personifies the casual, fun-loving, but adroit and commercial, way in which Virgin does business. The absence of neckties on male employees, for instance, is a symbol.

Both of these examples portray the leader as a visionary who personifies a style, culture or paradigm that is adopted by the organisation as their outlook on life. An incoming successor is faced with the choice of perpetuating this style, or substituting an alternative. Crisis may make a change necessary and acceptable to the organisation, and those being led may legitimise the introduction of a new paradigm. The leader can only be effective if the style he or she adopts is natural, arising from their natural traits and attributes.

These observations reinforce the views expressed by Johnson (1990, p. 184): 'that rational, linear . . . or synoptic models of decision making, so typical of normative models of strategic decision making, do not characterise management behaviour'. Such systems may be used to try to apply rationality whilst masking the true strategy process, which is relatively unstructured, iterative and a social process heavily influenced by leadership. The competencies of the strategic leader are the ability to conceive vision, to be master of their own milieu and to demonstrate interpersonal skills.

6.7 Leadership style and appropriateness

Westley and Mintzberg (1989) studied the style that various business leaders had, and Table 6.1 is adapted from their findings. They showed

Table 6.1   Varieties of leadership style

Characteristic style	Salient capacities	Content	Process	Organisation content
Creator (Edwin Land)	Inspiration, imagination, foresight	Product focus	Sudden, holistic, introspective, deliberate	Start-up, entrepreneurial
Proselytiser (Steven Jobs)	Foresight, imagination	Market focus	Emergent, shifting focus, interactive	Start-up, entrepreneurial
Idealist (René Levesque)	Imagination, sagacity	Ideals focus	Deliberate, deductive, introspective, incremental	Turnaround, public bureaucracy
Bricoleur* (Lee Iacocca)	Sagacity, foresight, insight	Product/ organisation focus	Emergent, inductive, interactive, incremental	Revitalisation, turnaround, private and public bureaucracy
Diviner (Jan Carlzon)	Insight, sagacity, inspiration	Service focus	Incremental, sudden, crystallisation, interactive	Revitalisation, bureaucracy

*The authors explain: 'the term "bricoleur" refers to a common figure in France; a man who frequents junkyards and there picks up stray bits and pieces which he then puts together to make new objects' (p. 27).
Source: Westley and Mintzberg (1989, p. 23).

Table 6.2   The five approaches in brief

Approach	The CEO's strategic question	CEO's role
Commander	How do I formulate the optimum strategy?	Rational actor
Change	I have a strategy in mind, now how do I implement it?	Architect
Collaborative	How do I involve top management to get commitment to strategies from the start?	Coordinator
Cultural	How do I involve the whole organisation in implementation?	Coach
Crescive	How do I encourage managers to come forward as champions of sound strategies?	Premise-setter and judge

Source: Brodwin and Bourgeois (1984).

that leadership style varied from individual to individual, and in response to different contexts.

This categorisation is firmly based on business needs, and it has proved difficult to draw exact parallels with the military. The predominant type of military commander is probably nearest to the 'Idealist' category, together with some elements of the 'Diviner'. Wellington's Peninsular Campaign had a 'Bricoleur' flavour, but is not typical of modern military practice.

Brodwin and Bourgeois (1984) suggested a different analysis of approaches to leadership, which they summarised as shown in Table 6.2.

The following is a brief summary of the five approaches:

(a) *The Commander approach.* The CEO concentrates on formulating strategy, and once he has the 'best' strategy, he passes it along to those who are instructed to make it happen.

(c) *The Organisational Change approach.* Once the CEO has decided on the strategy he or she puts it into effect using measures such as a reorganisation, changing financial incentives, or hiring new people.

(d) *The Collaborative approach.* The CEO enlists the help of senior managers to ensure that they will back the plan.

(e) *The Cultural approach.* The collaboration is extended to middle or lower organisational levels to ensure acceptance and to develop corporate culture.

(f) *The Crescive approach.* Strategy formulation and implementation proceed together, and the CEO guides managers to develop and champion strategies.

The obvious military parallel suggested by this description is the 'Commander', but modern practice seems to match better the 'Collaborative'. Furthermore, the British MOD method of defence strategy development (as described in the case study in Chapter 4 above) fits into the 'Culture' approach.

Rothschild (1996) raised the issue of the matching the leader's style and attributes to the requirements of the task. He links strategy and leadership style to the stage of development of a company (see Table 6.3).

He goes on to suggest that the leader should also be matched to the strategic differentiator adopted by the company: for example, if the company bases its strategy around products or applications, then an innovative, problem-solving strategist is required. This theory would suggest that strategists can only produce solutions that match their personal paradigm, and there would seem to be evidence to support this

Table 6.3   Linking leadership style to the stages of development

Life-cycle phase	Leader	Characteristics
Birth/Childhood: embryonic	Risk-taker	Is a visionary
		Is aggressive
		Is highly intuitive
		Creates dynamic change
		Has 'killer' instinct
Adult: rapid growth	Caretaker	Builds on strengths
		Creates gradual change
		Willing to commit to longer term
Maturity: slow growth	Surgeon	Is selective
		Knows what is attractive
		Is decisive
		Makes tough decisions
		Holds nothing sacred
Old age/death: decline	Undertaker	Selects the best
		Liquidates
		Is compassionate

Source: Rothschild (1996).

assertion. Steve Jobs was successful in the embryonic and adult stages of Apple, but has been less successful during the maturity phase. Sir Winston Churchill was fully supported as a war leader but rejected in peacetime. Lord Mountbatten was better equipped for the 'political' development of the defence organisation after the Second World War than Viscount Montgomery, the fighting field marshal. The problem that Rothschild identifies is replacing a successful leader when their style has become inappropriate. He pointed out (Rothschild, 1996, p. 19) that: 'IBM stayed with caretaking/evolutionary management too long. It was slow to recognize the PC revolution and then gave away the crown jewels and helped Microsoft and Intel become the leaders.'

Bennis (1999, p. 75) concluded that top-down leadership worked in only the simplest situations: 'The truth is that adaptive problems require complex and diverse alliances. Decrees, orders, etc., *do not work*.' Bennis went on (1999, pp. 77–8) to describe the four competencies that will determine the success of the new style of leadership he advocated:

1   The New Leader understands and practices [sic] the Power of Appreciation. They are connoisseurs of talent, more curators than creators.

2   The New Leader keeps reminding people of what's important.

LEADER'S SENSE OF URGENCY

	Low	High
	Orchestrated learning	Execute now
Sufficient	Managing interacting processes. Contributing ideas. Building vocabularies, shaping understandings. Empowering role models. Serving as coach, teacher, confessor.	Setting a vision and goals. Defining a strategic agenda. Moving quickly. Encouraging learning by doing. Intense personal involvement. Emphasis on implementation.
	Orderly transition	Shock treatment
Insufficient	Cultural evolution. Signalling the need for change and its implications. Arranging succession to new role models. Encouraging graceful exits. Protecting operating core and external dependencies	Cultural revolution. Quickly replacing key personnel. Centralising decision-making. Establishing performance goals and responsibilities. Redirecting resources.

DENSITY OF ADMINISTRATION AND TECHNICAL COMPETENCE

Figure 6.5 Alternative influence processes for leading organisational change.
Source: Lenz (1993, p. 158).

3   The New Leader generates and sustains trust.

4   The New Leader and the Led are intimate allies.

Lenz (1993, p. 158) devised the matrix shown in Figure 6.5. Lenz's analysis revealed that urgency leads to a centralisation of authority and a 'macho' leadership style. Replace 'urgency' with 'crisis' and the previous findings discussed on page 202 above are endorsed. The degree of competence of middle management can be a matter of conjecture, and may rest with the confidence in them felt by the leader and dominant coalition. 'Shock treatment' when the management *are* competent can be risky, because of the alienation that would be engendered, and yet what Lenz terms the 'Rambo' school of leaders tend to act in such a peremptory fashion. In addition to these perceptions of competence, the organisation's culture will affect the range of leadership processes that are acceptable. Lenz observed (1993, p. 166):

the distribution of power is known to vary systematically with the type of organization. In universities, hospitals and professional firms, such as law practices and consulting organizations, power is usually widely shared and the only viable leadership processes may be associated with ... low urgency conditions. Thus, 'execute now' and 'shock treatment' are not within the range of leaders' discretion.

In the military, however, professional organisation though it may be, 'execute now' and 'shock treatment' *are* available because of the hierarchical rank and power structures, and the danger then exists that they may be used inappropriately.

6.8   Handling organisational politics

Organisational politics, which have been discussed earlier, are a reality and the leader has to manage them successfully. Rumour and the manipulation of information thrive on ignorance of the real situation, and so openness is a remedy. Of course, some information may need to be held back temporarily since it may be incomplete, or its release may prejudice a plan, but the instinct to suppress and make secret is stronger than the willingness to make information available to all. Information is power, and the way to lessen this power in single hands or in a cabal is freedom of information. The leader must acknowledge that politics is endemic in organisations (not the least because transition to the upper reaches of organisations is competitive) but a damaging use of power in a way contrary to the best interests of the organisation must be dealt with firmly.

This remedy, however, calls into question who decides what the best interests of the organisation are, and it is important that this concept is not used as a means of the unfair use of power by the dominant coalition. The leader, by consultation, needs to resolve this question because it is, itself, strategic. Leaders themselves, being human, will have blind spots which will limit their vision, and these can only be overcome by sharing decision within a coalition. An organisation whose members seek, or acquiesce in, submission and which is led by a dominant personality is fraught with dangers, as the example of Adolf Hitler so clearly shows. On the other hand, the reflexive response to problems by forming a committee in the expectation that a sharing of ideas will inevitably produce a solution is equally false. Politics in organisations are likely to arise when there is a lack of confidence within the dominant coalition of their ability to solve problems in realistic ways.

6.9 Conflict

The leader is unlikely to work alone, except in the smallest, *ad hoc* organisations, and the senior executives of the organisation form a team (or a dominant coalition), which formulates, articulates and executes strategy. Eisenhardt *et al.*, (1997, p. 43) discovered: 'Top management teams typically face situations with high ambiguity, high stakes, and extreme uncertainty. Discord, contention, debate, disagreement – in short, conflict – are natural in such situations.'

This conflict is not necessarily to be regretted. On the contrary, the absence of a contrary view can lead to the dangers of group-think. Cutting and Kouzmin (2000, p. 495) gave the following definition: 'Group-think is where the group has ceased to learn and merely applies the prevailing concepts and solutions to whatever reality and facts present themselves.' They went on to suggest three possible patterns for this behaviour:

(a) A follower with a reasoning mode of thinking could believe that the executive group represent the company, and are, therefore, deserving loyalty.
(b) A follower with an assessing mode of thinking bows to the power that could be turned against them in the event of opposition.
(c) A follower with a willing mode of thinking wishes to retain the esteem of an executive group that seems to have the vision and ability to overcome any obstacle.

Under any of these circumstances, a poor decision may go unchallenged. The military can be seen to be particularly at risk to group-think: because loyalty is so heavily stressed, the commander has great power that could be exercised against the dissenter, and the effect of leadership is to confer great confidence in the commander. In the past, the dominance of leaders in the military was more often the norm, whereas in recent years the commander is likely to seek advice from his chief of staff and the staff themselves. Even so, the dissenter will need courage to challenge the view of the commander and staff.

The perceptive executive will recognise the value of disagreement:

Gentlemen, I take it we are all in agreement on the decision here . . . Then I propose we postpone further discussion of this matter until our next meeting to give ourselves time to develop dis-agreement and perhaps gain some understanding of what the decision is about. (Alfred P. Sloan, Chairman, General Motors: Cutting and Kouzmin, 2000, p. 493)

Table 6.4   Some studies of CEOs summarised

	No. of CEOs surveyed	Conclusions	Study
1981	20	Strategic awareness is positively related to hierarchical level	Hambrick
1982	24	Significant relationship between the nature of the corporate strategy and the personality of the CEO	Miller, Kets de Vries and Toulouse
1982	53	Background experience of CEO is significantly associated with the firm's diversification strategy	Song
1983	25	Revealed their increasing involvement in strategic decision-making	Steiner
1989	108	CEO has discernibly different characteristics from other members of the top management team	Norburn

Source: Harrison and Pelletier (1997).

Maverick leaders contribute to this healthy dissonance, but are often not welcomed. Organisations, generally, crave stability, but success is usually found in insightful change. Modern fighter aircraft are designed to be unstable, because high manoeuvrability is gained. The aircraft is made manageable by its electronic control system. So, better strategies often emerge from the intervention of questioning, destabilising, lateral thinkers, but organisations generally favour conformance, and mavericks are suppressed, or at least, prevented from reaching the top. Group-think is often more acceptable than the politically incorrect. When mavericks have been allowed to reach the top (Nelson, T.E. Lawrence, Wingate), they have been great contributors, but the awful example of Hitler remains as a warning.

6.10   Studies of chief executive officers

Harrison and Pelletier (1997) referred to the relatively small number of studies that have been conducted on CEOs, and a selection are summarised in Table 6.4.

These studies confirm that strategy and strategic decision are the concern of the CEO and that the personality and style of the leader influence the outcome of the formulation process.

6.11 Rank and ability

In the military, status is identified by the rank held by the individual. That rank is a sign of the power assigned to that individual, but is not necessarily a true indicator of their leadership ability *in that rank*. They will have shown leadership at lower ranks in order to be promoted (and also given indications of being able to perform at the next rank), but, owing to the different skills required at higher ranks, the candidate may not be able to make the transition to strategic leadership. This situation also pertains in industry.

Strategic leadership requires the ability to cope with complexity and uncertainty, whilst all the previous experience to date is likely to have been dealing with practical problems. Earlier in this chapter, statesmanship was given as a strategic leadership parallel, where individuals have to consider a much wider canvas than ever before, and be able to think through long and uncertain causal chains to foresee likely outcomes. Whereas most humans can exercise leadership skills, few can cope with these special demands.

Professor Mason (Interview, 14 November 2000) provided some examples of the shortcomings that can persist into high rank. The following are Napoleon's comments on some of his marshals:

MARSHAL MURAT: He was only brave when confronted by the enemy, and then he was the bravest man in the world . . . But, if he was placed in council he was a poltroon with no judgement and quite incapable of making a decision.

MARSHAL LANNES: His courage in the first place carried him further than his spirit, but each day his spirit rose to the occasion and restored the balance.

MARSHAL AGERAU: His courage, his outstanding virtues certainly elevated him far above the crowd, but, honours, titles and money plunged him back into it.

'A successful general must achieve concentration of force, display activity of body and mind, and be prepared to perish gloriously.'

The qualities required of strategic leaders are not demonstrated in positions below the top. Hints can be gained from observing performance against some of the criteria described above, but there will persist a doubt until the person is actually placed in that position. The loneliness of top command, the complexities and uncertainties may prove too much for someone who, until that point, has shown indications of the requisite talent.

6.12   Conclusion

Those who are responsible for the formation of strategy also head the organisation. They need, therefore, to be leaders, but their tasks are different from those facing executives lower down the hierarchy. Strategic leaders are required to develop and communicate a vision for their organisation that defines a channel for the energy of its members. Although leaders must inspire their followers, there is no one set of personality traits (such as extroversion) which they must have or acquire in order to secure the following of others. Although personality is existential, those aspiring to be strategic leaders must seek to develop the important leadership attributes, whilst remaining true to their own selves. Although business leaders are less likely than their military counterparts to need physical courage, there are no differences of mindset, attributes and abilities between those required to lead in business and those required to lead in the military. The next chapter considers the development of leadership.

7
Making Strategic Leaders

'The main job of organizational life . . . is to bring talented individuals into location for the legitimate uses of power.' Zaleznik (1970, p. 57)

7.1   Introduction

The study has identified the central importance of leadership in the strategy formulation process in both the military and business scenarios and has investigated the mindset of strategic leaders. Finally, the process by which strategic leaders are, or perhaps, could be identified and developed now needs to be addressed.

7.2   Producing strategic leaders

In Shakespeare's *Twelfth Night* (Act 2, Scene 5, italics in the original) Malvolio is the subject of a cruel joke, which is delivered in the form of a forged letter that contains the following lines:

> *be not afraid of greatness. Some are born great, some achieve greatness, and some have greatness thrust upon them . . . And, to inure thyself to what thou art like to be, cast thy humble slough and appear fresh. Be opposite with a kinsman, surly with servants: let thy tongue tang arguments of state; put thyself into the trick of singularity.*

It is still the case that accident of birth can predispose to leadership. The son of the owner of a company or of a field marshal will, from their earliest years, be exposed to expectations of leadership and grow up with the ideas of what is required. Leadership can be thrust upon someone by circumstance, but it is more likely that leadership (greatness) will be achieved through merit and training. The Shakespearean letter's advice on how to mark oneself out for selection for leadership may not be entirely fitting, but being singular and showing interest in matters strategic are still ways in which the aspiring will seek to be noticed.

Future strategic leaders, then, need first to prepare themselves. Then, their qualities need to be recognised and they need to be identified as suitable candidates. They need to have appropriate training and, perhaps, the support of a mentor. They must have appointments that provide the necessary opportunities and preparation for higher office. When they reach high office, they must retain and use the necessary qualities legitimately to the benefit of those they serve. Wick (1991, p. 211) summarised the American army approach: 'The Army method for development, as I understand it, contains three parts, as it were a stool with three legs. The first leg is academic, the second is self-development and the third is learning through experience.'

On the other hand, 'most companies are poor at developing their executives, and most of them acknowledge this: only 3 percent of the 6000 executives occupying the top 200 positions at 50 large US corporations examined by a recent McKinsey survey strongly agree that their organizations developed talent quickly and effectively' (Chambers *et al.*, 1998, p. 45). The differences between the military and business practice would seem to be significant.

7.3   Early training

The armed forces have long had their own colleges, since the beginning of the nineteenth century in some cases. These colleges combine the teaching of military skills and leadership, whilst inculcating a pride of service, loyalty, honour and discipline. This training focuses on preparations for a long-term military career. Naval, army and air force cadets will have practical training in the operations within their arm: for instance, air force cadets in the flying branch will graduate with pilot's wings. Professor Mason (Interview, 14 November 2000) stressed that service colleges need to broaden the perspective of their training beyond the mere military, to instil mental discipline, and to develop powers of analysis.

The business trainee is likely to read for an undergraduate degree in business studies that is likely to major in one of the business functions, such as marketing or finance. The student will learn much about the theory and practice of business, and may or may not consider the associated ethics of commerce. The studies are not conducted in a disciplined environment. Very few will consider issues of leadership and only a small proportion will have practical experience in companies on placement. Sir John Harvey-Jones gave his views on the limitations of a business degree:

> I am very much opposed to putting fresh-faced youths into business school. I believe that business schools should only take people who have actually been on the floor and got their feet wet. If they persist in seeing a business opportunity in conning keen-faced undergraduates into thinking they can learn the whole theory, then can go and put it into practice, they do two things. The business school itself gets out of touch, it is always teaching yesterday's war, and, secondly, it gets nowhere with the kids, because the moment the kids go out, they find that the theory is not, in fact, the way it works in practice ... you are much better with mature students, and sandwich courses are the best of the lot. (Interview, 21 April 1998)

On graduation, then, students in both fields will have much to learn, but, arguably, the military cadets are better prepared for future executive positions.

7.4   Self-preparation

The first requirement is for the young, potential leader to be master of his own *métier* (an aim stressed by General Meyer (1991)). For instance, the young naval officer will concentrate upon developing knowledge of seamanship. Young officers are unlikely to progress satisfactorily unless they are good at their primary job, but all will be given increasing amounts of responsibility as their career progresses. They will be expected to read about military history and achievements, and acquire knowledge of command and operations. On the other hand, none of those interviewed for this study gave other than grudging acknowledgement of the value of reading biographies, mainly because, though of interest, such books were felt to be too personality-specific to be useful guidance. The young officer has to come to terms with the paradox that, in the armed forces, conformity is valued as a source of reliability but, at the same time, exercise of initiative is essential *on the appropriate occasion*. Development of the powers of lateral thinking is encouraged, but only when judgement is also acquired.

The developing manager is likely to learn by observing senior managers and will need to differentiate good practice from bad. Some young executives keep notes of their observations and use these as a checklist for future guidance. Another valuable school is that of mistakes. Everyone makes mistakes, and it is important to use them to develop successful heuristics for future use. The attitude of employers is clearly important here, in that they should regard honest mistakes as learning experiences and not occasions for punishment. Repeated mistakes of the same type, however, are clearly indications of incompetence. Experience clearly is a valuable source of leadership development, particularly in developing the mind of the leader. Jacobs (1991, pp. 201–2) observed:

> strategic leaders must operate in terms of whole systems . . . Mapping ability is the capacity to build a cause-and-effect map of external reality from experience over time; this is what representational cognitive science is all about, the building of a meaning framework that can be used to interpret experiences . . . So what we see is that the leader has a cognitive map that he can use to make sense out of complexity. He is also able to use it to understand where the levers are, so that he can influence the flow of causality – the outcome. He can make things happen.

Robert Townsend's (1976) suggestion was that, if in a position in business below the top, when asked to make a decision, the aspiring leader should ask themself, 'What would I do if I ran this whole organisation?' In this way, Townsend averred, better decisions would be made, the developing manager would develop thinking strategically, and this behaviour would attract favourable attention from the bosses.

The aspiring leader will need self-knowledge, particularly to form some view as to his or her personality type, using some of the ideas and methods described above in Chapter 6. McCollum (1999) found a beneficial effect on leadership from the use of the Maharishi's Transcendental Meditation technique, but the sample was only 24 and from one company only (and where the CEO was already a user of the technique). It is unlikely that choosing a role model will succeed unless the aspirant is endowed with similar qualities and personality. Reading the many books on leadership and attempting to develop *all* the qualities that they list will lead to either utter confusion or sainthood. The chosen way to leadership must be consonant with the person's personality, and self-knowledge will be gained by those who look, and as a natural part of maturation. During this introspection, the aspiring leader needs to confront what Washbush and Clements (1999) called the darker side of leadership, the propensity to use other people for our own selfish ends. They quoted Palmer (1994, p. 25):

> Why must we go in and down? Because as we do so, we will meet the violence and terror that we carry within ourselves. If we do not confront these things inwardly, we will project them outward onto other people. When we have not understood that the enemy is within ourselves, we will find a thousand ways of making someone 'out there' into the enemy...

Finally, the aspiring leader needs to have realistic ambition and the self-confidence to exploit his or her ability and knowledge. Given these triggers, the candidate must set out to develop the required qualities and make sure that they become noticed.

7.5 Experience

Wick (1991) found from interviewing nine hundred Fortune 500 managers that 74 per cent of key developmental experiences were judged to have occurred on the job whilst only 7 per cent arose during training programmes. His full findings (1991, p. 220) were that key developmental experiences, usually:

- Occur on the job
- Are initiated or chosen by the individual
- Contain novelty, risk and challenge
- Happen at any age
- Last months or years

Some jobs are better at promoting development than others and a McKinsey survey produced the results shown in Table 7.1.

These results show that, in the main, the jobs that provided the most valuable experience were those that carried the greatest responsibility and challenge. The problem for the aspiring executive is that these are the jobs that are in limited supply. Handfield-Jones (2000, p. 118) identified from her study the following considerations for positions generating experience:

1 The executive should have authority and responsibility, and scope and variety inherent in the job.

Table 7.1   What kind of jobs develop executives?

Importance of the job as a source of valuable experience: percentage ranking by 200 top executives

Responsibility	
New position with large scope	72
Turning around a business	70
Starting a new business	63
Large, high profile special project	58
Expanding a business by 20% or more	53
International	
Working outside home country	58
International responsibilities while in home country	43
Colleagues	
Highly talented and competent boss	52
Line and staff positions	42
Seven or more direct reports	38
Subordinate with performance problem	26
A difficult boss	20
Novelty	
New business unit or industry	42
New functional area	40
Error	
Made high-profile business mistake	35

Source: Handfield-Jones (2000, p. 121).

2 People with high potential should move through challenging jobs every two or three years.
3 The series of jobs should provide a range of challenges.
4 Executives should learn their craft from highly skilled colleagues as well as superiors.

Sir John Harvey-Jones had typically trenchant views:

> You give them small units, small businesses, to play with and you give them a lot of headroom and you actually have to allow them to make mistakes. This, unfortunately, is what business is very bad at – business tends to be one mistake and you're out. The Services are the same in peacetime – you are allowed to be sick on the Admiral's shoes only once and that's it! (Interview, 21 April 1998)

Mr George held similar views: 'Experience and judgement remain key attributes of the strategist. Managers should take wide, long-term views from their earliest years' (Interview, 22 July 1998).

Mr Hooper (Interview, 8 December 1999) made a similar point but from a different standpoint. He said that the armed forces had a concern that was summed up in the question, 'Do we have enough people who are going to take charge of the next generation and have had experience of war?' He observed that, at the time of the Falklands War, those commanding ships were the last of the generation that had served in the Korean War.

The principle of progressive accumulation of experience accords with the practice of career development used by the armed forces. In general, those who are advancing in rank will spend two to three years in a post and, usually, one of the tours in a rank will be in a command position. The degree of autonomy afforded to officers in the military is more restricted than some in business, because of the inherently hierarchical form that is a feature of the military organisation.

7.6   Identifying strategic leaders

Any candidate who has thought about the issues of strategic leadership, aspires to become one, and has received some training, needs to be identified as a suitable prospect for higher rank. In the military, a detailed system of annual confidential reporting ensures a substantial database of opinions of the subject provided by several reporting officers higher in the organisation. Since the military move their men and women regularly to new jobs to ensure a breadth of experience, the confidential reports will have been prepared by a wide variety of reporting officers and in a number of different types of job. Although variations occur, probably through personal prejudices or a personality clash, a coherent, consistent picture of the individual usually emerges over time. Professor Mason observed that the system depended on the perceptiveness of the reporting officers and, on the occasions when the reporting system had failed, it was usually the inability to identify sycophancy and superficiality in the candidate. (Professor Mason, as an air vice-marshal, served as Air Secretary in the Royal Air Force, where he was responsible for officers' career development, promotion, training, and so on. He had a special responsibility for air rank appointments.) The confidential reports are used as the basis for appointments, selection for courses and for promotion and, in each case, the method used includes vetting or choice by a board of officers of similar rank, or in the case of promotion, officers two ranks senior to the candidate. Campbell (1991), a psychologist, reported the results of extensive work he had conducted into the validity of reporting on leadership traits. In addition to the assessments made by five colleagues, he also used data provided by the persons themselves as to how well they rated themselves as leaders, and compared these to the views of subordinates of the subject. He did this for people in the military, public service and commercial enterprises. His conclusions were:

> Leadership characteristics and the impact of leadership can be assessed by observers using standardized forms. The resulting scores are valid, reliable, and in conformity with common sense. Using such measures operationally raises a whole host of logistical, statistical, political, financial and psychological questions; therefore the adoption of these methods will be slow.
>
> Finally, these measures are currently proving useful in leadership development programs, where individuals can see their own scores and make plans for future improvements. (Campbell, 1991, p. 140)

Non-military organisations tend to use a system of appraisal that includes a discussion between the reporting officer and the subject. A shortcoming of this technique in comparison with the military system is that the assessment may be more subjective, in that there is not the same diversity of reporting officers, if regular moves to new posts are not made. It could be that a developing leader is trapped with an unsympathetic boss for a number of years and, if the candidate moves to a new company, the previous data are not available. A characteristic of those interviewed for this study (for example, Sir Peter Walters) was that in business the 'high-flyers' were moved as regularly to new, and testing, appointments as their military counterparts. Another problem of subjective judgement is that selection may favour the extrovert and the ambitious, rather than the quieter but talented. The qualities of good judgement, sound decision-making, common sense, integrity and knowledge of one's business are a sounder basis for selection. Alenia Marconi Systems identify 'People of Potential' to whose career special attention is paid (Interview with Mr Terry Soame, 24 January 2001). In this technology-based company, the candidates are often engineers with post-graduate qualifications, who have shown potential in technical posts and who are then given jobs that broaden their commercial experience. On the other hand, there is the view expressed by Dr King

(Interview, 1 November 1999) that the selection of strategists is Darwinian and only the fittest survive.

Professor Mason (Interview, 14 November 2000) identified the individual with 'spare capacity' (that is, the ability to do their job well, to look to improve their job, but still have time for wider activities) as a potential candidate for higher rank. Sir John Harvey-Jones (Interview, 21 April 1998) recalled a boss of his who spent much time out of the office shooting, but was always ahead of his job requirements. Mr Hooper made a similar observation: 'they [budding leaders] need to develop the habit of creating time to think – thinking is absolutely crucial. They need to develop the skill of communication, which involves, particularly at the strategic level, active listening, asking the right questions' (Interview, 8 December 1999).

The Royal Air Force makes a positive attempt to identify potential talent in the middle ranks and to assign them to demanding posts. Should they fail, they will drop out of the frame. If they succeed, their position amongst the 'fast-runners' will be confirmed. A possible criticism is that this system can become a self-fulfilling prophesy in that those that are assessed to have potential are given the posts that are particularly relevant to developing talent.

7.7 Training for top positions

The budding leader needs training to develop the required skills and qualities. Rausch (1999, p. 171), however, sounded a note of caution: 'It seems we can teach *about* 'leadership', but not how one can *become* a leader. No one can learn how to become a Lincoln, Joan of Arc, Napoleon, Hitler or Saddam Hussein.'

Lenz (1993, p. 173) also warned that the study of the lives of leaders is insufficient: 'Unless there is also taught a conceptual framework that relates such subjects [famous leaders] to various contextual conditions in which influence processes are executed, there may be no way to grasp important connections between context and administrative action.'

Teaching techniques of leadership may be necessary at one level, but the real problem for budding leaders is learning to cope with complexity and ambiguity in decision-making on the one hand, and, on the other, the interplay of people in organisations where politics and power are at work. The student must learn that there is a contextual appropriateness to leadership behaviour, as well as the need to reconcile the innate personality of the leader to the adopted style of behaviour. Mr Hooper's view was that leadership is almost impossible to teach and quoted a conversation with one of his students:

> 'I just want to check that I have got this right. You are not going to teach us very much, are you?' and I said, 'Quite right'. 'But we are going to learn a great deal, aren't we?' and I said, 'Yes'. 'Which means that I, personally, am going to work very hard.' And I said, 'Absolutely right!' (Interview, 8 December 1999)

The armed forces have a series of courses that are available for their men and women at an appropriate stage of their careers. We have seen that different forms of leadership are needed at the various levels of command, and these are catered for in courses for junior leaders, junior commanders, middle-rank officers and the most senior. The selection process is used to identify those most likely to benefit from such training and, generally, more are trained than is absolutely necessary to fill the posts in the higher ranks. This practice ensures that those who prove unsuitable in practice can be passed over, and other forms of wastage, such as death or incapacitating illness, do not prevent the filling of higher posts with suitable candidates. The significant course for those who are thought to have potential for high rank is the staff college. As the idea of a general staff was developed (see Chapter 3 above), so the need for staff training became evident. Staff colleges teach communications skills and logical thinking as basic attributes of the staff officer, but also widen the horizons of the young officer to include ideas of government, such as foreign policy, economics and civil administration. In the United Kingdom, the officers destined for 'star' rank can be selected to attend the year-long Royal College of Defence Studies course in London, which prepares the graduate for an executive strategic role. Selection for these courses is done by specially convened boards of officers on the basis of the annual confidential reports on the candidates. Professor Ann Robinson remarked:

> training is the one thing in a commercial organisation ... that gets left to the last, whereas in the military it is very important ... in the army, they will have been endlessly trained and have set down that this process of objectives and strategy is the way an army works, but nobody realises that that is the way a business works. (Interview, 5 September 1998)

In business, the principal option open to the rising executive is to return to university for a Master's degree in Business Administration.

These courses are designed to develop the overall, 'helicopter' view of business and the composition of the course generally provides an opportunity to develop analytical and advocacy skills. Leadership is not a subject which is universally given prominence. Academic bodies teaching leadership are growing in number as the realisation grows of the importance of the subject to business, and some, like Exeter, have a separate establishment for that purpose.

The armed forces have an advantage over business in developing leaders in that they usually have their officers on some form of formal commission, with penalties for early retirement. This stability should result in a payback for training given, which is often not the case in business. Companies have to find ways of retaining their talent in an environment where advancement is generally quicker by moving sideways and up to another company, rather than waiting for vacancies to arise in one's own company. Commercial organisations do not usually find the argument compelling that they are contributing to the overall strength of British management by paying for, often expensive, training. Sir Ian Pedder, however, gave the example of BP Amoco:

> my son-in-law is at BP Amoco. He is out in Australia now running the shipping business. He has had exactly the same training as a Service officer would. He went to sea, he drove a ship around, and they let him drive a ship – he had a big ship and a little ship, and they said, 'David, we'd like you to go ashore now, and we want you go on a course, do the Open University, and that sort of thing.' That was when he was 35, and he is [now] 43–44 but he was completely sent back to do as we would have done, put people to go on the proper sort of course. (Interview, 16 September 1999)

Yelverton (1997) gave his recipe for developing top managers:

1 Move them around into high-risk, high-visibility jobs.
2 Give them responsibility.
3 They must groom their replacements.
4 A good mentor is needed.
5 They should not try to manage their career.
6 They succeed who learn from their mistakes.
7 A leader needs strong personal values.

If they do not train, however, problems can occur. Mr Hooper (Interview, 8 December 1999) gave examples of Barclays and Reed Elsevier who took eight and eleven months respectively to appoint a leader and then had to go outside their own organisation to do so. Inevitably, those leaders coming from outside will need time to absorb the culture, which delays their reaching full effectiveness.

Calori *et al.* (1994) studied CEOs, whom they considered as 'cognizers' responsible for integrating the views of the top management team under conditions of situational complexity. They found that their data supported the view that those managers who had lengthy experience in diversified, multinational corporations have more complex cognitive maps of the structure of their environment than other CEOs. Furthermore, international experience was found to be important in influencing positively the ability of CEOs to handle complexity. The developing leader in both the military and the business field, it would seem, would benefit from being exposed to both complexity and the international dimension.

A further consideration in the development of the leader is the specialist/generalist argument. It was seen earlier that a requirement for a leader is to be expert, or, at least, highly competent, in their field. On the other hand, rising leaders must broaden their vision to understand other functions. Thus, the accountant that knows nothing of marketing, or the pilot that understands nothing of logistics, is unlikely to have sufficient breadth of knowledge to be able to make sound strategic decisions. Common sense is also based upon accumulated knowledge, such that it is impossible to be truly intuitive on matters of which one has no experience. At some stage the junior specialist must make the transition to a generalist who has breadth of knowledge and vision and who can handle complexity in information combined with political and organisational awareness. He or she must develop a statecraft mentality.

7.8   Mentoring

Formal training in leadership is widely practised and, presumably, fulfils the purposes expected of it. Zaleznik (1977), however, asserted that the most effective training of the talented is for a senior executive to mentor a talented junior. Mentor, in the *Odyssey*, was the old man (but often the goddess Pallas Athene who impersonated him) who guided the young Telemachus in the absence of his father Odysseus. The mentoring approach is recognised in the military who appoint middle-ranking officers to be Personal Staff Officers (PSOs) to star-ranking officers. In this way, officers who have been identified as having potential are exposed to the practice of command at high level, and this experience can be a turning point in the young officer's career (a view expressed by

Air Vice-Marshal Roser). Often, the PSO can help the senior officer by discussing problems and ideas in private before these issues are discussed in open forum with others. In business, the Personal Staff Officer system is not often practised and senior executives are more likely to regard their secretaries as confidantes and an alter ego. Those interviewed for this study had varying views on the value of the Personal Staff Officer system.

Colonel Gooderson thought that PSOs would be very useful but that the idea was not commercial, since such a person would be an expensive overhead. Sir John Harvey-Jones thought it 'a very bad principle – I have always been against personal staffs and PAs in business'. Sir Patrick Hine thought that the PSO position is more beneficial to the individual than to the organisation, so it becomes a judgement whether this is the most cost-effective method of developing strategists. The Chief Executive Officer of British Aerospace has a Personal Staff Officer.

General Meyer (1991, p. 159) put it even more forcefully: 'If there is no mentoring in a development program, it's not a leadership program.' In his view, the successful development of military leaders in the Second World War arose from the close-knit army organisation between the wars in which it was possible to know one's contemporaries through having served with them in units. One might add that, in such circumstances, networking was available for the sharing of views and the seeking of advice.

Mentoring can be informal or formal. Informally, a senior member of the organisation can decide to help a junior with advice and guidance. Formally, someone will be appointed to look after a junior and the mentor will be paid for providing this service. Megginson (2000) addressed the issue of training for mentors and he suggested that the consensus of opinion of those studying in this field was that a thousand hours of preparation were necessary before a mentor could undertake a formal programme. It is likely that only the largest companies will undertake a formal system of this nature.

7.9 The person/organisation tension

Personal development can cause a tension within an organisation that is seeking to solve problems through teamwork. On the one hand, organisations are tending to empower individuals, and the rising executives may seek autonomy as a means of differentiating themselves from the competition. On the other hand, organisational life is relational and cooperative. Janssens and Steyaert (1999, p. 130) followed Schein in suggesting that an individual is a set of social selves that modify behaviour for appropriateness. This style will, then, be suited to particular situations and tasks. Company doctors, for instance, specialise in turning round ailing companies, and 'hatchet men' are sent in when draconian measures are deemed to be necessary. The executive with an innate desire to collaborate is unlikely to make a successful 'macho' autocrat. Does the aspiring executive, then, need to develop acting skills so that an appropriate role can be played as the situation demands? Such lack of integrity is usually discovered and despised. Polonius' advice to Laertes, 'to thine ownself be true' (*Hamlet*, Act 1, Scene 3) is sound, but leadership development is largely self-discovery and the budding leader may need to experiment to find the style that best suits his or her personality.

The aspiring leader, then, must resolve the individual/group dichotomy by collaborating effectively in groups, whilst displaying those individual qualities that will gain notice.

7.10   Conclusion

The path to strategic leadership requires self-development and self-awareness. The identification and development of leadership traits are a necessary precursor to practising them. The young leader must be an acute observer of all around, noting bad practice as well as good. Training courses can point the way, but experience is the only sure source of knowledge, even though risk of failure is ever present. The military system is more formal and relies heavily on confidential reporting, but is more organised than that in business. The more enlightened companies identify potential executives and develop them, but the majority seem to promote from those who survive the deep end. Business can learn from military practice, even though expense would be incurred. This cost has to be weighed against the losses caused by incompetence and inexperience at the strategic level.

8
Conclusion

The aim of this study is to assess whether the strategy process in the business field also prevails in the military context, and to identify areas of similarity and difference. The following hypotheses were proposed:

1 That 'strategy' is a concept that is used similarly both in business and the military.
2 That the process by which strategy is devised is broadly comparable in each context.
3 That the process is affected by contextual factors, particularly crisis, in a similar way in both business and the military.

The first task in this study was to determine whether the concept and nature of strategy were sufficiently similar in the contexts of business and military to permit a valid comparison. Although the application and outcomes of strategy were found to be different, because war and business are conducted in a different manner, the fundamental idea of strategy as a means of achieving one's aims, whilst frustrating those of the opposition, was the same in both fields. The process requires broad vision and pragmatism in the formulation and final choice of strategy, and these qualities suggested the behaviour of statesmen. The complexity of the task creates problems for the human mind, and may be too great for rational analysis alone, leading to the additional use of intuition.

Strategy, then, means the same in business and the military, so the next task was to design the research method that would lead to answers to the research question. An important part of any research is to review the existing literature on the subject and, in this case, researching two contexts, strategic management theory and military strategy, necessitated access to many sources. The original part of the research, however, was based upon comparative case studies and interviews of strategists from both fields. Although there is no standard by which to determine the amount of research required, two pairs of case studies and 24 interviews were deemed to be sufficient to permit drawing valid conclusions. The case studies were written as two pairs, with one from each of business and military in each pair to aid comparison. Analysis of the data collected concentrated on:

(a) The influence of organisation
(b) The influence of leadership
(c) The attitude to risk
(d) The underlying theory and practice
(e) The influence of context

These sub-questions provided a framework for the analysis, but it also became evident that they were drivers of the strategy process. The nature of the subject and the type of evidence collected resulted in a phenomenological, non-quantitative approach.

The third chapter moved on to describe and compare military and business strategy, seeking to identify the paradigms and controversies that have emerged from scholarly activity in these fields. Much less has been written on military strategy process than in the field of business strategy studies, so the conclusions on military practice tended to be more inferential. The literature suggests that there are various forms of process which can be used by an organisation needing a strategy, and the context in which the strategy is decided is influential. For instance, the degree of uncertainty present in the environment will affect the confidence that can be placed on strategies extending into the longer term. Furthermore, the effect of context is that strategies that are copied from others are unlikely to succeed, since the many environmental factors are unlikely to be exactly the same in each case. The concepts of strategic management proved to be useful in comparing military strategy process, even though the military do not explicitly use this theory. The language used in strategic studies is often indicative of the mindsets of the theorists, so a semantic comparison ended this section of the chapter. Again, the language used in the two fields has marked similarities, since both acknowledge that strategy is concerned with ends, ways and means. Strategists are humans who require to think laterally, and with clarity and subtlety. Great strategies usually break the mould of conventional thinking.

Chapter 4 concentrated upon the strategy formulation process, which was seen to end in a decision. Decision can be the result of a deliberate process of thinking using an institutional system at regular times in the year, or it can be associated with an emergent style in which strategy is chosen as and when required. Since strategy process involves the interplay of ends, ways and means, the resources available have to be sufficient to achieve the desired ends, given the contextual factors, such as the environment, which bear upon the ways that are available and appropriate. At the limits, thinking about strategy can be highly rational, logical and based upon facts, or it can be intuitive and heuristic. The military process is more likely to be deliberate and rational, although there is flexibility enough in their thinking for emergent solutions to arise. The military are less likely to take intuitive decisions than some businessmen, particularly entrepreneurs. Strategy is seen to be an art rather than a science, so intuition and judgement are the factors that separate the good strategist from the mediocre. The literature in both fields acknowledges that an aim is the starting point of the process, and the military place great stress on determining a precise aim. Strategy depends on tactics for its implementation, and it is important that those involved in the strategy process know the boundary between the two and allow the trusted organisation to implement strategies without oppressive interference from above.

In Chapter 5, the evidence gathered for this study was compared to the foregoing analysis of the theory in the literature. The sub-questions listed in p. 191 above were used as a framework for the discussion of the findings.

8.1   The influence of organisation

Larger organisations tend to be hierarchical and bureaucratic. Military organisations operate with greater formality than businesses. The large organisations favour deliberate strategy processes, but the British Ministry of Defence routinely uses emergent methods, when necessary. There is a bias towards top-down influence on strategy in both fields, but the process was mainly described as 'iterative', and thus involved a degree of bottom-up.

Organisation politics were seen as a natural outcome of collecting talented, ambitious people to work together. Interviewees spoke of 'baronies' and 'fiefdoms' within organisations, and saw these as being to do with power and territory. The problem was seen to be that the best interests of the total organisation and the baronies did not necessarily coincide. For instance, the introduction of air power into warfare stimulated internecine struggle within the military, where none had existed during the period when the army and navy generally did not have designs on each other's operations. Air power, however, bridged the gap between land and sea using an element that covered the entire globe, and, when coupled with increasing financial constraints for defence as a whole, the newcomer generated vicious arguments as to the allocation of resources. These inter-service struggles are now less evident, but resources are still an important strategic factor. The effect on the strategy process can be a distortion of the final decision in favour of the powerful. The powerful, however, are not always right.

8.2   The influence of leadership

Leadership was found to be central to the whole subject of strategy so Chapters 6 and 7 were devoted to this subject. The findings are reviewed on p. 258.

8.3   The attitude to risk

Risk was accepted as a fact of life in both business and the military, and both fields were usually cautious and risk-averse. The military commander has to face the possibility of large losses of people and *matériel*, now unacceptable to society, and the business leader can lose the company entirely, an eventuality not likely to gain favour with the stakeholders. As always, the risk has to be commensurate with the expected return. The military system discourages risk-taking, and only the more entrepreneurial in business are likely to make risky decisions. Strategy, though, since it deals with the future, is uncertain and can never be truly safe, and sensitivity analysis can be used as a method of reducing the risk of being caught out by events. Luck, too, is an ever-present factor, but not one that can be built into the strategy process. Measures may be taken to reduce the effect of chance (and the military uses war-gaming for this purpose), but stochastic methods still require that the probabilities themselves often have to be estimated. Strategists are in the hands of fate like the rest of us.

8.4   The underlying theory and practice

The military stress the overriding importance of the aim, and much effort is expended in ensuring that it is precisely stated and represents the most that can be done with the resources available. Business, on the other hand, seems to accept less precise, more general aims, and thus risks devising a poorly focused strategy. Businesses will produce vision or mission statements whose value is diminished by the inclusion of vague, but impressive, statements of intent. The strategy cannot be devised until a clear idea of what is to be achieved is stated with precision.

Vision, though, is important and the leader must be responsible for developing it. The statement of a desired future state (vision) is an important guide to the organisation's activities and must be embedded in the consciousness of the people involved. Clear lines of communication ('a two-way road without traffic lights': Sir Christopher Benson, Interview, 8 July 1999) in the company are essential to gaining ownership and sharing in this vision. Wide involvement in strategic issues by everyone in the group aids this acceptance and internalisation of the vision. The role of leadership in the strategy process became of sufficient importance to this study as to justify the final part of this thesis concentrating upon leaders and their development.

The evidence suggests that the strategy process is generally an iterative process that gradually refines ideas, leading to endorsement by the dominant coalition. The majority of military interviewees saw these iterations as being started mainly from the top of the organisation, although the staff was seen as a source of both ideas and detailed plans. The entrepreneur in business is more likely to operate in this mode, although, even then, they stressed the need for involvement by their subordinates. The actual techniques used for evolving strategy varied. Large bureaucratic organisations (for example, the British Ministry of Defence (MOD) and IBM) were more likely to use formal methods using a set programme of actions related to the calendar. Some of these bureaucracies found it difficult to incorporate the ideas welling up from the lower reaches of their organisation, although the MOD cycle began with inputs from individual branches at the lowest level. Large, divisionalised companies were faced with the problem of control of their operations and clearly feared a descent into chaos if strict methods were not employed. Several interviewees reported that their experience was that 'away days' were used as a means of encouraging staff involvement, strategic thinking and communication. No single, 'best' method was found because the culture of the organisation and the personalities of its leaders make each strategy process unique. Communication within the organisation can lead to the identification of good ideas which, when thoroughly worked out, can be presented to the board for modification or approval. Purely top-down strategising seems to have mainly been replaced as societies themselves have become more liberal (although autocrats have not disappeared entirely).

Investigating whether the thought process of strategy is rational or intuitive proved to be difficult. The military have a logical thought sequence, the appreciation, which seeks to prevent jumping to conclusions before a proper appraisal of the facts. This method can be used in business situations and does seem to condition the military mind, but its formal application in real war situations is not guaranteed. Intuition proved to have an undefined place, because, although the bright idea can always occur, neither the military nor business were prepared to accept them without a rational consideration of the implications, usually in a plan. Even so, it was accepted that the future has to be uncertain, since there are no facts beyond the present. Thus, it may be that the decision-maker, having taken all prudent steps to evaluate the proposal, is left with making an intuitive judgement, and operating in a coalition with other executives may serve to reduce the personal risk to reputation and the perceived risk of the plan. There was general agreement amongst interviewees that common sense, 'nous', was the most valuable attribute of the strategist. Intuitive common sense is the unconscious encapsulation of the knowledge acquired by experience. All the mistakes and scars endured or observed in the past are accumulated and stored by the wise, and wisdom is the *sine qua non* of the strategist.

8.5   The influence of context

Crisis was seen by all as leading to a centralising of decision. Although probably inevitable, this drawing of control to the top was not viewed as necessarily desirable. A tactical crisis can be addressed by the dominant coalition, whereas it would be better practice for the subordinate managers to be allowed to solve the problem. The more devious might declare a crisis to exist so that they can assert (or regain) control. Crisis can cause panic and a view that a quick decision is vital, whereas, in truth, there probably remains time for consultation. The macho manager may actually enjoy crisis, but the wise manager or military leader still consults widely before making a decision.

Chapter 6 delved further into the issue of strategic leadership and considered some of the theories on this difficult and imprecisely understood human activity. Strategic leaders play a key role in the strategy process. They are principally a source of vision for the organisation, and infuse subordinates with a sense of purpose and determination. Modern leaders consult widely within their own organisations, and network through contacts in similar or related fields. Leaders involve their subordinates and exploit their talents, avoiding domination unless the situation demands a temporary exercise of power. Leaders do not need to be superhuman, but they cannot succeed without personal values and virtues. Leaders, as such, are made, but the truly great strategic leaders are probably born.

Chapter 7 then turned to the issue of finding and developing strategic leaders. The military have always valued leadership and, to this day, spend much time and effort in identifying and training their future leaders. The development of *strategic* leadership is more difficult than developing tactical leaders, because the wider perspective demands more the Renaissance man than the narrow, excellent specialist. The candidate for high office should have a breadth of interests, be thinking strategically from early days, and always have a reserve of time and talent. This preoccupation with leadership is not so pronounced in business, but leaders in this field are recognised and, generally, valued. The major difference between the military and business, however, in this field is the resources applied to identification, selection and training of leaders. The military provide progressive training throughout an officer's career preparing him or her for posts before they take up an appointment. Business, on the other hand, can see training as an expense for which there is not necessarily any direct return. As a person becomes better qualified, so they are subject to predation by 'head hunters' and the recruiting company can reap the benefit of the training paid for by another. The military usually insist that the recipient of training will serve for a specified period afterwards to amortise the cost, but business would find that hard to enforce. Some businesses, however, do value progressive training and an interviewee gave BP as an example. Promotion in the armed forces is highly competitive. Progression to the top in business is again very competitive but more haphazard, which may account for the political activities within these organisations of the ambitious.

The findings have been summarised in Table 8.1. Because of the wide variety of contexts and strategy content, these should be seen as *tendencies* rather than positive generalisations. The evidence is insufficient to go further.

Three hypotheses were proposed at the outset:

1 That strategy is a concept that is used similarly in both business and the military.

Table 8.1   The strategy formulation process: a summary of findings

Factors	Military	Business
Process	Iterative	Iterative
Direction	Mainly top-down	Mainly top-down
Crisis	Centralises decision	Centralises decision
Risk	Risk-averse	Mainly risk-averse
Aims	Strong emphasis	Weaker emphasis
Organisational politics	In peace, but not in war	Active
Leadership	Positive effect	Positive effect
Implementation planning	Always used	Some use, more in larger companies
Rational/intuitive	Rational, occasional intuition	Rational, but more use of intuition
Deliberate/emergent	Deliberate, but some emersion in peace	Varies widely, but large companies more likely to use deliberate methods

2 That the process by which strategy is devised is broadly comparable in each context.
3 That the strategy process is affected by contextual factors, particularly crisis, in a similar way in both business and the military.

All of these hypotheses have been found to be true. Significant differences do, however, occur in the two fields in the areas of training for strategic leadership, and in the selection of the aim of the enterprise. In both of these activities, the military act more formally and attach greater importance to them than does business.

The strategy process is an iterative human activity undertaken in a particular context to devise a way to achieve an aim. Every company or military force, in every situation, with every set of human beings, will devise their own strategy process. Although there are general patterns of strategic behaviour from which generalised theories are formed, none can completely encapsulate each and every variation and nuance occurring in essentially unique, real-life situations. Groups needing a strategy should seek guidance from general theory, but must work out for themselves in detail how it is to be devised.

Bibliography

Adair, John (1988) *Effective Leadership*, London, Pan Books.

Allen, R.W., Madison, D.L., Porter, L.W., Renwick, P.A. and Mayes, B.T. (1979) 'Organizational politics: tactics and characteristics of its actors', *California Management Review*, vol. 21, no. 1, pp. 77–83.

Allison, Graham T. (1971) *Essence of Decision*, New York, HarperCollins.

Alvesson, Mats and Willmott, Hugh (1996) *Making Sense of Management*, London, Sage.

Andersen, Jon Aarum (2000) 'Intuition in managers. Are intuitive managers more effective?', *Journal of Managerial Psychology*, vol. 15, no. 1, pp. 46–67.

Ansoff, H.I. (1968) *Corporate Strategy*, Harmondsworth, Penguin.

Ansoff, H. Igor (1991) 'Critique of Henry Mintzberg's "The Design School" reconsidering the basic premises of strategic management', *Strategic Management Journal*, September, pp. 449–61.

Ansoff, H. Igor and McDonnell, E. (1990) *Implanting Strategic Management*, 2nd edn, Englewood Cliffs, NJ, Prentice-Hall.

Ansoff, H. Igor and Sullivan, Patrick A. (1993) 'Optimizing profitability in turbulent environments: a formula for strategic success', *Long Range Planning*, vol. 26, no. 5, pp. 11–23.

Bailey, Andy and Johnson, Gerry (1992) 'How strategies develop in organisations', in David Faulkner and Gerry Johnson (eds), *The Challenge of Strategic Management*, London, Kogan Page, pp. 147–78.

Barber, Herbert F. (1992) 'Developing strategic leadership: the US Army War College experience', *Journal of Management Development*, vol. 11, no. 6, pp. 4–12.

Barnet, Richard J. (1972) *Roots of War*, New York, Penguin.

Barnett, Corelli (1975) *Strategy and Society*, The Spenser Wilkinson Memorial Lecture 1974, Manchester, Manchester University Press.

Barney, Jay (1991) 'Firm resources and sustained competitive advantage', *Journal of Management*, vol. 17, no. 1, pp. 99–120.

Baylis, John, Booth, Ken, Garnett, John and Williams, Phil (1975) *Contemporary Strategy*, London, Croom Helm.

BBC2 (1998) *A Paper War: Inside Robertson's Defence Review*, screened 31 May.

Beach, Lee Roy, Mitchell, Terence R., Paluchowski, Thaddeus F. and van Zee, Emily H. (1992) 'Image theory: decision framing and decision deliberation', in Frank Heller (ed.), *Decision-Making and Leadership*, Cambridge, Cambridge University Press.

Becher, A. (1989) *Academic Tribes and Territories: Intellectual Enquiry and the Cultures of Discipline*, The Society for Research into Higher Education and the Open University Press (in Tranfield and Starkey, 1998).

Bellamy, Christopher (1997) *Knights in White Armour*, London, Pimlico.

Bennis, Warren (1999) 'The end of leadership: exemplary leadership is impossible without full inclusion, initiatives and cooperation of followers', *Organisational Dynamics*, vol. 28, no. 1, pp. 71–80.

Bennis, W. and Nanus, B. (1985) *Leaders: The Strategies for Taking Charge*, New York, Harper & Row.

Berger, Peter L. and Luckmann, Thomas (1966) *The Social Construction of Reality. A Treatise in the Sociology of Knowledge*, Garden City, NY, Doubleday.

Bernstein, Alvin H. (1994) 'The strategy of a warrior-state: Rome and the wars against Carthage, 264–201 B.C.', in Williamson Murray, Macgregor Knox and Alvin Bernstein (eds), *The Making of Strategy: Rulers, States and War*, Cambridge, Cambridge University Press.

Bettis, Richard A. and Prahalad, C.K. (1995) 'The dominant logic: retrospective and extension', *Strategic Management Journal*, vol. 16, pp. 5–14.

Billings, Robert S., Milburn, Thomas W. and Schaalman, Mary Lou (1980) 'A model of crisis perception: a theoretical and empirical analysis', *Administrative Science Quarterly*, vol. 25 (June), pp. 300–16.

Boar, Bernard (1995) 'Sun Tzu and Machiavelli on strategy', *Journal of Business Strategy*, vol. 16, Issue 1, (Jan/Feb), pp. 16–18.

Bodner, William C. and Thomas, Howard (1993) 'The role of competitive groups in strategy formulation: a dynamic integration of two competing models', *Journal of Management Studies*, vol. 30, no. 1, pp. 51–67.

Bogdan, Robert and Taylor, Steven J. (1975) *Introduction to Qualitative Research Methods*, New York, John Wiley & Sons.

Brandenburger, A. and Nalebuff, B. (1995) 'The right game: use game theory to shape strategy', *Harvard Business Review*, vol. 73, issue 4, pp. 57–71.

Brinton, Crane, Craig, Gordon A. and Gilbert, Felix (1967) 'Jomini', in Edward Mead Earle (ed.), *Makers of Modern Strategy: Military Thought from Machiavelli to Hitler*, New York, Atheneum.

Brodwin, David R. and Bourgeois III, L.J. (1984) 'Leadership styles', from 'Five steps to strategic action', *California Management Review*, vol. 26, no. 3, pp. 176–90, in Cynthia Hardy (1994), *Managing Strategic Action*, London, Sage, pp. 143–56.

Brown, Shona L. and Eisenhardt, Kathleen M. (1998) *Competing on the Edge*, Boston, Mass., Harvard Business School Press.

Bryant, Arthur (1957) *The Turn of the Tide*, London, Collins.

Bryant, Arthur (1959) *Triumph in the West*, London, Fontana.

Bryman, Alan (1996) 'Leadership in organizations', in Stewart R. Clegg, Cynthia Hardy and Walter C. Nord (eds), *Handbook of Organization Studies*, London, Sage.

Bullock, Alan (1993) *Hitler and Stalin: Parallel Lives*, London, Fontana.

Bulmer, Martin (1984) 'Introduction: problems, theories and methods in sociology – (how) do they interrelate?', in Martin, Bulmer (ed.), *Sociological Research Methods: An Introduction*, New Brunswick, NJ, Transaction Books.

Burrell, Gibson and Morgan, Gareth (1979) *Sociological Paradigms and Organisational Analysis*, Aldershot, Ashgate.

Calori, Roland, Johnson, Gerry and Sarnin, Philippe (1994) 'CEOs' cognitive maps and the scope of the organization', *Strategic Management Journal*, vol. 15, pp. 437–57.

Camerer C. (1991) 'Does strategy research need game theory?', *Strategic Management Journal*, vol. 12, pp. 137–52.

Campbell, Andrew (1991) 'Brief case: strategy intuition – a conversation with Henry Mintzberg', *Long Range Planning*, vol. 24, no. 2, pp. 108–10.

Campbell, Andrew and Yeung, Sally (1991) 'Creating a sense of mission', *Long Range Planning*, vol. 24, no. 4 (August), pp. 10–20.

Campbell, David (1991) Address in *Strategic Leadership Conference: Proceedings*, US Army War College, Carlisle, Pa., pp. 99–146.

Campbell, J.P., Daft, R.L. and Hulin, C.L. (1982) *What to Study. Generating and Developing Research Questions*, Beverley Hills, Calif., Sage.

Carey, Robert (1996) 'From the barracks to the boardroom', *Performance Strategies*, March, pp. 28–32.

Cawood, David (1984) 'Managing innovation: military strategy in business', *Business Horizons*, no. 27 (Nov/Dec), pp. 62–6.

Chaffee, Ellen Earle (1985) 'Three models of strategy', *Academy of Management Review*, vol. 10, no. 1, pp. 89–98.

Chakravarthy, Balaji S. and Dos, Yves (1992) 'Strategy process research: focusing on corporate self-renewal', *Strategic Management Journal*, vol. 13, pp. 5–14.

Chakravarthy, Balaji S. and Lorange, Peter (1991) *Managing the Strategy Process*, Englewood Cliffs, NJ, Prentice-Hall.

Chambers, Elizabeth G., Foulon, Mark, Handfield-Jones, Helen, Hankin, Steven M. and Michaels III, Edward G. (1998) 'The war for talent', *McKinsey Quarterly*, no. 3, pp. 44–57.

Chen, Min (1994) 'Sun Tzu's strategic thinking and contemporary business', *Business Horizons*, March–April, pp. 42–8.

Chorn, N.H. (1991) 'Organisations: a new paradigm', *Management Decision*, vol. 29, no. 4, pp. 8–11.

Christensen, C.R., Andrews, K.R., Bower, J.L., Hamermesh, R.G. and Porter, M.E. (1987) *Business Policy: Text and Cases*, 6th edn, Homewood, Ill., Irwin.

Cohen, M.D., March, J.G. and Olsen, J.P. (1972) 'A garbage can model of organizational choice', *Administrative Science Quarterly*, vol. 17, pp. 1–25.

Command 3999 (1998) *The Strategic Defence Review*, London, The Stationery Office.

Coulson-Thomas, Colin (1992) 'Strategic vision or strategic con? Rhetoric or reality?', *Long Range Planning*, vol. 25, no. 1 pp. 81–9.

Cowan, David (1994) 'Good information – generals cannot do without it: why do CEOs think they can?', *Marketing Intelligence and Planning*, vol. 12, no. 11, pp. 16–21.

Coyne, Kevin P. and Subramanian, Somu (1996) 'Bringing discipline to strategy', *McKinsey Quarterly*, no. 4, pp. 14–25.

Craig, Gordon A. (1967) 'Delbrück: The Military Historian', in Edward Mead Earle (ed.), *Makers of Modern Strategy: Military Thought from Machiavelli to Hitler*, New York, Atheneum.

Cray, David, Mallory, Geoffrey R., Butler, Richard J., Hickson, David J. and Wilson, David C. (1991) 'Explaining decision processes', *Journal of Management Studies*, vol. 28, no. 3, pp. 227–51.

Cummings, Stephen (1995) 'Pericles of Athens – drawing from the essence of strategic leadership', *Business Horizons*, vol. 38, Issue 1, (Jan/Feb), pp. 22–7.

Cutting, Bruce and Kouzmin, Alexander (2000) 'The emerging patterns of power in corporate governance', *Journal of Managerial Psychology*, vol. 15, no. 5, pp. 477–511.

Cyert, Richard M. and March, James G. (1963) *A Behavioral Theory of the Firm*, Englewood Cliffs, NJ, Prentice-Hall.

Daft, Richard L. and Weick, Karl E. (1984) 'Toward a model of organizations as interpretation systems', *Academy of Management Review*, vol. 9, no. 2, pp. 284–95.

Dandeker, Christopher (1990) *Surveillance, Power and Modernity*, Cambridge, Polity Press.

Dandeker, Christopher (2000) 'The United Kingdom: the overstretched military', in Charles C. Moskos, John Allen Williams and David R. Segal (eds), *The Postmodern Military*, Oxford, Oxford University Press, pp. 32–50.

Davidson, Mike (1995) *The Grand Strategist*, London, Macmillan – now Palgrave.

Dean, James W. and Sharfman, Mark P. (1996) 'Does decision process matter? A study of strategic decision-making effectiveness', *Academy of Management Journal*, vol. 39, no. 2, pp. 368–96.

Deetz, Stanley (1996) 'Describing differences in approaches to organization science: rethinking Burrell and Morgan and their legacy', *Organization Science*, vol. 7, no. 2 (March/April), pp. 191–207.

Defence Committee (2000) *Fourteenth Report: Lessons of Kosovo, Volume 1 Report and Proceedings of the Committee, 23 October 2000*, London, The Stationery Office.

de Wit, Bob and Meyer, Ron (1994) *Strategy: Process, Content, Context*, 1st edn, Minneapolis/St Paul, Main., West.

de Wit, Bob and Meyer, Ron (1999) *Strategy Synthesis: Resolving Strategy Paradoxes to Create Competitive Advantage*, London, International Thomson Business Press.

Director of Air Force Plans and Programmes (1997) 'RAF Guide to the Long Term Costings', Ministry of Defence, Air Force Department.

Dixon, Norman F. (1976) *On the Psychology of Military Incompetence*, London, Pimlico.

Dodgson, Mark (1993) 'Organizational learning: a review of some literatures', *Organization Studies*, vol. 14, no. 3, pp. 375–94.

Drucker, Peter (1980) *Managing in Turbulent Times*, London, Pan Books.

Dupuy, Colonel Trevor N. (ed.) (1993) *International Military and Defence Encyclopedia*, vol. 5 (P to S), Maclean, Va., Brassey's US.

Dutton, Jane E. (1993) 'Interpretations on automatic: a different view of strategic issue diagnosis', *Journal of Management Studies*, vol. 30, no. 3, pp. 339–57.

Earle, Edward Mead (ed.) (1967) *Makers of Modern Strategy: Military Thought from Machiavelli to Hitler*, New York, Atheneum.

Easterby-Smith, Mark, Thorpe, Richard and Lowe, Andy (1991) *Management Research: An Introduction*, London, Sage.

Eccles, R.G. and Nohria, N. (1992) *Beyond the Hype. Rediscovering the Essence of Management*, Boston, Mass., Harvard Business School Press.

Eden, Colin and Ackerman, Fran (1998) *Making Strategy*, London, Sage.

Ehrman, John (1956) *Grand Strategy*, vol. V, London, Her Majesty's Stationery Office.

Eisenhardt, Kathleen M. (1989a) 'Building theory from case study research', *Academy of Management Review*, vol. 14, no. 4, pp. 532–50.

Eisenhardt, Kathleen M. (1989b) 'Making fast strategic decisions in high-velocity environments', *Academy of Management Journal*, vol. 38, no. 3, pp. 543–78.

Eisenhardt, K. M. and Zabaracki, M.J. (1992) 'Strategic decision making', *Strategic Management Journal*, vol. 13, pp. 17–37.

Eisenhardt, Kathleen M., Kahwajy, Jean L. and Bourgeois III, L. J. (1997) 'Conflict and strategic choice: how top management teams disagree', *California Management Review*, vol. 39, no. 2 (Winter), pp. 42–62.

Eisenhower, Dwight D. (1977) *Crusade in Europe*, New York, Da Rapo Press.

Elton, Robert M. (Covering signatory) (1987) *Executive Leadership*, Department of the Army Pamphlet 600–80, Washington DC, Department of the Army.

Farrago, Ladislas (1979) *Patton: Ordeal and Triumph*, London, Mayflower Books.

Feurer, Rainer and Chaharbaghi, Kazem (1995) 'Strategy development: past, present and future', *Management Decision*, vol. 33, no. 6, pp. 11–21.

Feurer, Rainer and Chaharbaghi, Kazem (1995) 'Strategy formulation: a learning methodology', *Benchmarking for Quality Management and Technology*, vol. 2, no. 1 pp. 38–55.

Feurer, Rainer, Chaharbaghi, Kazem and Wargin, John (1995) 'Analysis of strategy formulation and implementation at Hewlett-Packard', *Management Decision*, vol. 33, no. 10, pp. 4–16.

Fiedler, Fred F. (1996) 'Research on leadership selection and training: one view of the future', *Administrative Science Quarterly*, no. 41, pp. 241–50.

Finlay, Paul (2000) *Strategic Management: An Introduction to Business and Corporate Strategy*, Harlow, Pearson Education.

Foss, General John W. (1997) 'Command', *Military Review*, Jan/Feb, in www-cgsc. army.mil/milrev/english/janfeb97.

Fredrickson, James (1986) 'The strategic decision process and organizational structure', *Academy of Management Review*, vol. 11, no. 2 pp. 280–97.

Freedman, Lawrence (1981) *The Evolution of Nuclear Strategy*, London, Macmillan – now Palgrave.

Galbraith, Craig, Stiles, Curt and Galbraith III, Oliver (1996) '"Blood and guts" strategy: military and corporate strategic theory', in Carl L. Swanson, Abbass Alkhafaji and Mike H. Ryan (eds), *International Research in Business Disciplines*, vol. 2, Greenwich, Conn., JAI Press, pp. 213–35.

Garthoff, Raymond L. (1966) *Soviet Military Policy*, New York, Praeger.

Garud, Raghu and Van der Ven, Andrew H. (1992) 'An empirical evaluation of the internal corporate venturing process', *Strategic Management Journal*, vol. 13, pp. 93–109.

Gerstner, Louis V. (1994) Chairman's Letter, IBM Annual Report (www.ibm.com/ ibm/ibmar94/letterbody.html).

Gerstner, Louis V. (1996) Chairman's Letter, IBM Annual Report. (www.ibm.com/ annualreport/1996/htmljs/ChairmansLetter).

Ghoshal, Sumantra and Bartlett, Christopher A. (1994) 'Linking organizational context and managerial action: the dimensions of quality management', *Strategic Management Journal*, vol. 15, pp. 91–112.

Gilbert, Felix (1967) 'Macchiavelli: the renaissance of the art of war', in Edward Mead Earle (ed.), *Makers of Modern Strategy: Military Thought from Machiavelli to Hitler*, New York, Atheneum.

Giles, William G. (1991) 'Making strategy work', *Long Range Planning*, vol. 24, no. 5, pp. 75–91.

Gilmore, William S. and Camillus, John C.(1996) 'Do your planning processes meet the reality test?', *Long Range Planning*, vol. 29, no. 6, pp. 869–79.

Glaser, B. and Strauss, A. (1967) *The Discovery of Grounded Theory: Strategies for Qualitative Research*, London, Weidenfeld & Nicolson.

Goddard, Jules and Houlder, Dominic (1995) 'Beyond magic: conjectures on the nature of strategy in the late 1990s', *Business Strategy Review*, vol. 6, no. 1, pp. 81–107.

Goerlitz, Walter (1953) *History of the German General Staff*, New York, Praeger.

Golub, Andrew Lang (1997) *Decision Analysis: An Integrated Approach*, New York, John Wiley & Sons.

Goold, Michael and Campbell, Andrew (1987) 'Many best ways to make strategy', *Harvard Business Review*, November/December, pp. 70–6.

Graeger, Colonel Rudiger (1998) 'Field Marshal Günther von Kluge as C-in-C West in 1944', *Journal of the Royal United Services Institution*, vol. 143, no. 5, pp. 59–66.

Grant, Robert M. (1997) *Contemporary Strategy Analysis*, Oxford, Blackwell.

Groner, Rudolf, Groner, Maria, and Bischof, Walter F. (1983) 'The role of heuristics in models of decision', in R.W. Scholz (ed.), *Decision Making under Uncertainty*, Amsterdam, Elsevier Science.

Grundy, Tony and King, Dave (1992) 'Using strategic planning to drive strategic change', *Long Range Planning*, vol. 25, no. 1, pp. 100–8.

Hamel, Gary (1996) 'Strategy as revolution', *Harvard Business Review*, July/August, pp. 69–82.

Hamel, Gary and Prahalad, C.K. (1989) 'Strategic intent', *Harvard Business Review*, May/June, pp. 2–15.

Hamel, Gary and Prahalad, C.K. (1993) 'Strategy as stretch and leverage', *Harvard Business Review*, March/April, in de Wit and Meyer (1994) p. 244.

Hammer, Michael and Stanton, Steven (1999) 'How process enterprises *really*, work', *Harvard Business Review*, November/December, pp. 108–18.

Hammond, John S., Keeney, Ralph L. and Raiffa, Howard (1998) 'The hidden traps in decision making', *Harvard Business Review*, September/October, pp. 47–58.

Hampden-Turner, Charles (1990) *Charting the Corporate Mind*, Oxford, Basil Blackwell.

Handfield-Jones, Helen (2000) 'How executives grow', *McKinsey Quarterly*, no. 1 pp. 117–23.

Handy, C. (1980) *Understanding Organizations*, Harmondsworth, Penguin.

Handy, C. (1990) *Inside Organizations*, London, BBC Books.

Handy, Charles (1995) *Gods of Management*, London, Arrow.

Hardy, Cynthia and Clegg, Stewart R. (1996) 'Some dare call it power', in Stewart R. Clegg, Cynthia Hardy and Walter R. Nord (eds), *Handbook of Organization Studies*, London, Sage, pp. 622–41.

Harris, Simon and Ghauri, Pervez (2000) 'Strategy formation by business leaders', *European Journal of Marketing*, vol. 34, no. 1/2, pp. 126–42.

Harrison, E. Frank (1996) 'A process perspective on strategic decision making', *Management Decision*, vol. 34, no. 1, pp. 46–53.

Harrison, E. Frank and Pelletier, Monique A. (1997) 'CEO perceptions of strategic leadership', *Journal of Managerial Issues*, Fall, pp. 299–317 (from http://proquest. umi.com).

Harrison, E. Frank and Pelletier, Monique A. (1998) 'Foundations of strategic decision effectiveness', *Management Decision*, vol. 36, no. 3, pp. 147–59.

Hart, Stuart L. (1992) 'An integrative framework for strategy-making processes', *Academy of Management Review*, vol. 17, no. 2, pp. 327–51.

Hart, Stuart and Banbury, Catherine (1994) 'How strategy-making processes can make a difference', *Strategic Management Journal*, vol. 15, pp. 251–69.

Hausman, Eric and Burke, Steven (1995) 'A behind-the-scenes look at Big Blue board', *Computer Reseller News*, 24 April, p. 112.

Hax, Arnoldo (1998) 'Redefining the concept of strategy', in B. de Wit and R. Meyer (eds), *Strategy: Process, Content, Context*, 2nd edn, London, International Thomson Business Press, pp. 28–32.

Hellegren, B. and Melin, L. (1993) '"The role of strategists", ways-of-thinking in strategic change processes', in J. Hendry *et al.* (eds), *Strategic Thinking: Leadership and Management of Change*, Chichester, Wiley, pp. 161–92.

Heller, Frank (ed.) (1992) *Decision-Making and Leadership*, Cambridge, Cambridge University Press.

Henderson, Bruce D. (1989) 'The origin of strategy', *Harvard Business Review*, November/December, pp. 139–43.

Hermann, Charles F. (1963) 'Some consequences of crisis which limit the viability of organizations', *Administrative Science Quarterly*, vol. 21, pp. 41–65.

Hermann, Charles F (1972) 'Threat, time and surprise: a simulation of international crises', in Charles F. Hermann (ed.), *International Crises: Insights from Behavioral Research*, New York, Free Press, pp. 187–211.

Hersey, P. and Blanchard, K.H. (1969) *Management of Organizational Behavior*, Englewood Cliffs, NJ, Prentice-Hall.

Herwig, Holger H. (1994) 'Strategic uncertainties of a nation state (Prussia–Germany, 1871–1918)', in Williamson Murray, Macgregor Knox and Alvin Bernstein (eds), *The Making of Strategy*, Cambridge, Cambridge University Press, pp. 242–77.

Hindess, Barry (1977) *Philosophy and Methodology in the Social Sciences*, Hassocks, Harvester Press.

Hinterhuber, Hans and Levin, Boris (1995) 'Management by war – a helpful way to view the competition', in D.E. Hussey (ed.), *Rethinking Strategic Management*, New York, Wiley & Sons, pp. 107–22.

Hodgkinson, Gerard P. and Bown, Nicola J. (1998) 'Towards a cognitive model of strategic decision processes', conference paper, Strategic Management Conference, Orlando (quoted with permission).

Hofer, C.W. (1973) 'Some preliminary research on patterns of strategic behaviour', *Academy of Management Proceedings*, pp. 46–59.

Hofer, C.W. and Schendel, D. (1978) *Strategy Formulation: Analytical Concepts*, Minneapolis/St Paul, Main., West.

Hofstede, Geert (1993) 'Cultural constraints in management theories', *Academy of Management Executive*, vol. 7, no. 1, pp. 81–94.

Holsti, Kalevi (1991) *Peace and War: Armed Conflicts and International Order 1648–1989*, Cambridge, Cambridge University Press.

Hooper, Alan and Potter, John (1997) *The Business of Leadership*, Aldershot, Ashgate.

Hopkinson, William (2000) *The Making of British Defence Policy*, London, The Stationery Office.

Hoskin, Keith (1990) 'Using history to understand theory: a re-consideration of the historical genesis of strategy', conference paper for the ETASM Workshop on Strategy, Accounting and Control, Venice. October.

Howard, Michael (1970) *Studies in War and Peace*, London, Temple Smith.

Howard, Michael (1983) *Clausewitz*, Oxford, Oxford University Press.

Howard, Michael and Paret, Peter (eds) (1976) *Vom Kriege*, Princeton, NJ, Princeton University Press.

Hussey, Jill and Hussey, Roger (1997) *Business Research*, London, Macmillan – now Palgrave.

Idenburg, P.J. (1993) 'Four styles of strategy development', *Long Range Planning*, vol. 26, no. 6, pp. 132–7.

Inge, General Sir Peter, (1993) in Simon Caulkin, 'The lust for leadership', *Management Today*, November, pp. 40–3.

Irving, David (1982) *The War between the Generals*, Harmondsworth, Penguin.

Isabella, Lynn A. (1990) 'Evolving interpretations as a change unfolds: how managers construe key organizational events', *Academy of Management Journal*, vol. 33, no. 1, pp. 7–41.

Isenberg, Daniel J. (1984) 'How senior managers think', *Harvard Business Review*, November/December, pp. 81–90.

Itami, Hirovuki and Numaqami, Tsuvoshi (1992) 'Dynamic interaction between strategy and technology', *Strategic Management Journal*, vol. 13, pp. 119–35.

Jablonsky, David (1993) 'Why is strategy difficult?', in Gary L. Guertner (ed.), *The Search for Strategy*, Westport, Conn., Greenwood Press.

Jackson, Bill and Bramall, Edwin (1992) *The Chiefs*, London, Brassey's UK.

Jacobs, Dr T.O. (1991) Address in *Strategic Leadership Conference: Proceedings*, US Army War College, Carlisle, Pa., pp. 183–205.

James, Barrie G. (1984) *Business Wargames*, Harmondsworth, Penguin.

Janis, Irving (1992) 'Causes and consequences of defective policy-making: a new theoretical analysis', in Frank Heller (ed.), *Decision-Making and Leadership*, Cambridge, Cambridge University Press, pp. 10–45.

Janssens, Maddy and Steyaert, Chris (1999) 'The world in two and a third way out? The concept of duality in organization theory and practice', *Scandinavian Journal of Management*, vol. 15, pp. 121–39.

Johnson, Gerry (1990) 'Managing strategic change: the role of strategic action', *British Journal of Management*, vol. 1, pp. 183–200.

Johnson, G. and Scholes, K. (1997) *Exploring Corporate Strategy*, 4th edn, Hemel Hempstead, Prentice-Hall Europe.

Joint Service Publication (JSP) 101 *Manual of Service Writing*, London, HMSO.

Joyce, Paul and Woods, Adrian (1996) *Essential Strategic Management*, Oxford, Butterworth Heinemann.

Jungermann, Helmut (1983) 'The two camps on rationality', in R.W. Scholz (ed.), *Decision Making under Uncertainty*, Amsterdam, Elsevier Science.

Kahn, Herman (1960) *On Thermonuclear War*, Princeton, NJ, Princeton University Press.

Kaplan, Abraham (1964) *The Conduct of Inquiry: Methodology for Behavioral Science*, San Francisco, Chandler.

Kaufmann, William W. (1964) *The McNamara Strategy*, New York, Harper & Row.

Kennedy, Major-General Sir John (1957) *The Business of War*, London, Hutchinson.

Kiersey, D. and Bates, M. (1978) *Please Understand Me: Character and Temperament Types*, Del Mar, Calif., Prometheus Nemesis Books.

Kiesler, S. and Sproull S, (1982) 'Managerial responses to changing environments: perspectives and problems sensing from social cognition', *Administrative Science Quarterly*, vol. 37, pp. 548–70.

Knights, David (1992) 'Changing spaces: the disruptive impact of the new epistemological location for the study of management', *Academy of Management Review*, vol. 17, no. 3, pp. 514–36.

Knights, David and Morgan, Glenn (1991) 'Corporate strategy, organizations, and subjectivity: a critique', *Organization Studies*, vol. 12, no. 2, pp. 251–73.

Krause, Donald G. (1995) *The Art of War for Executives*, London, Nicholas Brealey.

Kuhn, T.S. (1962) *The Structure of Scientific Revolution*, Chicago, Ill., University of Chicago Press.

Langley, Ann (1995) 'Between "Paralysis by Analysis" and "Extinction by Instinct"', *Sloan Management Review*, Spring, pp. 63–76.

Lee, Robert and Lawrence, Peter (1991) *Politics at Work*, Cheltenham, Stanley Thornes.

Lengnick-Hall, Cynthia A. and Wolff, James A. (n.d.) 'Conceptual maps for strategy formulation', Conference Paper.

Lenz, R. Thomas (1993) 'Strategic management and organizational learning: a meta-theory of executive leadership', in John Hendry and Gerry Johnson (eds), *Strategic Thinking: Leadership and the Management of Change*, Chichester, John Wiley & Sons.

Levy, D. (1994) 'Chaos theory and strategy: theory application and managerial implications', *Strategic Management Journal*, vol. 15, pp. 167–78.

Liddell-Hart, B.H. (1970) *History of the Second World War*, London, Cassell.

Liedtka, Jeanne M. (1998) 'Strategic thinking: can it be taught?', *Long Range Planning*, vol. 31, no. 1, pp. 120–9.

Lindbergh, Charles A. (1953) *The Spirit of St Louis*, Dublin, Poolbeg Press.

Lindblom, Charles E. (1959) 'The science of "muddling through"', *Public Administration Review*, vol. 19, pp. 79–88.

Lloyd, Glyn and Phillips, Mike (1994) 'Inside IBM: strategic management in a federation of businesses', *Long Range Planning*, vol. 27, no. 5, pp. 52–63.

Longford, Catherine (1967) *Wellington: Years of the Sword*, London, Weidenfeld & Nicolson.

Luecke, Richard (1994) *Scuttle Your Ships before Advancing*, New York, Oxford University Press.

Luttwak, Edward (1976) *Grand Strategy of the Roman Empire*, Baltimore, Md., Johns Hopkins University Press.

Luttwak, Edward N. (1987) *Strategy: The Logic of War and Peace*, Cambridge, Mass., Belknap Press.

Lynn, John A. (1994) 'A quest for glory: the formation of strategy under Louis XIV, 1661–1715', in Williamson Murray, MacGregor Knox, and Alvin Bernstien (eds), *The Making of Strategy*, Cambridge, Cambridge University Press.

McAlpine, Alistair (2000) 'The servant', in Alistair McAlpine (ed.), *The Ruthless Leader*, New York, John Wiley & Sons.

McCabe, Douglas M. (1981) 'Strategy and tactics: analogies for human resources managers', *Personnel Journal*, December, pp. 958–63.

McCaskey, Michael (1982) 'Conceptual mapping', in B. de Wit, and R. Meyer (eds), *Strategy: Process, Content, Context*, 2nd edn, London, International Thomson Business Press, pp. 120–30.

McCollum, Bruce (1999) 'Leadership development and self-development: an empirical study', *Career Development International*, vol. 4, No. 3, pp. 149–54.

Machiavelli, Niccolò (1958) *The Prince* (translated by W.K. Marriott), London, Dent.

McNulty, Terry and Pettigrew, Andrew (1999) 'Strategists on the board', *Organization Studies*, vol. 20, No. 1, pp. 47–74.

McWilliams, Abigail and Smart, Dennis T. (1995) 'The resource-based view of the firm: does it go far enough in shedding the assumptions of the S–C–P paradigm?', *Journal of Management Inquiry*, vol. 4, no. 4 (December), pp. 309–16.

Magee, Roderich R. II (ed.) (1998) *Strategic Leadership Primer*, Carlisle Barracks, Pa., Department of Command, Leadership and Management, US Army War College.

Mahoney, Joseph T. (1993) 'Strategic management and determinism: sustaining the conversation', *Journal of Management Studies*, vol. 30, pp. 173–91.

Mair, Andrew (1997) 'Reconciling managerial dichotomies at Honda Motors', in Bob de Wit, and Ron Meyer (eds), *Strategy: Process, Content and Context*, 2nd edn, London, International Thomson Business Press, pp. 893–911.

Marsh, John (1993) *The Strategic Toolkit*, Bedford, IFS International.

Mason, Richard and Mitroff, Ian (1981) *Challenging Strategic Planning Assumptions*, New York, Wiley.

Mee, J.F. (1965) 'Objectives in a management philosophy', in W.E. Schlender, *et al.* (eds), *Management in Perspective*, Boston, Mass., Houghton Mifflin.

Megginson, David (2000) 'Current issues in mentoring', *Career Development International*, vol. 5, Issue 4/5, pp. 256–60.

Meyer, General Edward C. (1991) Address in *Strategic Leadership Conference: Proceedings*, US Army War College, Carlisle, Pa., pp. 151–60.

Miles, Matthew B. and Huberman, A. Michael (1994) *An Expanded Sourcebook of Qualitative Data Analysis*, London, Sage.

Miller, Danny (1992) 'The Icarus paradox', *Business Horizons*, January/February, in de Wit and Meyer (1994) pp. 454–67.

Miller, Susan J., Hickson, David J. and Wilson, David C. (1996) '*Decision-Making in Organizations*', in Stewart R. Clegg, Cynthia Hardy, and Walter R. Nord (eds), *Handbook of Organization Studies*, London, Sage.

Mintzberg, Henry (1978) 'Patterns in strategy formation', *Management Science*, vol. 24, No. 9, pp. 934–48.

Mintzberg, Henry (1987a) 'Crafting strategy', *Harvard Business Review*, July/August, pp. 66–75.

Mintzberg, Henry (1987b) 'The strategy concept: five Ps for strategy', *California Management Review*, Fall, pp. 11–24.

Mintzberg, Henry (1990a) *Schools of thought*, in W. Frederickson (ed.), *Perspectives on Strategic Management*, New York, Harper, pp. 105–235.

Mintzberg, Henry (1990b) 'The Design School: reconsidering the basic premises of strategic management', *Strategic Management Journal*, vol. 11 (March), pp. 171–95.

Mintzberg, Henry (1991) 'The effective organization: forces and forms', *Sloan Management Review*, Winter, pp. 54–66.

Mintzberg, Henry and Lampel, Joseph (1999) 'Reflecting on the strategy process', *Sloan Management Review*, Spring, pp. 21–30.

Mintzberg, Henry and Waters, James A. (1985) 'Of strategies, deliberate and emergent', *Strategic Management Journal*, vol. 6, pp. 257–72.

Mintzberg, Henry, Ahlstrand, Bruce and Lampel, Joseph (1998) *Strategy Safari*, Hemel Hempstead, Prentice-Hall.

Mintzberg, Henry, Quinn, James Brian and Ghoshal Sumantra (1998) *The Strategy Process*, rev. European edn, Hemel Hempstead, Prentice-Hall.

Mintzberg, H., Raisinghani, D. and Théorét, A. (1976) 'The structure of "unstructured" decision processes', *Administrative Science Quarterly*, vol. 21, pp. 246–75.

Montgomery of Alamein, Field Marshal Viscount (1958) *The Memoirs*, London, Collins.

Morris, Betsy (1997) 'He's smart, he's not nice, he's saving Big Blue', *Fortune*, 14 April, pp. 40–51.

Morris, William T. (1969) 'Management decisions – art or science?', in Gordon Yewdall, (ed.), *Management Decision-Making*, Newton Abbot, David & Charles.

Moskos, Charles C., Williams, John Allen and Segal, David R. (2000) 'Armed forces after the Cold War', in Charles C. Moskos, John Allen Williams, and David R. Segal (eds), *The Postmodern Military*, Oxford, Oxford University Press.

Murray, Williamson, Knox, Macgregor and Bernstein, Alvin (eds) (1994) *The Making of Strategy: Rulers, States and War*, Cambridge, Cambridge University Press.

Musashi, Miyamoto (1993) *The Book of Five Rings* (trans. Thomas Cleary), Boston, Mass., Shambhala.

Narayanan, V.K. and Fahey, Liam (1982) 'The micro-politics of strategy formulation', *Academy of Management Review*, vol. 7, no. 1, pp. 25–34.

Nickols, Fred (1999) *Eight Maxims of Strategy* (http://home.att.net/Nnickols/maxims).

Norman, Richard and Ramirez, Rafael (1993) 'From value chain to value constellation: designing interactive strategy', *Harvard Business Review*, July/August, pp. 65–77.

Nutt, Paul C. (1990) 'Strategic decisions made by top executives and middle managers with data and process dominant styles', *Journal of Management Studies*, vol. 27, no. 2, pp. 173–94.

Ohmae, Kenichi (1982) *The Mind of the Strategist*, New York, McGraw-Hill.

Palmer, P.J. (1994) 'Leading from within: out of the shadows into the light', in J.A. Conger (ed.), *Spirit at Work: Discovering the Spirituality in Leadership*, San Francisco, Jossey-Bass.

Palmer, R.R. (1967) 'Frederick the Great, Guibert, Bulow: from dynastic to national war', in Edward Earle Meade (ed.), *Makers of Modern Strategy*, New York, Atheneum, pp. 49–75.

Papadakis, Vassilis, Kaloghirou, Yiannis and Iatrelli, Maria (1999) 'Strategic decision making: from crisis to opportunity', *Business Strategy Review*, vol. 10, Issue 1, pp. 29–37.

Papadakis, Vassilis M., Lioukas, Spyros and Chambers, Davis (1998) 'Strategic decision-making processes: the role of management and context', *Strategic Management Journal*, vol. 19, pp. 115–47.

Pappas, James L. and Brigham, Eugene F. (1979) *Managerial Economics*, 3rd edn, Hinsdale, Ill., Dryden Press.

Parker, Geoffrey (1994) 'The making of strategy in Hapsburg Spain: Philip II's "bid for mastery" 1556–1598', in Williamson Murray, MacGregor Knox and Alvin Bernstein (eds), *The Making of Strategy*, Cambridge, Cambridge University Press, pp. 115–40.

Parker, Martin (1992) 'Post modern organizations or post modern organization theory', *Organization Study*, vol. 13, no. 1, pp. 1–17.

Parker, R.A.C. (1990) *The Struggle for Survival*, Oxford, Oxford University Press.

Parks, Bill, Pharr, Steven W. and Lockeman, Bradley D. (1994) 'A marketer's guide to Clausewitz: lessons for winning market share', *Business Horizons*, July/August, pp. 68–73.

Peattie, Ken (1993) 'Strategic planning: its role in organizational politics', *Long Range Planning*, vol. 26, no. 3, pp. 10–17.

Pennings, Johannes M. (1985) 'Introduction: on the nature and theory of strategic decisions', in Johannes M. Pennings *et al.* (eds), *Organizational Strategy and Change*, London, Jossey-Bass.

Peters, Tom and Waterman, Robert H. (1982) *In Search of Excellence*, New York, Harper & Row.

Pettigrew, Andrew (1977) 'Strategy formulation as a political process', *International Studies of Management and Organizations*, vol. 7, no. 2, pp. 78–87.

Pettigrew, A. (1988) *The Management of Strategic Change*, Oxford, Basil Blackwell.

Pettigrew, Andrew (1992a) 'Guest editor's introduction', *Strategic Management Journal*, vol. 13, pp. 8–16.

Pettigrew, Andrew (1992b) 'On studying managerial elites', *Strategic Management Journal*, vol. 13, pp. 163–82.

Pfeffer, J. (1981) *Power in Organizations*, Marshfield, Mass., Pitman, in Hardy and Clegg (1996).

Phillips, Major Thomas R. (1943) 'Frederick the Great: military instructions for generals', in Major Thomas R. Phillips (ed.), *Roots of Strategy*, London, Bodley Head, pp. 163–218.

Porter, Michael E. (1980) *Competitive Strategy*, New York, Macmillan – now Palgrave.

Porter, Michael E. (1991) 'Towards a dynamic theory of strategy', *Strategic Management Journal*, vol. 12, pp. 95–117.

Porter, Michael E. (1996) 'What is strategy?', *Harvard Business Review*, November/December, pp. 61–77.

Portillo, Michael (ed.) (1997) *British Defence Doctrine: JWP 0–01*, London, Her Britannic Majesty's Stationery Office.

Pound, Ezra (1934) *The ABC of Reading*, 1.1 in Tripp, Rhoda Thomas (1970), *The International Thesaurus of Quotations*, Harmondsworth, Penguin.

Prahalad, C.K. and Bettis, R.A. (1986) 'The dominant logic: a new linkage between diversity and performance', *Strategic Management Journal*, vol. 7, pp. 485–501.

Prahalad, C.K. and Hamel, Gary (1990) 'The core competence of the corporation', *Harvard Business Review*, May/June, pp. 79–91.

Prahalad, C.K. and Hamel, Gary (1994) 'Strategy as a field of study: why search for a new paradigm?', *Strategic Management Journal*, vol. 15, pp. 5–16.

Quinn, James Brian (1978) 'Strategic change: logical incrementalism', *Sloan Management Review*, Fall, reprinted Summer 1989, pp. 45–60.

Rapaport, Anatole (ed.) (1968) *Clausewitz: On War*, Harmondsworth, Penguin.

Rausch, Edwin (1999) 'The paradigm for leadership development: simple guideline questions that serve as reminders of issues to consider in every decision', *Career Development International*, vol. 4, no. 3, pp. 170–4.

Rawson, Hugh (1998) 'The strategist's strategist', *Across the Board*, vol. 35, no. 4, p. 11.

Rittenhouse, John D. (1991) Address in *Strategic Leadership Conference: Proceedings*, US Army War College, Carlisle, Pa., pp. 55–96.

Roberts, Wess (1989) *The Leadership Secrets of Attila the Hun*, London, Bantam Books.

Rothenburg, Gunther E. (1986) 'Moltke, Schlieffen and the doctrine of strategic envelopment', in Peter Paret (ed.), *Makers of Modern Strategy*, Oxford, Oxford University Press.

Rothschild, William E. (1996) 'A portfolio of strategic leaders', *Planning Review*, vol. 24, no. 1 (January/February) pp. 16–19.

Rumelt, Richard P., Schendel, Dan and Teece, David J. (1991) 'Strategic manage-ment and economics', *Strategic Management Journal*, vol. 12, pp. 5–29.

Russell, Bertrand (1961) *History of Western Philosophy*, 2nd edn, London, Routledge.

Schelling, Thomas C. (1980) *The Strategy of Conflict*, Cambridge, Mass., Harvard University Press.

Schoemaker, Paul (1992) 'How to link vision to core capabilities', *Sloan Management Review*, Fall, pp. 67–81.

Schwarzkopf, General H. Norman (1993) *The Autobiography: It Doesn't Take a Hero*, London, Bantam Books.

Scott, W.G. (1967) 'Decision concepts', in F.G. Castles, D.J. Murray, and D.C. Potter (eds), *Decisions, Organizations and Society*, Harmondsworth, Penguin.

Sekaran, Uma (1992) *Research Methods for Business: A Skill Building Approach*, 2nd edn, New York, John Wiley & Sons.

Short, Lt. Gen. (1999) 'PBS Interview with Lt. Gen. Short', further details unknown. Transcript supplied by Air Vice-Marshal Professor A.R. Mason.

Simon, H.H. (1965) *Administrative Behaviour*, London, Free Press/Macmillan – now Palgrave.

Simpson, Peter and Burnard, Hugh (2000) 'Leaders achieving focus in the place of not knowing', *Leadership and Organization Development Journal*, vol. 21, no. 5, pp. 235–42.

Slim, Field Marshal Sir William (1957) 'Leadership in management', *Australian Army Journal*, (held in notes issued by the Royal Air Force Staff College, 1965).

Solomon, Caryn (1998) 'Resolving conflict', *Family Business*, London, Director Publications.

Stacey, Ralph (1993) 'Strategy as order emerging from chaos', *Long Range Planning*, vol. 26, no. 1, pp. 10–17.

Stacey, R. (1996) 'Emerging strategies for a chaotic environment', *Long Range Planning*, vol. 29, no. 2, pp. 182–9.

Stacey, Ralph D. (2000) *Strategic Management and Organisational Dynamics*, 3rd edn, Harlow, Pearson Education.

Stalk, George (1988) 'Time the next source of competitive advantage', *Harvard Business Review*, July/August, in de Wit and Meyer, (1994) p. 225.

Stalk, George, Evans, Philip and Shulman, Lawrence E. (1992) 'Competing on capabilities: the new rules of corporate strategy', *Harvard Business Review*, March/April, pp. 57–69.

Stogdill, R.M. (1950) 'Leadership, membership and organization', *Psychological Bulletin*, no. 47, pp. 1–14.

Strategic Defence Review (1998) *Essay 1: The Strategic Defence Review Process*, London, The Stationery Office.

Strauss, A.L. and Corbin, J. (1990) *Basics of Qualitative Research – Grounded Theory Procedures and Techniques*, London, Sage.

Strawson, John (1971) *Hitler as a Military Commander*, London, Sphere Books.

Stumpf, Stephen A. and Mullen, Thomas P. (1991) 'Strategic leadership: concepts, skills, style and process', *Journal of Management Development*, Vol. 10, no. 1, pp. 42–53.

Sullivan, Gordon R. and Harper, Michael V. (1996) *Hope is not a Method*, New York, Random House.

Sun Tzu (1983) *The Art of War* (trans. James Clavell), New York, Delacorte Press.

Teece, David J., Pisano, Gary and Shuen, Amy (1997) 'Dynamic capabilities and strategic management', *Strategic Management Journal*, vol. 18, no. 7, pp. 509–33.

Thorngate, Warren (1976) '"In general" vs. "it depends"', *Personality and Social Psychology Bulletin*, no. 2, pp. 404–10.

Thucydides (1954) *The Peloponnesian War* (trans. Rex Warner), Harmondsworth, Penguin.

Thurman, Maxwell, US Army Ret. (1991) Keynote Speech, *Strategic Leadership Conference: Proceedings*, US Army War College, Carlisle Barracks, Pa., pp. 5–52.

Townsend, Robert (1976) *Up the Organisation*, a video in the 'Management Classics', series produced by the BBC.

Tranfield, David and Starkey, Ken (1998) 'The nature, social organisation and promotion of management research: towards policy', *British Journal of Management*, September, and at conferences in 1995 and 1997.

Verity, John W., Peterson, Thane, Depke, Deidre and Schwartz, Evan I. (1991) 'The new IBM', *Business Week*, 16 December, pp. 36–41.

Volkema, Roger J. and Gorman, Ronald H. (1998) 'The influence of cognitive-based group composition on decision-making process and outcome', *Journal of Management Studies*, vol. 35, no. 1, pp. 105–21.

Waldron, Arthur (1994) 'Chinese strategy from the fourteenth to the seventeenth centuries', in Williamson Murray, Macgregor Knox, and Alvin Bernstein (eds), *The Making of Strategy: Rulers, States and War*, Cambridge, Cambridge University Press.

Washbush, John B. and Clements, Christine (1999) 'The two faces of leadership', *Career Development International*, vol. 4, no. 3, pp. 146–8.

Westley, Frances and Mintzberg, Henry (1989) 'Visionary leadership and strategic management', *Strategic Management Journal*, vol. 10, pp. 17–32.

Weston, Hilary (1991) 'IBM – make it your business', *Harvard Business School Case no. 9-190-137*, (revised 17 June 1991).

Wheelen, Thomas L. and Hunger, J. David (1992) *Strategic Management and Business Policy*, 4th edn, Reading, Mass., Addison-Wesley.

Whittington, Richard (1993) *What is Strategy – and Does it Matter?*, London, Routledge.

Wick, Calhoun (1991) Address in *Strategic Leadership Conference: Proceedings*, US Army War College, Carlisle Barracks, Pa., pp. 211–28.

Wise, D. (1984) 'Apple's new crusade', *Business Week*, 26 November, pp. 146–56.

Yelverton, Jerry (1997) 'Adaptive skills: seven keys to developing top managers', *Vital Speeches of the Day*, vol. 63, no. 23, pp. 725–7.

Yoffie, David B. and Pearson, Andrall E. (1990) 'The transformation of IBM', *Harvard Business School Case no. 9–391–073*, (revised 9 September 1991).

Zaleznik, A. (1970) 'Power and politics in organizational life', *Harvard Business Review*, May/June, pp. 47–60.

Zaleznik, A. (1977) 'Managers and leaders: are they different?', *Harvard Business Review*, vol. 55, May/June, pp. 67–78.

Appendix: List of Persons Interviewed

General Sir Hugh Beach, GBE, KCB, MC, DL, DCL, MA, MSc: Past Master General of the Ordnance

Dr Christopher Bellamy, MA, PhD, AIL, FRUSI: Security Studies Institute, Cranfield University

Sir Christopher Benson: Past Chairman, Boots plc, and Chairman, Royal Sun Alliance

Mr Kevin Bounds: Consultant, KPMG

Ms Therese Bradley: Co-Founder and Chief Executive, Software Paths Ltd, Dublin

Field Marshal Lord Bramall, KG, GCB, OBE, MC, JP: Past Chief of General Staff and Past Chief of Defence Staff

Professor Lawrence Freedman: Professor of War Studies, Kings College, London

Mr Tony George: Past Company Secretary of GKN plc; Joint Honorary Colonel, Royal Monmouthshire Royal Engineers

Colonel Peter Gooderson, TD: Managing Director, LoadLok Ltd, and Chairman, Territorial, Auxiliary and Volunteer Reserves Association of Wales

Sir John Harvey-Jones, MBE: Past Chairman of ICI

Mr Richard Hatfield: Deputy Under-Secretary of State (Policy), Ministry of Defence, London

Air Chief Marshal Sir Patrick Hine, GCB,GBE: Past Commander-in-Chief Strike Command, Joint Commander British Forces 'Desert Storm' and currently Military Adviser to British Aerospace plc

Mr Alan Hooper, MA, FRSA, FIMgt: Director, Centre for Leadership Studies, University of Exeter

Brigadier John Hooper, OBE, DL, FIMgt: Ex-Royal Engineers and Past Chief, Executive Airships International

Dr Tim King: Founder and Past CEO, UK Online Ltd

Mr Charles Mackie: Past Chairman, Stewart and Lloyds Ltd; Past Colonel

Air Vice-Marshal Professor R.A. Mason, CB, CBE, DFC, MA: Director, Centre for Studies in Security and Diplomacy, Birmingham University

Mr B.J.W. Mayers: Founder and Head of Dundridge College

Admiral of the Fleet Sir Julian Oswald, GCB: Past Chief of Naval Staff and currently Military Adviser, SEMA Group plc

Air Marshal Sir Ian Pedder, KCB, OBE, DFC, RAF: Past Controller, National Air Traffic Control Organisation, and past Director, DanAir Ltd

Professor Ann Robinson, MA, PhD: Director General, National Association of Pension Funds; Past Policy Director, Institute of Directors

Air Vice-Marshal P.W. Roser, MBE, FRAeS, RAF: Senior Directing Staff (Air), Royal College of Defence Studies

Mr Terry Soame: Strategic Director (Technical), Alenia Marconi Systems

Sir Peter Walters: Chairman, SmithKline Beecham plc

Index